WISDOM LITERATURE AND POETRY

THE SERIES

Volume I
The Pentateuch

Volume II
Old Testament History

Volume III
Wisdom Literature and Poetry

Volume IV
The Major Prophets

Volume V
The Minor Prophets and the Apocrypha

Volume VI
The Gospels

Volume VII
Acts and Paul's Letters

Volume VIII
Revelation and the General Epistles

INTERPRETER'S CONCISE COMMENTARY

WISDOM LITERATURE AND POETRY

A COMMENTARY ON
JOB, PSALMS, PROVERBS, ECCLESIASTES,
THE SONG OF SOLOMON

By
Hugh Anderson
Lawrence E. Toombs
Robert C. Dentan
Harvey H. Guthrie, Jr.

Edited by Charles M. Laymon

Abingdon Press
Nashville

Interpreter's Concise Commentary
Volume III: WISDOM LITERATURE AND POETRY

Library of Congress Cataloging in Publication Data

Main entry under title:
Wisdom literature and poetry.
(Interpreter's concise commentary; v. 3)
Includes bibliographies.
1. Bible. O.T. Hagiographa—Commentaries. I. Anderson, Hugh, 1920– . II. Laymon, Charles M. III. Series.
BS491.2.I57 1983 vol. 3 220'.07s 83-8827
[BS1308]

ISBN 0-687-19234-X (pbk.)

(Previously published by Abingdon Press in cloth as part of *The Interpreter's One-Volume Commentary on the Bible*, regular ed. ISBN 0-687-19299-4, thumb-indexed ed. ISBN 0-687-19300-1.)

MANUFACTURED BY THE PARTHENON PRESS AT NASHVILLE, TENNESSEE, UNITED STATES OF AMERICA

EDITOR'S PREFACE

to the original edition

A significant commentary on the Bible is both timely and timeless. It is timely in that it takes into consideration newly discovered data from many sources that are pertinent in interpreting the Scriptures, new approaches and perspectives in discerning the meaning of biblical passages, and new insights into the relevancy of the Bible for the times in which we live. It is timeless since it deals with the eternal truths of God's revelation, truths of yesterday, today, and of all the tomorrows that shall be.

This commentary has been written within this perspective. Its authors were selected because of their scholarship, their religious insight, and their ability to communicate with others. Technical discussions do not protrude, yet the most valid and sensitive use of contemporary knowledge underlies the interpretations of the several writings. It has been written for ministers, lay and nonprofessional persons engaged in studying or teaching in the church school, college students and those who are unequipped to follow the more specialized discussions of biblical matters, but who desire a thoroughly valid and perceptive guide in interpreting the Bible.

The authorship of this volume is varied in that scholars were chosen from many groups to contribute to the task. In this sense it is an ecumenical writing. Protestants from numerous denominations, Jews, and also Roman Catholics are represented in the book. Truth cannot be categorized according to its ecclesiastical sources. It is above and beyond such distinctions.

It will be noted that the books of the Apocrypha have been included and interpreted in the same manner as the canonical writings. The value of a knowledge of this body of literature for understanding the historical background and character of the Judaic-Christian tradition has been widely recognized in our time, but commentary treatments of it have not been readily accessible. In addition, the existence of the Revised Standard Version and the New English Bible translations of these documents makes such a commentary upon them as is included here both necessary and significant.

The commentary as a whole avoids taking dogmatic positions or representing any one particular point of view. Its authors were chosen throughout the English-speaking field of informed and recognized biblical scholars. Each author was urged to present freely his own interpretation and, on questions where there was sometimes a diversity of conclusions, each was also asked to define objectively the viewpoints of others while he was offering and defending his own.

Many persons have contributed to the writing and production of this volume. One of the most rewarding of my personal experiences as editor was corresponding with the authors. On every hand there was enthusiasm for the project and warmth of spirit. The authors' commitment to the task and their scholarly sensitivity were evident in all of my relationships with them. The considerate judgments of the manuscript consultants, Morton S. Enslin, Dwight M. Beck, W. F. Stinespring, Virgil M. Rogers, and William L. Reed, were invaluable in the making of the character of the commentary. The copy editors who have worked under the careful and responsible guidance of Mr. Gordon Duncan of Abingdon Press have contributed greatly to the accuracy and readability of the commentary.

—Charles M. Laymon, Editor

PUBLISHER'S PREFACE

The intent of *The Interpreter's Concise Commentary* is to make available to a wider audience the commentary section of *The Interpreter's One-Volume Commentary on the Bible.* In order to do this, the Publisher is presenting the commentary section of the original hardback in this eight-volume paperback set. At the same time, and in conjunction with our wish to make *The Interpreter's One-Volume Commentary* more useful, we have edited the hardback text for the general reader: we have defined most of the technical terms used in the original hardback text; we have tried to divide some of the longer sentences and paragraphs into shorter ones; we have tried to make the sexually stereotyped language used in the original commentary inclusive where it referred to God or to both sexes; and we have explained abbreviations, all in an attempt to make the text more easily read.

The intention behind this paperback arrangement is to provide a handy and compact commentary on those individual sections of the Bible that are of interest to readers. In this paperback format we have not altered the substance of any of the text of the original hardback, which is still available. Rather, our intention is to smooth out some of the scholarly language in order to make the text easier to read. We hope this arrangement will make this widely accepted commentary on the Bible even more profitable for all students of God's Word.

WRITERS

Hugh Anderson
Professor of New Testament, University of Edinburgh, Scotland

Lawrence E. Toombs
Professor, School of Religion, Waterloo Lutheran University, Waterloo, Ontario, Canada

Robert C. Dentan
Trinity Church Professor of Old Testament Literature and Interpretation, General Theological Seminary, New York, New York

Harvey H. Guthrie, Jr.
Dean, Episcopal Theological School, Cambridge, Massachuseetts

CONTENTS

THE BOOK OF JOB

Hugh Anderson

Introduction

Literary Character

Job is one of the noblest works of world literature. It should be classed with the Greek tragedies of Aeschylus and Sophocles, with Dante's *Divine Comedy*, Milton's *Paradise Lost*, and Goethe's *Faust*. Tennyson called Job "the greatest poem of ancient or modern times."

There is no doubt about the supreme literary grandeur of Job. But there is a question about what kind of literature it is. Is it primarily a drama? Is it epic or lyric poetry? Is it a philosophical composition? Or is it didactic, intended to teach and instruct?

Perhaps the wisest course is not to try to fit Job into any one literary category but to acknowledge it for what it is—a vast literary complex. In addition to a prose narrative (chapters 1–2; 42:7-17), it contains a remarkable variety of poetic pieces, many of which could be read as separate literary units complete in themselves. The range of the author's poetic imagination is extensive. It is expressed in such forms as hymns of praise to the Almighty, Job's laments over his fate, proverbs, and descriptions of the blessedness of the righteous and the destruction of the wicked.

The last two of these literary forms are part of the stock in trade of the so-called "wisdom" writers of the Old Testament. Job is usually grouped with Proverbs and Ecclesiastes under the heading of "wisdom literature." The wise men or sages of Israel were a special class characterized by their rationalistic approach to ethics, religion, and the problems of human life. When Elihu addresses Job's three friends as wise men (34:2), the title is to be understood in this specialized sense. In their disputation with Job his friends often appeal to an apparently well-established norm of wisdom.

We must, however, exercise some caution about calling Job a book of wisdom in the same sense as Proverbs or Ecclesiastes. In this book the bits of proverbial wisdom and the contrasting destinies of the righteous and the wicked nearly always come from the friends. The hero himself tirades in vehement protest against the cold calculations of their wisdom point of view. So we see here what may be called an anti-wisdom strain. Yet, on the positive side, the author's theology resembles that of the wisdom literature in general, in that it is expressed in utterances about creation (chapters 38–39). We may be sure that he was very much influenced by contact with the wise men or sages.

Wisdom, in the technical sense indicated above, went far beyond the boundaries of the nation of Israel. The wise men of Israel had their counterparts in Egypt and beyond the eastern borders of Palestine (cf. I Kings 4:30-31). Each of the four main human characters in Job is a foreigner. Eliphaz, one of the friends, comes from Teman in Edom, and Edom apparently had a special reputation for wisdom (cf. Jeremiah 49:7).

Fortunately modern archaeological discoveries have increasingly clarified for us the wider cultural background of Job. We recognize today that the book belongs to a family of literary works of the ancient Near East. These were generally constructed as dialogues with complaints about suffering—especially innocent suffering. Basically they dealt with the problem of theodicy, which may be roughly defined as the problem of how to square belief in a good God with the existence of evil in the world.

An example of this type of writing is the Babylonian psalm "I

Will Praise the Lord of Wisdom"—often called the Babylonian Job. It is a prayer of thanksgiving for deliverance from misfortune. The author tells how he was wrongfully removed from his priestly office, banished from home, and reduced to slavery. He called on the gods for help. When they did not respond, he concluded that their idea of goodness must be different from that of humans. He was smitten with a serious illness for which no cure could be found, and his enemies rejoiced.

Then he had two visions promising him both help and cure. In the sequel his health was restored, his innocence vindicated, and he was released from slavery. The god Marduk took him by the hand and his persecutors were punished. He went back to Babylon, and in the temple of Marduk the people joined him in praising god for his mercy.

Alongside this psalm we may place a Babylonian dialogue between a sufferer and his friends, who address each other as scholars eminent for their wisdom and insight. Another earlier poem from the same background is entitled "A Pessimistic Dialogue Between Master and Slave." This is concerned with the seeming meaninglessness of life. There is a comparable Egyptian work, written probably before 2000 B.C., in which a sufferer converses with his own soul. He contemplates suicide as a justifiable way out of the afflictions of this life.

Of all these ancient works perhaps the one most closely related to Job is a Sumerian poem from Nippur dating from soon after 2000 B.C. Sumer was the land which came to be known in classical times as Babylonia. It was the scene of probably the first high civilization in history. The hero of the Sumerian poem is a nameless man who was suddenly reduced from health, wealth, and happiness to severe illness and pain. Though he laments his fate, he does not blame his god for it. Rather he confesses his own guilt, and the god delivers him from his ordeal.

The author of Job may not have been directly dependent on such writings as these. Nevertheless he inherited their tradition and outlook. In terms of both literary form and content, therefore, his book was not produced "out of the blue." It should not be viewed as coming from a purely Hebrew environment.

Authorship

Despite our richer acquaintance with the background of Job, the name of the author remains unknown to us. We do not have any information about him except the few hints we can gather from the book itself. One of the most striking features of the book is that its setting is not Hebrew and that it is filled with foreign elements. The action and characters are most closely associated with Edom, the land on the southeast border of Israel. It was inhabited by a seminomadic people who were in touch with both the Arabian peninsula and Egypt.

The author seems to avoid both the divine name Yahweh and the other common Hebrew designation for God, Elohim. Instead he uses such "outside" names as El, Eloah, and Shaddai. The civil and moral customs alluded to do not appear to be specifically Hebrew in character, but were common to all ancient civilized nations. As we have seen, ancient wisdom writings furnished a literary, poetic, and religious background for the author. His Hebrew language has been greatly influenced by Arabic. Accordingly, a few scholars have argued that he could hardly have been a Jew at all. Indeed he was most probably an Edomite.

On the other hand, the author does show some familiarity with the prophetic and wisdom literature of the Old Testament. For example, Job's dirge in chapter 3 recalls Jeremiah 20:14-18 and certain psalms of lamentation (Psalms 38; 88; and 102). Therefore, since we do not have sufficient concrete evidence to connect the author with a particular foreign locale, it is perhaps better to assume that he was a Jew.

He was, however, a Jew who had traveled very widely and had amassed an encyclopedic knowledge of the lore of the ancient Near East. Evidently he was especially well versed in the lore of Egypt. His work contains a number of Egyptian loan words and many echoes of Egyptian language. Moreover the whole tone of chapter 31 is reminiscent of the so-called "negative confession" of the Egyptian Book of the Dead.

The author was also a keen observer of the natural world. He had a remarkably scientific understanding of its working, as we can see in the majestic nature poem of chapter 38 and the portrayal of the wonders of the animal world in chapter 39.

His gifts of intellect appear to have been matched by his gifts of heart. The whole book bears the stamp of a profoundly religious spirit, sensitive to the world's sin and sorrow. Job's violent reaction to his ordeal is depicted with such realism that we feel the author himself knew what it was to be "battered with the shocks of doom." He poured himself into his hero's doubts and fears and protests.

Date

The question of when Job was written is a very open one. The difficulty is compounded by the fact that the book consists of two separate portions. 1:1–2:13 and 42:7-17 are prose and may be recognized as the beginning and end of an old folk story. The long section in between is in poetic form. The prose narrative takes us back to a great antiquity, reflecting the genuine coloring of the patriarchal age—for example, wealth consisting of cattle and slaves and Job's great age. Therefore there arose an ancient view that the author of Job was Moses himself. But we have no means whatever of confirming this tradition. There is in fact one feature of the prose prologue—the prominent part played by Satan—that may be as late as the sixth or fifth century, a time when Persian influences were infiltrating Hebrew religious thinking.

Probably the safest inference is that the author—or as some believe, the editor—employed a very old folk legend regarding a pious sufferer. This, as we have seen, had ancient Sumerian-Babylonian and Egyptian parallels. He then adapted it slightly as a setting for the poetical composition.

Can we define a date for the extensive poetical section of Job? Significantly enough, there is not a single allusion in it to any event in Hebrew history. Yet this very lack may give us some clue to the time of writing. It implies that the earlier faith in God's rulership over the history of Israel had broken down. This had been replaced by the questioning and anxiety that followed the destruction of Jerusalem in 586, when God's judgment on the nation was executed. Since the book was known to Ben Sira (Ecclesiasticus 49:9) it can scarcely be later than 250. Thus we may tentatively place the writing somewhere between the sixth and third centuries.

Structure

The Hebrew text of Job as it has come down to us is the most corrupt of all biblical documents. There is abundant evidence that the original has repeatedly been worked over and revised by a number of different editors. The poetical portion is in the form of a dialogue. This consists of a soliloquy by Job, followed by three cycles of six speeches—one from each of Job's friends in turn and an immediate reply to each by Job himself. The third cycle of speeches, however, is confused and incomplete. Chapters 24–27 are particularly garbled. Bildad's third speech (chapter 25) is very brief and is not in accord with his earlier utterances. Job's reply (chapters 26–27) brings forward ideas to which he had previously been opposed. Zophar's third speech is missing altogether.

The poem that follows in praise of wisdom (chapter 28) is a separate literary unit. Though it may possibly be from the hand of the author, it is certainly out of context where it stands. It is generally recognized as an addition to the original poem.

Most scholars also agree that the speeches of Elihu in chapters 32–37 are an addition to the original work. The youthful Elihu (32:6) takes up the better part of two chapters apologizing for his intrusion into the debate. When he does eventually say something positive, he mainly reiterates or supplements points already made by Job's three friends. Then again the words of Elihu in chapters 36-37 simply anticipate God's reply out of the whirlwind in chapters 38–40. Accordingly we may assume that the Elihu speeches were composed and inserted by an editor who felt called upon to counter Job's defiance more effectively than the friends had done and to improve on the arguments presented in the divine discourse. They should not be dismissed as entirely insignificant, however. They provide us with an interesting early commentary on certain aspects of the original poem by someone who did not share the author's philosophy.

There are many problems connected with the structure of the book. The most critical is that of the relationship between the prose prologue and epilogue (1:1–2:13; 42:7-17) and the great poem of 3:1–42:6. At first sight they seem to be quite separate from and contradictory to each other. The prose narrative centers on a pious sufferer who remains faithful to God's will and is rewarded in the end for showing patience. The Job of this folktale must have been widely known in antiquity as an outstanding example of quiet and brave endurance under trial.

The Job of the poem, on the other hand, is a rebel. Even after his confrontations with God, he seems to be left in his distress and suffering. The poem is hostile to the notion of the final reward of the suffering righteous. The prose epilogue endorses it. Because of this conflict many scholars have concluded that the original author wrote only the poem. They think the prose prologue and epilogue were added later by some editor or editors out of a wish for a happy ending and a desire to encourage the afflicted.

Nevertheless there are good reasons for thinking that the author of the poem was himself responsible for combining it with the prose narrative. The result is a "framework-poem," patterned after early Sumerian-Babylonian and Egyptian models. In the prose section the "plot" is unfolded. We are allowed a glimpse of the righteous Job in the days of his prosperity (1:1-5) and are introduced to the actions taken in the heavenly court for his trial. Against the background of this prelude the disintegration of Job's faith and his desperate cry in chapter 3 are all the more heartrending. So at the end, after the Job of the poem has been silenced by his encounter with the God of the whirlwind (42:1-6), the epilogue appears to make good sense by drawing down the curtain on his misery and depicting his final restoration (42:7-17). The whole book, therefore—prose narrative and poem together—may be taken as a single and unified work of great dramatic force and urgency.

Theme

If Job is a dramatic unity, is there also one great theme running through the whole work? The question is not so simple as might at first appear. Modern readers have great difficulty with the long poetical section. We are troubled by the lack of any logical progression of thought. Further, the poet does not seem to define any clearly fixed subject for conversation in the speeches. Job's speeches range rapidly from topic to topic and are marked by sudden changes of tone and mood. The speeches of the friends do not consist of rationally developed arguments. Rather they seem to be a series of loosely connected sections. For example, Eliphaz offers Job five different and largely separate propositions to think over in chapters 4 and 5.

The difficulties presented by the poetical portion may partly account for the traditional interpretation of the book. The popular view has fastened on the prose folk story's simple saint—one whose faith in God remains undimmed through every tribulation. This view sees the real theme of the work as "the fortitude of a good person under testing." But we can take that to be the theme of Job only at the cost of ignoring or neglecting what the poetry actually says. The poem shows us one who shakes a fist against God in fiery *impatience* and gives vent to blasphemous utterance.

There is also the view that the author is dealing with the problem of suffering, especially innocent suffering, and its meaning. This is nearer the point. The reader is told in the prologue that Job was an innocent man and that this innocent man was smitten with a dread physical disease. How is this seeming injustice to be explained? In the body of the poem the friends move around this question. They attempt to answer it out of their own traditional belief in a God who rewards or punishes according to one's moral deserts. They assert that, in face of the majesty of this "tit-for-tat" God, Job must simply resign himself to the calamities that have befallen him.

But is this all the author of Job intends to say? Not if the Job of the poem himself, rather than the friends, speaks for the author. The question raised by this Job is both broader and deeper than the question of how to account for the infliction of physical suffering on the innocent. His physical predicament has become merely the outward symbol of an intense inward agony. It is the agony of all humanity in those tortured hours when they feel themselves the victims of a meaningless and evil universe, when faith is swallowed up in the abyss of doubt and God seems to have vanished.

The anguished Job speaks the language of those whose complacency has been shattered by staggering events that reason cannot grasp: "What kind of God is this who hides from me?" "Let me but meet God face to face that I may justify myself." What is at stake for Job—and for the author—is the twofold question of the justice of God and the justice and honor of a person before God.

Job's longing to recover his justification before God—which he thinks has been lost—finally finds its answer in his direct encounter with the Most High God of the whirlwind. Before this God Job is silenced. He has not one plea or claim left; he has no longer any merit of his own. He has found the God *who is God,* who is higher than all human reckoning, who can only be adored, and in whose presence one is fit only to repent. Through his repentance Job's estrangement from God and the world is ended. He is restored; he has become a "new person."

So the basic theme of Job is the possibility of finding the sovereign God amid the whirlwind of despair, anxiety, and desolation. The book is peculiarly relevant to our own age. The hero is an angry man, an insubordinate campaigner against conventional doctrine. In the darkness of his night of agony Job protests, with Promethean arrogance, against heaven. He cannot endure the consolations of his friends, with their glib utterances about a God who metes out justice, reward, and punishment by human rather than divine standards. Indeed, he violently rejects them. Vanished for him is the little God whose only role in the world is thought to be that of guarding our inferior ethical judgments and adjusting our human grievances.

Job is living in that awful period between the demise of the old gods of formal religion and the coming of that other God who is higher than all human systems and deeper than all human anguish. Only at last, in the pit of despair, is Job given his reply. The answer he receives is not an all-embracing philosophical solution to his torment of soul. Rather, it is an experience, a direct confrontation with the sovereign God. In this presence Job's self-righteousness and pride are broken, so that he is now given a new power of being and a new self.

In our own day, we too, like Job, are living precariously between the times. We have lost the support of the old gods of culture, history, and progress. No God created in a human image can satisfy our hunger. No version of religion that equates it simply with human wishes and ambitions or with the cult of individual happiness and success can meet our need. Job speaks to our situation because it speaks of the God who is found, through the night of doubt and sorrow, at the center of the storm.

I. The Prologue (1:1–2:13)

1:1-5. ***The Righteous and Prosperous Job.*** The opening is in true folk-story style: **There was a man in the land of Uz.** Uz probably lay in the desert **east** of Palestine and northeast of Edom. The author, though a Jew, has given his work a foreign setting. That is fitting. The problems Job faces transcend national boundaries. Job, the sheik of Uz, is depicted in his heyday. He is sustained by an enlightened moral conscience and by religious faith. He is rich in his possessions and blessed in his family. No father is more devoted to his children. When they feast together in celebration of a birthday, Job—fearful of some irreverent conduct on their part—**continually** makes sacrifices to God on their behalf. The curtain rises then on an idyllic scene—Job in the day of his affluence and faithfulness. Set against this, how stark are the tragedies that are to invade his life!

1:6-12. ***Conspiracy in Heaven.*** The scene now shifts suddenly from earth to heaven. The **sons of God** are the "angelic beings." Here they are assembled before the divine Presence. **Satan**—literally "the Adversary"—has slipped in among them. Here Satan stands on the side of the servants of God and plays the part of prosecuting attorney for the heavenly court. But the reader can hardly avoid picturing Satan as the fiendish "devil" of later centuries. Sensing the challenge in God's inquiry about the **blameless** Job, Satan retorts that Job would not be the good and pious man he is if there were no profit in it. So Satan is commissioned to strike down **all that he has.**

1:13-22. ***The Testing of Job.*** A grim series of disasters hammers Job's prosperity into the dust. All his wealth, his flocks, and his servants are destroyed. The **fire of God**—that is, lightning—falls upon his sheep. Marauders come miraculously at Satan's command—**Sabeans** from Sheba in the south and **Chaldeans** from Babylonia in the east. But even the crowning blow—the death of all his children—leaves Job's faith in his God unshaken. When Job speaks about returning **naked,** he means to the earth, which is the common **womb** of all people. Job's superb refusal to relinquish his faith has become a rallying call for countless people in days of catastrophe.

2:1-13. ***Further Testing.*** Job's initial victory is followed by a repetition of the opening scene in heaven. God points out that Job has so far remained steadfast. Satan's reply, **Skin for skin!** is usually taken to refer to bargaining or exchange. More likely it is a very terse popular proverb meaning that "the heart of a man is enclosed by skin after skin." Satan is therefore saying that if Job's fidelity is to be taken away, every protection he has must be penetrated and access gained to his inmost soul.

So the new strategy afflicts Job himself with a dreadful illness. He is brought near to death, for the fact that he sits **among the ashes** is a mark of mourning. Yet, despite his wife's entreaty, he will not renounce his faith. Finally his **three friends** arrive from neighboring desert tribes. They have heard of his misfortune and come to **comfort him** and to mourn with him. **Seven days** was the time appointed for mourning.

Though there are discrepancies between them (see Introduction) the indroductory folk story perpares us for the poem to come in two ways:

(1) It connects God with Job's agony. Though the Job of the poem is unaware of what has occurred in the heavenly court, the reader knows, and this intensifies Job's predicament.

(2) It shows us a man who has reached the last limits of human endurance and who yet remains secure in his faith in God. Just when the prologue has prompted us to ask whether this faith of Job's can last forever, we are shocked by his discordant outcry in chapter 3.

II. The First Round of Speeches (3:1–11:20)

3:1-26. *The Flint in Job's Heart.* The Job of the poem first speaks in a mood vastly different from the pious utterances of the prologue. The flint has struck into his soul. He curses his life in the way we frequently do in our darkest hours: "I wish I had never been born!"

3:4-10. From the shelter of his former God-protected life Job has now passed into the depths of apparent abandonment by God. His once peaceful and ordered existence has become a chaos, and he summons the powers of chaos to join him in his cursing. **Leviathan** was the primeval serpent monster of the sea, a symbol of confusion. Job is probably conjuring up the notion of the war of the forces of **darkness** and disorder against the God of heaven and light—or the notion of the return of chaos.

3:11-19. Job's life has become a terrifying and meaningless void. He would prefer the ghostly existence of the departed shades in the underworld of Sheol, where death is the great leveler.

3:20-26. Verses 20-22 revert to the question of verse 11: **Why did I not die at birth?** In his agony of body and soul Job feels trapped—as one **whom God has hedged in.** His first tentative charge against God's justice is implicit in verse 23. This will subsequently become a raging storm of protest.

Verse 24 should probably be translated "moans are served as my food and groans poured out as my drink."

4:1–5:27. ***Eliphaz' Reply.*** The seven days and nights of silent mourning observed by the three friends (2:13) are now ended. Eliphaz feels constrained to reply to Job's outburst.

The author makes little attempt to develop the character of any of the three friends as individuals. They appear simply as special pleaders, each coming to court with already fixed ideas and set speeches. There is hardly any interchange of ideas, nor do the speakers really pick up the threads of conversation from one to the other. Within each speech there is a good deal of detail not strictly relevant to the main issue. The speeches are in fact mostly composite. They are made up of separate or loosely connected units and lack any rationally developed argument. The author's method is to use the word images of the friends as so many windows. Through these we may look at the chief problem raised by Job—and at the end come to understand it better.

4:1-11. Eliphaz' first speech illustrates a number of these points. He offers for consideration several largely unrelated propositions. First he reminds Job that a man of faith and uprightness, who has once been a tower of strength to the **weak,** should be the last person to succumb to despair. In verses 7-8 he states the philosophy that the righteous retain their prosperity in this life while the wicked are brought down to ruin **by the breath of God.** Eliphaz thus insists that history makes sense and that the universe is ruled by God on moral lines (cf. 5:13; 8:3, 20). Verses 10-11 apparently portray the breaking up of a den of **lions.** They are usually understood to refer to the sudden downfall of the wicked.

4:12-21. Verses 12-17 purport to be Eliphaz' account of his ecstatic visionary encounter with God in the waking hours **of the night.** The question put by the divine visitor makes clear that no **mortal man** can make a convincing case for his own righteousness **before God.** But this really contradicts the whole viewpoint of Eliphaz in the remainder of his speech. Eliphaz is arguing that the good person *is* just in the sight of God and will as surely be rewarded for righteousness as the guilty will be punished. Throughout the dialogue it is not the friends but Job himself who is apprehensive that he will never be able to convince God of his righteousness.

Probably, therefore, the night vision was originally related by Job (cf. 7:14, where he speaks of being "scared by dreams"). If so, verses 18-21 should also be taken as Job's words. He is saying that humans have little chance to persuade God of their merits when God will not recognize those even of his **angels,** the heavenly attendants. Certainly verses 12-21 accord more with Job's situation and philosophy than with the friends'.

5:1. If the night vision of the **spirit** or **form** of God (4:15-16) was told by Job, then this is Eliphaz' jeer at one who claims to have visits from supernatural beings.

5:2-27. Eliphaz now presents a series of pictures. The theme is the reward of the good and the ruin of the evil. One who murmurs against one's lot comes at last to a sorry end and suffers dire calamities. For example, **his sons . . . are crushed in the gate**—the city gate being the place where justice was administered. God is portrayed as the great adjuster (verses 8-16), who dispenses a retributive justice. Eliphaz then seems to address Job more directly in verses 17-27. He is saying that if Job will accept his affliction as a merited divine **chastening,** he can yet win the favor of God and enjoy a life of peace and plenty. The **stones** will not accumulate to spoil his fields nor the wild **beasts** raid his farm. But the promise of a long and happy life if only he will acknowledge his guilt before God can only outrage Job. He now believes that the processes of divine justice have miscarried in his case.

6:1–7:21. *Job's Alienation.* There is a greater progression of thought in the speeches of Job than in those of the friends. In his first speech there was the hint that his desire for death was a charge against God and God's justice. Now in this long second speech his words become increasingly bitter and irreverent.

They convey with gripping realism the horror of his journey into the twilight zone of human existence. Job's tragic situation is one not only of physical suffering but of complete disruption of his existence. He is cut off from his friends. They do not understand him (6:24-27). He has become—for no reason he can discover—the victim rather than the favorite of heaven (6:4; 7:20).

6:1-7. The vehemence of his words, Job claims, matches the awful severity of his sufferings. His outcry is against God as the grand inquisitor who tortures him. It is an instinctive reaction, as natural as the protest of animals against an unaccustomed diet or the complaint against insipid and repulsive food.

6:8-13. These verses reveal the nature of Job's struggle with God. He still accepts the reality of **the Holy One.** He cannot admit that he has broken the old relationship by any sin. But at the same time he knows God now as his crushing enemy, who is pushing him beyond all human capacity to bear pain.

6:14-23. Job has to wage this struggle with God in awesome loneliness. These verses convey the dereliction of one estranged completely from his friends. He has never asked from them any gifts or benefits (verses 22-23). But he has had every reason to expect their sympathy, and they are a bitter disappointment to him. He compares them to a wadi—a stream that runs full in winter but in summer, when the thirsty traveler's need is greatest, has not a drop of water to offer.

6:24-30. Job asks that the friends regard him not according to his **words,** which are born of despair and are no true index of his normal state (verses 25-26). Instead they should regard his life, which is innocent and free from error (verse 24). There is nothing in it, so far as he is able to **discern,** to justify the disasters that have come to him.

7:1-10. Job speaks for all disillusioned people. He protests vehemently how empty life is, and how puny is one's standing before God. He contrasts himself with the laborer who waits longingly for the evening to get some rest and receive his **wages** for the day. All that Job has got for waiting is sleepless nights that remind him of the hopelessness of life and the near approach of death (verses 1-6). He therefore looks on death as the grim underscoring of life's futility (verses 7-10).

7:11-21. These verses are important for understanding what is at issue for Job in his struggle. His anguish of soul arises, not from feeling Godforsaken, but from being God-haunted. He cannot understand why the all-powerful God does not mercifully overlook frail **man**—why instead he maintains a close watch over him and lies in wait to **test him. Why will he not let me alone till I swallow my spittle?** Verses 17-18 are a bitterly ironical reminiscence of Psalm 8. The psalmist rejoices over the gracious care of God the friend. Job bewails the inescapable care of God the enemy. The question posed in chapter 7 is the question of how God deals with a person—or the question of human existence before God.

8:1-22. *Bildad's Reply.* Bildad is indignant at Job's violent complaints against God. He enters the lists as champion of the **justice** of God. For Bildad there is no problem. People's destinies are measured by God exactly according to their merits; the good fare well, the wicked ill. After the storm of Job's speech, Bildad's utterance is like a great calm. The simplicity of his words reveals the simplicity of his theology. Those who suffer must have sinned; those who sin receive their due reward. As an advocate of this simple orthodox philosophy Bildad appeals to the tradition of the ancients to support his view (verses 8-10).

9:1–10:22. *Job's Contention with God.* Job does not take up in detail any of the points made by the friends. He has already shown that he has encountered God as an enemy. Nevertheless he seeks to communicate with God and is clearly thinking of engaging God in a legal contest (9:3, 15-16, 19-20, 32-33). Job clearly feels that in such a lawsuit he will not stand a chance (9:15-20). But he still wishes to bring God into court and face God there (10:2).

9:1-12. The friends have offered the picture of a God who unfailingly rewards the righteous and punishes the guilty. Job now sees that they are really scaling God down to human size by making God dispense justice according to their own concept of morality. Over against the too-small God of the friends, the God whom Job describes here is an absolute Lord, whose deeds cannot be controlled by any human reason. So Job appeals to God's irresistible might in initiating natural calamities (verses 5-7) and in creating and controlling the heavenly constellations (verses 8-10). Before God's fearful workings in nature a human being is helpless.

9:13-31. But the main question Job has to face is whether his suffering is God's verdict of guilt. He simply will not allow himself to be declared guilty in this way (verses 15, 20, 21; cf. 10:2, 7). He defends his own integrity and innocence. Job is pointing to himself as a good man who has suffered affliction. Thus he is demolishing the friends' notion that God deals with humanity in terms of a retributive justice. The God of whom and to whom Job speaks here has the incomparable freedom to root justice wherever he pleases. He has vanquished even the chaos dragon of the sea (here called **Rahab**; see above on 3:1-26) and her retinue of deities. How could Job ever hope to stand before this God in a legal contest?

9:32-35. Newly aware of the awful gap between himself and God, Job feels the need for an **umpire**—an arbiter or referee who might listen to the complaints of both sides. Verses 32-33 may be taken as expressing his longing for an intermediary between the inaccessible God and the person who feels the need to communicate with God. But his plight is that he knows there can be no arbiter. The absolute God is so powerful that God determines cases and is always in the right.

10:1-2. Even so Job refuses to be silent. Life has so little left to offer him that he may as well speak out. The whole of the speech which is introduced by **I will say to God** tells us what Job would say to God if there were any opportunity. We are to picture Job, in his fevered imagination, picturing himself in a face-on encounter with God in the law court. It is as if a jilted lover, fancying himself in his beloved's presence, were seeking her explanations of her quarrel with him.

10:3-7. These verses are somewhat disjointed and difficult to interpret. Job's rhetorical question in verse 5 implies a hypothetical shortness of God's life. But this is hardly a probable reason for the pursuit of God's quarrel with Job in verse 6. Some have understood God's being short-lived in the sense of his being limited in experience, but that is a forced interpretation. Possibly, therefore, in the process of editing verse 5 has been misplaced from its proper context alongside verses 20-22. Verse 4 connects well vith verse 6: **Dost thou see as man sees . . . that thou dost seek out my iniquity?**

10:8-22. Job goes on to charge God with fickleness toward God's creature. Why should God bestow such lavish care on bringing Job to birth and yet be intent to brand him as guilty and convict him of sin? Why should God become his terrible enemy and hunt him like a wild beast? Why should the God who gave him birth not leave him alone at least to go down to the grave in peace?

Knowing that there is no umpire between God and himself (9:33), Job's only option is to confront directly his opponent. The poignant questions he puts to God arise from his yearning to understand the secrets of God's dealings with him. They express the perennial human need for a mediator with God. It is instructive to contrast Job's portrayal of God as the great enemy, who chases us endlessly for a verdict of guilty against God, with Francis Thompson's poem "The Hound of Heaven." There, from the standpoint of Christian faith, God appears as the great lover, pursuing sinful humanity forever with God's mercy.

11:1-20. *Zophar's Cold Comfort.* Angered by Job's long-winded speech, Zophar takes him to task. Like Bildad, Zophar is one of those who must have neat, practical, and easily understood explanations for life's problems. Job's claim to be innocent, as Zophar thinks, is without foundation. Job cannot measure his innocence or guilt, for a human has no access to **wisdom,** the place of which is known only to God (verses 4-6). In verse 6*a* Zophar says in effect that if Job but knew it—if he could but stand on God's side—he would realize that he has in fact got off much more lightly than he deserves. We can guess what the reaction of a person in Job's position would be.

11:7-12. In this series of questions Zophar is reminding Job that God's ways are inscrutable. Therefore he must simply accept what has come to him without blasting the gates of heaven as he is doing. Verse 12 is difficult to translate. The meaning may be that the stupidity of a man like Job has as much chance of being remedied as a **wild ass's colt** has of being **born a man.** By a slight change in the Hebrew text, however, we get another translation: "And man is an offspring which a donkey produces; an ass begets a man." The verse would then be a harsh verdict on human ignorance (the ass being the symbol of ignorance) in contrast with God's omniscience. Clearly this verse is an old proverb. It's original form and meaning are not now easy to recover.

11:13-20. Zophar addresses a nice little sermon to Job. Here is the friends' favorite theme of God's treatment of the righteous and the wicked. The wicked perish without **hope.** However, if Job will only rid his household of all **iniquity,** then he will enjoy a new day of security and blessedness. But the promise of a "better day coming if you're good" is cold comfort indeed to a man in desperate torment of body and soul. The medicine of forgetfulness offered by Zophar (verse 16) can only sharpen the anguish of one who has lost all his children, his property, his health.

There is a radical inconsistency in Zophar's whole speech. But this never dawns on him. He is too sure of his own belief in the divine distribution of rewards and punishments according to one's deserts. He insists that neither Job nor any person can understand the ways of God (verses 4-12). Yet at the same time he goes on to make his own fairly rigid mathematical calculations about how God dispenses justice (verses 13-20). So it becomes clear that Job, in his agony, is pressing toward a more adequate view of God's ways than the friends seem to possess.

III. The Second Round of Speeches (12:1–20:29)

12:1–14:22. ***Job's Plea for Life.*** With biting sarcasm Job asks whether his friends think they are the whole **people** and so have a monopoly of all **wisdom.** He then pours cold water on their intellectual arrogance by reminding them that their ideas are merely part of the common stock of human knowledge. In chapter 12 Job is not expressing any fresh thought or any new presentation of his case before God. Rather he is echoing the views and opinions expressed by the friends.

12:4-25. The text of verses 4-6 is so disordered that it is almost impossible to achieve a translation that makes sense. A number of indications—for example, the use of Yahweh in verse 9*b*—suggest that verses 7-12 may be an interpolation. Verses 13-25, however, clearly show that in this early part of Job's third speech he is alluding to the views of the friends rather than developing his own thought. In verse 13 he makes a concession to the friends' opinion that **wisdom and might** belong only to God. Then he proceeds to make his own ironic summary and extension of some of the friends' arguments. "You tell me God is wise and mighty," Job appears to be saying; "I will show you just how mighty." Then in a sequence of graphic images he describes how God intervenes indiscriminately and destructively in history, swiftly and unexpectedly changing the normal course of things.

13:1-19. But talk of God's irresistible might is irrelevant to the **case** Job wants to **argue** with **the Almighty.** Indeed the friends have been no better than quack doctors (**worthless physicians**). Job is convinced that his contest with God is unequal enough without his so-called friends' taking up arms on God's side (verses 5-12). He entreats them to be silent so that he may, at whatever cost, further state his case against God (verses 13-15). He dares to go on only because he believes that his very readiness to confront God is the sign of his innocence and the pledge of his ultimate victory (verses 16-19).

13:20-28. Job is back once again in the law court with God, so to speak, and addresses God directly. He asks only that his case be decided in a fair and legal way—not by the arbitrary divine power which holds him prisoner (verse 27).

14:1-12. This book is marked by swift changes of mood and feeling. Throughout the dialogue with the friends Job both rails against and presses on toward God. He both utters fiery protests against God's ordering of life and holds on to the lingering hope that justice will prevail (cf. 6:2; 13:18). So within this chapter he seems to waver between despair and hope. His lament over the dreadful futility that overshadows human life recalls the cynicism of the Preacher's cry "All is vanity" (Ecclesiastes 1:2). Job's entreaty for a brief snatch of happiness before death arises from his certainty of the finality of death. This present life can never be restored beyond death. A human being is not like a **tree,** able to regenerate life from the wasted **stump** of a dead body.

14:13-22. But then suddenly into the darkness of his brooding pessimism there breaks the light of a new expectation (verses 13-15). There comes the hope of a personal reconciliation with God, in the end, beyond death. Job asks for life, the real life of unbroken communion with God instead of the death of alienation from God. He is willing to be hidden in **Sheol** (see above on 3:11-19) for ages—if only he can be sure of a **time** appointed for the end of God's wrath and the granting of mercy. However, Job's dream of future restoration is immediately abandoned. He turns in a moment to bemoan the sure and steady decay of human hopes.

15:1-35. ***Eliphaz' Hardening Toward Job.*** The gently persuasive tone of Eliphaz' first speech now gives way to caustic criticism. Job is accused of consummate arrogance (verses 7-8). He has become the foe of true religion by his blasphemous talk (verses 4-6). He claims to possess an innocence before God which not even God's angels have (verses 14-16).

15:17-19. Accordingly Eliphaz tries to "convert" Job by frightening him with a terrifying picture of the fate of the wicked. As is usual with the friends, Eliphaz first appeals to the wisdom of the ancients for corroboration. In verse 19 he may be alluding, in good Arab fashion, simply to the earliest and purest days of his own tribe of Teman. But the Hebrew of this verse allows us to take it together with verses 17-18, in another way: "I will declare what wise men have told, and their fathers have not hidden: 'To them alone the land is given, and no stranger passes among them.' " Verse 19 then becomes the quotation of an old saying about the prosperity of the righteous, who may dwell peacefully in the land without any strangers or enemies to disturb them.

15:20-24. Eliphaz now tells Job that while on the surface the **wicked** may appear to prosper, they are in reality troubled in their inward life and haunted by the thought of their impending doom. Eliphaz' argument here is of course a weak one—just as weak as the argument that the wicked always suffer and the righteous always prosper in this life. As we know, many of the arch evildoers in the history of our twentieth century have by no means been plagued with remorse or conscience.

15:25-28. As if to strike further terror into Job's heart, Eliphaz confronts him with a picture of wickedness on a monstrous scale. The images of these verses may be taken as metaphorical descriptions of the rampant evil of the godless person (verses 25-26). Such a one is insolent in pride (verse 27; **fat** is often a symbol of arrogance in the Old Testament), at home amid ruin and devastation (verse 28). On the other hand Eliphaz may here be describing some mythological king, taking up arms against God (verses 25-26), smearing himself with grease to swim the sea (verse 27), making his quarters in ruined cities (verse 28).

15:29-35. After this picture of evil Eliphaz returns to the customary theme of the friends—the impermanence of the wicked.

16:1–17:16. *Job at His Tether's End.* Job rejects the futile consolations of his friends. Indeed he is outraged by them (16:1-5). Now he reaches an unsurpassable dread of God. Here the God of Job's experience is portrayed as a demon-God who has **gnashed his teeth** at Job and **sharpens his eyes** over him—the Septuagint speaks of "eye-daggers." God has become his devilish enemy, setting him up as a **target** for practice. He is staggered at the incompatibility between his own innocence (16:16-17) and the fiendish persecutions of this devil-God. Job has now apparently sunk down into an abyss of complete estrangement from the God he once knew as friend.

16:18-21. The tension of Job's struggle is nowhere more clear than when he implores the **earth** not to let his **blood** trickle away, that his **cry** may not come to rest. The ancients believed that blood which soaked into the ground became silent. If it lay on a rocky place unabsorbed, it cried out to heaven perpetually for vengeance. In appealing to God as the avenger of blood, Job is therefore harking back to the very old idea that God is the owner of all life. Wherever life is threatened or taken by violence, God must concern himself with it—as when the blood of Abel calls to God (Genesis 4:10).

From this Job suddenly comes to the startling confidence that he has after all a **witness . . . in heaven.** In chapter 16 Job is thus appealing *to* God *against* God—to the God whom, even at the last limit of his rebelliousness, he still can recognize as friend against the God who, in the bitterness of his experience, has become his foe.

Other explanations of these verses are possible. But they are obscure, largely because of textual difficulties. We cannot base on them, as some interpreters have done, the notion that Job is here expressing the hope that in a life beyond death he will come to know a heavenly Redeemer.

16:22–17:16. In the remainder of his speech Job returns to a mood of extreme pessimism. The whole passage presents us with many complex textual problems. For example, the meaning of 17:3-5 is most uncertain, especially verse 5. This has received widely different interpretations. One commentator translates: "To flattery he said: 'Friends!'—and the eyes of his children failed." He takes it to refer to the ancient fable of the fox who by flattery cajoles a pair of birds into trusting him and thus giving him a chance to kill their young. Job's mocking friends are like the fox. Others understand the verse to be a proverb by which the friends are compared to a man who invites guests to share his goods while "the eyes of his children languish"—that is, while they are starving.

Aside from textual difficulties, some sections of chapter 17 have obviously been displaced. Verses 8-9, for example, seem to be out of place on Job's lips and would be much more typical of the friends.

However, we can gather with some assurance that, in his estrangement from God, Job feels himself also alienated from time. He is severed from his **past.** He knows no future—**Where then is my hope?** Without any past and without future, with only a seemingly meaningless present, Job has in fact suffered the same shattering of existence as many of the displaced persons of our time.

18:1-21. ***Bildad's Description of the Wrongdoer's Downfall.*** Bildad begins by taunting Job about his interminable talk (verse 2). Job has treated the friends as dolts, when all the time he himself is like the angry fool who destroys himself in his wrath (verses 3-4*a*; cf. 5:2-5). Apparently he wants God to change the natural order of things just for his sake (verse 4*bc*). What Bildad implies here is that the law of suffering as the result and proof of sin is inexorable. No exception can possibly be made in Job's case.

18:5-21. For the rest Bildad confines himself to a gloomy account of the fate of the wicked. They are harried by all manner of adversity during life (verses 5-13). They disappear completely in death without remembrance or posterity (verses 14-21).

18:15*b*. The **brimstone** may refer to the sulphur **scattered** as a disinfectant on the house of the wicked man smitten with leprosy (verse 13). The ancients were well acquainted with the curative properties of sulphur. More probably this line depicts destruction of a house through brimstone falling on it from heaven. This would be a mark of the curse of God and recalls the story of the destruction of Sodom and Gomorrah (Genesis 19:24). Indeed throughout Bildad's whole description of the fearful destiny of the wicked there may well be features drawn from some old story of wicked primeval people destroyed by God in punishment for their sin.

19:1-29. ***Job's Fleeting Moment of Trust.*** Job suggests that by their supposed consolations the friends are only shattering him the more. They have repeatedly construed his suffering as God's just punishment on his wickedness (verses 3-5). Job himself is still convinced that God is in fact perverting justice and is waging cruel war against him (verses 6-12).

19:13-22. Alienated from God and from time, Job now reveals his alienation from his fellow humans. He is filled with that eerie feeling which calamity often brings of not belonging. His account of his abandonment by the whole human community ends in a vain plea for his friends' pity.

19:23-29. Job begs that his words be **graven in the rock for ever** and declares **I know that my Redeemer lives.** At this point we instinctively feel that Job has reached the climax of his struggle. Nowhere else do such solace and certainty seem to enfold him.

Christian interpreters have long seen here a positive belief in the resurrection of the body. In many editions of the King James Version we find over this chapter the heading "He believeth in the resurrection." Unfortunately, however, the Hebrew of verses 25*b*-26*a* is too obscure to draw any sure conclusion from it. In verse 26*b* the ambiguous phrase "from my flesh" can mean either "away from my flesh" (i.e. after death) or "from the vantage point of my flesh" (i.e. in this present life). Nor do verses 27-29 afford any help in determining the meaning of verses 25-26. The text is so corrupt that we can only conjecture what the original may have been. Accordingly we cannot infer from this passage that Job hoped for a resurrection of the body.

We have also been inclined to look at Job's assertion **my redeemer lives** from the standpoint of faith in Jesus Christ as Savior. But in order to grasp the real force of Job's words here we should compare them with other passages in which his ongoing struggle *against* God is at the same time a pressing on *to* God. Job momentarily expresses the wistful hope that through a heavenly friend justice will prevail for him, especially in 9:33 and 16:19.

The umpire for whom Job appeals in 9:33 is not to be connected with the Jewish Messiah nor taken as a prophetic signpost pointing to Jesus Christ. Rather there probably lies behind Job's appeal for an umpire the ancient Sumerian idea of a personal god on whom humans relied to present their cause to the greater gods in the divine assembly. So also it is a mistake to see in the ally or witness of 16:19 or in the Redeemer of 19:25 the figure of Christ. In fact the word translated "Redeemer" is better rendered as "vindicator." The Hebrew word refers to the next of kin who has the duty of avenging the blood of a brother or protecting his title to property after his death. The role of the vindicator is to insure justice for his own kinsfolk, bound to him by ties of blood.

In this passage then, so far as we can be at all sure of the text, Job first insists on the strength of his case. Since the friends have shown no sympathy with his words, and God has made no response, he wishes his case to be preserved, as if engraved with **an iron pen** in the rock forever. And in the same instant, in a bright flash of expectancy, he believes that if only his case is fairly represented in the divine court his claims for justice must eventually be fulfilled and he himself vindicated.

For all the comfort to which Job has won through here, the matter is not ended yet. This assurance of ultimate justice is not the last word of the book. Job has still to discover that he is living in the fateful period between the twilight of the old God of formal moralism, who dispenses justice as we measure it and understand it, and the dawn of that other God who is higher than all human reckoning.

20:1-29. ***Zophar's Speech on the Fate of the Wicked.*** Zophar's opening speech is somewhat obscure. He appears to be expressing his inward agitation and frustration with Job. For the most part he concentrates on the thought that the success and prosperity of the wicked are short-lived. They are not given long to enjoy the fruits of their shameful labors (verses 6-11, 16, 20-21). In their earlier descriptions of the terrible fate of the wicked the friends have been concerned mainly with crimes against God. Zophar is concerned chiefly with crimes against society. His arrows are directed at the racketeer who thinks nothing of crushing the poor for profit (verse 19). But Job, like we of today, cannot derive much comfort from Zophar's view that the racketeer is doomed to get no pleasure from his stolen riches.

IV. THE THIRD ROUND OF SPEECHES (21:1–31:40)

21:1-34. *Job's Refutation of the Friends' Philosophy.* Job rejects the consolations of the friends and asserts his right to speak. Then he expresses his resentment and impatience that—contrary to the friends' philosophy of just divine retribution—the evildoers prosper in all their undertakings. In fact they enjoy a gay life despite their open defiance of God's commandments.

21:16-22. Two pious expressions have clearly been inserted into Job's speech (verses 16*b* and 22). These are out of context on his lips and can be traced rather to some devoutly orthodox editor or scribe. Aside from these pious intrusions, the rest of the chapter shows that Job has begun to reflect on the general injustices found in the world. He refutes the contention of the friends that a day of doom is always in store for the wicked (verses 17-18). He refuses to be taken in by the argument that even if the wicked seem to prosper now, **God stores up** calamity for their children or their homes after their death. **What do they care,** Job asks ironically, when they are dead?

21:23-33. In verses 23-26 Job is not so much complaining that the divine justice is unfairly distributed as bemoaning the emptiness and irrationality of all existence. Dusty death awaits all people, rich and poor. Then he maintains that anyone could tell the friends that, far from the homes of the wicked being invariably destroyed, they very often remain safe and secure (verses 27-31). He goes on to say that the wicked may even have a lovely funeral, a most honorable burial, and a pleasant last resting place.

21:34. In this chapter it becomes clear that the theme of the book cannot be restricted to the problem of human suffering. Grievously offended by the friends' belief that the wicked inevitably are punished—which is demonstrably untrue to the facts of experience—Job is obsessed with the question of justice. He has been just, but he has been unjustly treated.

22:1-30. *Eliphaz' Indictment.* Eliphaz reveals the shallowness of his theology. He maintains that it is of no profit to God whether people are good or bad. Only people themselves stand to gain from being righteous. So Eliphaz confronts Job with what seems to him to be an irrefutable logic: the righteous reap benefits, the wicked losses. Job is wicked and therefore a loser. Eliphaz brands Job as indeed a very antisocial man (verses 6-7, 9). But from all we learn elsewhere of Job's highly sensitive social conscience (for example, chapter 31) we can only suppose that Eliphaz is carried away by the logic of his theology—that a big loser must be a big sinner. He must conjure up out of his imagination the most dastardly crimes for Job.

22:8-20. Verse 8 can hardly be taken to mean that part of Job's crime against society has been to join forces with the powerful. This verse should probably be transferred to the end of verse 14 and be understood as part of Job's words cited by Eliphaz. Job holds, observes Eliphaz, that God is indifferent to human deeds (verses 13-14). One practical consequence of God's indifference is that the powerful lord it on the earth (verse 8). Eliphaz tries to counter Job's argument in the only way he knows: the proof of God's interest is that the good are automatically blessed with prosperity and the bad punished (verses 15-20).

22:21-30. Eliphaz apparently believes that Job still has some chance. He proceeds to preach him a neat little sermon on repentance and its fruits: "Turn, Job, humble yourself. Find all your riches in God and God will restore to you your old prosperity." But—as we discover from his next speech—what Job really wants is not the return of his old prosperity. He wants to engage in such conversation with God as would make genuine reconciliation possible.

23:1–24:25. ***Job's Quest for God.*** The friends have their God in their hand, so to speak. They presume to know exactly how God orders and measures the world's affairs. By contrast, in his anguish of spirit Job is awaiting the coming of a high and unknown God far above the small God of the friends: **Oh, that I knew where I might find him.** Job is thus among the number of those profounder souls of the Bible who wait for God to come toward them in a revelation (cf. Isaiah 45:15; Matthew 5:3-6; Luke 2:25, 38).

23:4-17. In his moment of waiting for that other God, Job almost thinks himself into God's presence (verse 4). In another of his outbursts of confidence, he asserts that if he could once get God's ear he would win acquittal (verses 5-7). But, as previously, his hope of being vindicated in a fair trial (verses 10-12) is quickly swallowed up in his continued terror in the presence of God—the unsearchable God of arbitrary and inflexible judgments (verses 8-9, 13-17).

24:1-25. In this chapter Job reverts to his theme of chapter 21: the wicked all too often get off scot-free. In the midst of his account of the various crimes of the wicked (verses 2-4*a*, 13-17) there comes a series of poignant pictures of the terrible plight to which the **poor** are reduced by their cruel persecutors (verses 4*b*-12). Verses 18-24 are, through textual corruption, quite obscure or ambiguous. Following the Revised Standard Version rendering we may take it that in verses 18-20 Job is quoting the friends' view that evildoers are quickly destroyed. Then he refutes this in verses 22-23. But that in verse 24 Job should immediately contradict himself by speaking of the transitoriness of the wicked seems impossible. This verse must be out of place.

25:1–27:23. ***The Dialogue Continued.*** This subject heading is vague. But the text of this final part of the third cycle of speeches is badly dislocated. We can only say that the dialogue is going on.

25:1–26:14. The six verses of chapter 25 are clearly only a fragment of Bildad's original speech. Chapter 26 is assigned to Job. But though the utterances about God's marvelous works in verses 5-14 could come from either Job or the friends, verses 2-4 present a problem. Only by interpreting them in a most unnatural way—as Job's ironical acknowledgment of the help he has received from Bildad's speech—can we attribute them to Job. It seems better to take verse 1 as an editorial insertion and think of chapter 26 as a continuation of Bildad's address in chapter 25.

Thus Bildad is sarcastically charging Job with scaling God down to such a pygmy size that Job, a mere human, can dare to instruct God. James Moffatt translates verse 2: "What a help you are to poor God! What a support to his failing powers!" Verses 2-4 then connect naturally with what follows in verses 5-14. After teasing Job about his presuming to help "poor God," Bildad chastens him with an account of the might and majesty of God in nature. **Abaddon** (26:6) is a poetic synonym for **Sheol** (see above on 3:11-19). On **Rahab** see above on 9:13-31.

27:1-23. In this chapter verses 2-6 do sound like another genuine cry from Job—**Till I die I will not put away my integrity from me.** But verses 7-23 once again express the philosophy of the friends that the wealth amassed by the wicked is taken away from them overnight. Perhaps they are the words of the missing Zophar, who does not appear at all for the third round of speeches. Some scholars accept the text as it is—that is, chapter 25 as Bildad's and the whole of chapters 26–27 as Job's. They suggest that the author has greatly abbreviated Bildad's speech and has left Zophar out in order to show that the friends are now running out of arguments. The suggestion is more ingenious than convincing.

28:1-28. *A Hymn of Praise to Wisdom.* Most scholars agree that this chapter is completely out of accord with its context. The frame of mind represented here is too tranquil and submissive to be Job's. In fact, we find him as rebellious as ever in his next speech (cf. 30:20-23). Moreover, if Job had already attained to his view of things, he would have reached his "conversion." There would be no need of the divine speeches in chapters 38–41, since Job would already have learned the lesson contained in them.

Though we must regard chapter 28 as an interpolation, we should certainly have been the poorer for not having it. It ranks with Proverbs 8 as one of the most magnificent poetical pieces in the whole range of wisdom literature. The author of the poem—whether the author of the book or some other writer—is clearly an expert in ancient mineralogy and mining (verses 2-11).

The poem draws a sharp contrast between the unlimited human genius for material achievement and our strictly limited understanding of the ways in which God orders the world. Thus it has a direct applicability to our own age. We have come to exult in our technological genius and in our ever-increasing mastery and control over the physical universe. But **wisdom** eludes us—that wisdom which consists in the **fear of the Lord** and empowers us **to depart from evil.** The poet reminds us that that wisdom is with God, and is always and only God's gift.

Assuming that this chapter is an interpolation, we have to ask why some editor should have inserted it at this point in the dialogue. Was there a reply by Job to Zophar's speech in 27:7-23 which he found so outrageous that he deleted it and substituted this poem? Or did he think of this as a suitable place in the dialogue for a pause for quiet reflection before God's direct confrontation of Job? A few scholars believe that the divine speech of chapters 38–41 is incomplete and affords no real solution to Job's problem. Accordingly they propose that chapter 28 is the true conclusion of God's address to Job and should follow chapter 41. But that is only a surmise, and a rather unlikely one.

29:1-25. ***Job's Remembrance of Happier Days.*** There is a deep pathos in Job's reminiscences of the days of his prosperity, when God looked on him with favor. He was then secure in the companionship of his family and the possession of his wealth, and was highly respected on every hand, even by the **princes** and **nobles** of the land. He championed the cause of the afflicted and outsmarted their oppressors. He dreamed hopeful dreams of a serene and peaceful end to his life. In verses 21-25 he returns to the theme of verses 7-11—the esteem in which he was once everywhere held. This prepares the way for the contrast he is about to make in chapter 30—the contempt now poured on him. It makes that contrast the more poignant.

30:1-31. ***The Contrast of His Present Misery.*** In the course of his speeches, as we have seen, Job takes up an abundance of themes, and often changes rapidly from one to the other. So in verses 1-15 it is not easy to grasp the real point of his long description of the rogues and vagabonds who, excommunicated from all normal society, live like animals in the wilderness (verses 3-8) and sally forth to attack him (verses 9-15). Perhaps we should take these verses as yet another indication of how acute is Job's sense of alienation not only from God but from people. He is despised now even by the meanest of them.

30:16-19. Job turns next to what most interpreters take to be an account of his own grievous bodily **affliction.** But the Hebrew of these verses, especially verse 18, is so confused that we can scarcely recover the original. The eminent Jewish scholar N. H. Tur-Sinai translates verse 18: "In my cloth he disguiseth himself as an attorney; as 'my mouth' he clotheth himself in my coat." Tur-Sinai thinks of a figure "disguised" as God's attorney, who in fact makes Job accuse himself.

30:20-31. With verses 20-23 we are on surer ground. Job once more addresses God directly. He charges God with deliberately turning a deaf ear to his pleas and making sport of him by tossing him around on the winds of suffering. In verses 24-31 Job defends his right to **cry** to God for **help.** Who, left pitilessly to bear the burden of his own suffering, would not moan or howl like **jackals** or **ostriches?**

31:1-40. ***Job's Final Challenge to God.*** This chapter is one of the most significant and moving in the whole book. Job issues his final challenge to God. This is not, as we might have expected from his previous outbursts, a last gigantic thrust of the battering-ram against the ramparts of heaven. Instead it is the more effective weapon of a quiet and sensitive defense of the honor and integrity of his own character and life. Job here utters his "negative confession"—so called because it resembles that found in the ancient Egyptian Book of the Dead—or his "oath of purgation." The chapter embodies a most exalted ethic. It highlights genuine obedience to God's demand rather than outward fulfillment of the prescriptions of a moral code or exercise of a formal piety diligent in prayers and sacrifices. In this respect indeed it is worthy to be set beside the Sermon on the Mount.

Job's stress throughout is on his own abiding concern for the welfare of others. He would not assault the honor of any woman (verse 1), least of all the honor of his **neighbor**'s wife. He has not refused to listen to the case of his servant, or closed his eyes to the needs of the **poor.** He would not make money his god nor secretly worship the **sun** and the **moon.** He has taken no joy in the downfall of his enemies. He has not been hypocritical nor impelled by **fear** of what the public might say. He has been honest and faithful in his dealings with his **land.**

Armed with this goodness that goes beyond the line of duty or any written code, Job is ready to approach God with head held high, **like a prince** rather than a worm (cf. 25:6). Here is the climax of Job's contention with God. By a majestic self-assertion he even lords it over God. Job's whole defense of his honor and integrity in fact implies his conviction that he has dealt more faithfully with *his* world than God has done with **God's** world.

Job's ultimate protest should really set the stage for God's reply. Chapter 38 follows most naturally immediately after this chapter. The continuity is broken, however. God's reply is held up for six chapters by the interruption of the long-winded Elihu.

V. Elihu's Speech (32:1–37:24)

Nearly all scholars are now agreed that the Elihu speech has been interpolated into the original poem of Job. Elihu is mentioned nowhere else in the book. In the rest of the dialogue the friends' speeches alternate with those of Job. Elihu stands out on his own and continues for six chapters without a break.

Most likely these chapters were composed by a later poet—one whose point of view was quite different from that of the original author. The editor felt the need to build a bridge between Job's challenge and God's response. It may be that the editor was dissatisfied with both the friends' efforts at countering Job (32:3, 5) and the terms of God's reply.

32:6–33:7. ***Elihu States His Right to Speak.*** Protocol has up to now imposed silence on Elihu. But now that the friends and Job are through, he seizes his chance to talk. The friends have apparently given in to Job's arguments as unanswerable (32:13). But Elihu will not. With irrepressible bombast he declares himself to be **full of words** and bursting to speak. He does not doubt that he has something new and relevant to contribute—something communicated directly to him from God and superior to the traditions of the past (32:8-10).

Job has asked for an umpire to mediate between God and himself (9:33). We may reasonably suppose that the author of this interpolation intends Elihu to fulfill some such role. Elihu is presented as a skilled interpreter of God's ways on the one hand (32:8-9), and on the other as sympathetic in his understanding of humanity. **Behold, no fear of me need terrify you.**

33:8-33. *God's Communication.* With his right to speak established, Elihu goes on to answer Job's assertion that God does not answer him (verses 12-13). He insists that God does have ways of communicating with us, even though we may not understand them—for example, by dreams or visions (verses 15-17) or by the discipline of suffering (verses 19-22). One of Elihu's most distinctive emphases is the disciplinary aspect of suffering. It is part of his defense of God's overall strategy in human affairs. Elihu is prepared to argue that in human suffering God is not absent but may be speaking most profoundly and effectively just there and then. He maintains that an **angel** of God may enable one even on the threshold of death to grasp the logic of God's ways. So a person may see in suffering the hand of God and God's call to that repentance which leads to the recovery of new life and health. Eventually the healed and forgiven penitent will sing songs of thanksgiving.

34:1-37. *God's Justice.* But the foundation of Elihu's whole argument is his exposition of the impartial justice of God, over against Job's complaint that God had **taken away** his **right.** God is no ordinary despot (verses 10-12). He is the one who deigns to govern the universe (verses 13-15). All his works are absolutely just, since in no way does he show regard to **human** pretensions (verses 16-28).

34:29-37. This is another of those sections where the text is so corrupt it is almost impossible to reconstruct it. For example, the Hebrew of verse 31 reads literally "For to God one says, 'I have carried; I will not act corruptly.' "

35:1-16. *God's Independence.* In chapter 9 Job argued that it is all the same whether one is righteous or wicked. The limitless power of God makes justice for human beings impossible. Elihu now inverts Job's argument. He asserts that the very fact which insures the impartiality of God's justice is God's majestic detachment from the world (chapters 35–37). God is higher than the **clouds.** God can be neither affected nor coerced by **wickedness** or **righteousness.** Our actions have consequences only for ourselves (verses 5-8). But our actions do have consequences, as Elihu seems to argue in the rest of this chapter (the text of verses 9-16 is once again confused). In human relationships there are both oppressors and victims of oppression. If the victims cry to God for help and are not answered, that is not so much a slur on God's justice as a sign that the victims—like Job—lack genuine religious feeling.

36:1-23. ***God's Revelation in Affliction.*** Elihu maintains that the storms of affliction blow on the **wicked** and **righteous** alike. Everything depends on the temper in which the suffering person receives affliction. Those who perceive God's **instruction** in their anguish are turned away from impending moral disaster. But if they do not hear the call of God within the urgency of pain itself, they separate themselves from God and become broken and defeated (verses 12-15). Job's great fault, declares Elihu, has been his inability or unwillingness to see past his struggle to the reality of God or to sense the meanings of God in his agony (verses 17-23).

36:24–37:24. ***God's Power.*** Elihu calls Job to turn and magnify the God whose works are ineffably great. His description of the irresistible force of storms and the grandeurs of the natural world anticipates the speech of God in chapters 38–41, where God describes the wonders of the cosmos. But there is significant difference. The speech of God simply sets forth the glories of nature in staggering array and leaves the hearer to draw his own conclusions. Elihu philosophizes and makes his own applications. For example, the **lightning** brings warning of God's judgment. God uses **clouds** either to reveal the flashing of anger or to dispense showers of blessing.

The author of the Elihu speech aimed to go deeper than the

friends in meeting Job's case. In a measure he succeeds. He is less naïve about God's retribution than the friends (35:3-16). He appeals to the human rational capacity for discerning in suffering the very hand of God. For him Job's error lies in his ignorance; he does not know how to decipher the communications from God in his agony (34:35-36). But the Elihu author's solution could never have satisfied the original author. In that author's view what Job is seeking is not a moralizing answer to the problem of his suffering. As a representative of all humanity, he seeks the recovery before God of that justification of himself which he feels has been lost.

VI. God's Confrontation of Job (38:1–42:6)

Originally, Job's challenge to God (31:35-37) must have been immediately followed by God's answer (see above on 31:1-40). The response of God, when it does come, issues from the **whirlwind,** the traditional accompaniment of God's appearances in the Old Testament. Job has complained about God's silence. God now breaks the silence and addresses Job—but not really on equal terms, for the divine voice is wrapped in the mystery of the storm's center. If anything, the unbridgeable distance between God and humanity is increased. Job, who wants to come before God like a prince (31:37), is dwarfed by the opening fusillade of God's questions.

38:2–41:34. ***God's Majesty and Mystery in Creation.*** As God's speech develops, it becomes clear that the divine voice is strangely noncommittal. God passes no verdict on Job as either innocent or guilty. Nor does God prescribe any medicine of salvation or immortality for him. Instead God simply overwhelms Job with infinite power. God describes this power. It is manifested first in majestic control of all natural phenomena: in measuring the earth at creation's dawning (38:4-7); in command over the chaos monster of the **sea** (see above on 3:4-10), **light** and **darkness,** and **snow** and **rain** and **ice;** in ordering of the movements of the constellations (38:31-33) and of the **clouds.**

38:39–39:30. The divine discourse has its own shape and form. The veil is lifted on one riddle of the cosmos and Job is challenged to penetrate it—only to find another more baffling riddle lying behind the first, waiting to stretch his comprehension and imagination to the utmost. From the marvels of earth and sky Job is drawn on to contemplate the marvels of the animal creation—the **lion, raven, mountain goats, wild ass, wild ox, ostrich** hen, **horse, hawk,** and mountain **eagle.** All these creatures are beyond human ken but within the universal scope of God's providential care (cf. Psalms 104; 145:16).

40:15–41:34. Two other marvels of the animal creation are described at length in terms partly realistic and partly mythological. **Behemoth** seems to be the hippopotamus—known in the Nile but not the **Jordan. Leviathan** is apparently the crocodile (see above on 3:4-10). Many scholars believe part or all of these two descriptions to be a later addition to the book.

The first instinct of the modern reader is to wonder what kind of sublime irrelevance all this is. And perhaps our first inclination is to "Christianize" the conclusion of Job. Such interpretations of the book have tended to translate the Christian's saving experience of the grace of God in the cross of Jesus Christ into Job's situation. We would have Job too, through the divine encounter, become the recipient of God's grace and love. But this would transgress the proper limits of the book by moving it some centuries ahead of its own true time and place.

We have in fact to acknowledge that the whole of the divine speech betrays nothing of God's loving concern for humans or of the possibility of restoration. The "solution" of Job's plight seems to consist only in God's finally stretching out before him the canvas of the incomprehensible cosmos. If such a solution seems inadequate to the present-day reader, we must remember that the theology of the author moves within the same orbit as that of the wisdom literature generally. Wisdom theology expressed itself in utterances about the greatness of God in creation.

There is, however, a more positive—if yet not Christian—

side of the divine discourse. Job's yearning to be confronted with God is answered. God does speak to him. The questions are harsh and intimidating, but they are demands for a response. God's recognition of Job's freedom to respond is at the same time an acknowledgment of his responsibility. The dignity of his being is thus respected by God; he counts enough to be approached and questioned.

More than that, the God who questions him is the one whose face is turned in concern toward the whole of creation. This is implicit in the picture of God's limitless power over the works of nature. From God's just governance of all creatures there may also be inferred justice toward the greatest of God's handiworks—the human person. Of course we cannot comprehend this overarching universal justice of God. We can only adore it, like the morning stars which sang together when God laid the foundation of the earth (38:7).

42:1-6. *Job's Response.* The divine discourse has offered nothing to support Job's faith that human righteousness would be vindicated in the end. Instead its import has been that the measurements of the Creator are not those of God's creature. God is not the custodian of our human systems or the guardian of our inferior ethical judgments.

Before the God of the whirlwind the friends' little God of retributive justice has been reduced to what he really is—an idol we have made to adjust life's inequalities and to administer justice as we understand it. Before the God of the whirlwind Job's hopes of a vindicator have been dashed. The insistent defender of his own self-righteousness is crushed by the conviction of his own creaturely finitude. Before this Most High God he has no claim left, no merit of his own. He has found the God before whom all conditioned questions and complaints and pretensions disappear. In confrontation with this God he can only **repent in dust and ashes.**

42:3-4. In two lines of this final brief speech Job uses almost the very words with which God first questioned him out of the whirlwind (verses 3*a*, 4*b*; cf. 38:2, 3*b*). Conceivably Job repeats the opening question which God addressed to him as if to admit the rebuke implied in it—"Yes, I have hidden counsel without knowledge." Conceivably he cites the challenge to **declare** the answers to God's questions before confessing his inability to meet it. But the intrusion of these short segments mars the poetic structure here. It is more probable that some scribe wrote them down as marginal comments beside Job's own final words and they were incorporated into the text by a later copyist.

42:5-6. Unfortunately the last two lines of Job's recantation, **Therefore I despise myself, and repent in dust and ashes,** are of very uncertain translation. It is not impossible to take the words in a quite different way: "Therefore, though I am melting away, I am comforted in regard to dust and ashes." Perhaps the best translation is: "Therefore I abhor and repudiate [all my words, sitting] on dust and ashes" (on ashes as a sign of grief and mourning see above on 2:1-13).

However, the general sense of Job's confession and submission is not in doubt. It is well summed up in the quite unambiguous verse 5: **I had heard of thee by the hearing of the ear, but now my eye sees thee.** In the outcome, through the dark night of anxiety and despair, Job has encountered the answer to his predicament. The answer Job finds is no theoretical or philosophical or moralistic solution to his problem, but an experience. The vision spoken of is not, of course, the actual sight of any form or appearance of God. Job could not "see" the God shrouded in the mystery of the storm's center. What is meant is that for him hearsay has now been transformed into firsthand personal confrontation. He has confronted the God who, on the last frontier of Job's existence, bestows on him a new power in a new way.

VII. The Epilogue: Job's Recovery of Self (42:7-17)

The majority of interpreters hold that the prose narrative of the epilogue, which belongs to the same folk-tale world as the prologue, cannot have been part of the original book and in fact ruins its unity. They claim that its fairy-story ending, with all living happily ever after, flagrantly contradicts the message the author intended to convey—his condemnation of the friends' theory of divine reward and punishment. There is moreover, a radical inconsistency. In the divine speech climaxing the poem Job is condemned, but in the epilogue he is praised (verse 7).

But this view that the prose epilogue is not an integral part of the original work may be questioned first on literary grounds. We may account for any inconsistency by the assumption that in adopting the old folk tale as the framework for his own composition the author was working with prefabricated materials which he did not feel free to alter too extensively.

The majority view may also be questioned on thematic or theological grounds. The hard reality of Job's plight has been his alienation. Alienated from his family, from his friends, from time, from God, Job's anguish is the anguish of the dissolution of his existence, the anguish of self-estrangement. When Job's tragedy is understood thus, the epilogue can be construed as a meaningful conclusion to his encounter with the Absolute Being of the whirlwind.

The epilogue may be taken as symbolizing Job's recovery of his own true existence through his meeting with this transcendent Being. His family is restored. The people and things from which he was alienated are returned to him. Time is no longer excruciatingly out of joint for him, for he lives happily for many years. The dislocation of his existence is healed. Before God he has become a whole man once more. He has recovered his own being through his experience of Being.

Among Old Testament books this is perhaps most of all a book for our time. Job could find no solace in the traditional little predictable God of the friends. No more can our generation find any genuine solace in a small God who is no bigger or better than the perpetuator of our human values, the custodian of our particular way of life, the preserver of our national prosperity, the protector of our religious denomination. Such idol-gods as this have died a thousand deaths in our century. Craving an answer in our darkening history as Job did in his own thick darkness, we may remember that Job's answer was found, not in the friends' talk about a God who puts everything to right in the world's affairs—nor even in what God says and does—but in God's very self.

Precisely at this point, where the book shows us a man encountering, to the recovery of his true life and selfhood, the God who is God out of the darkest places of anguish and despair, it both speaks a trenchant word to us and anticipates the heart of the New Testament message. The Most High God is to be found in unexpected ways and places, and none more unexpected than Golgotha, where there is neither comfort nor security but a great agony, where Jesus of Nazareth is crucified and God may be met in grace and truth.

THE BOOK OF PSALMS

Lawrence E. Toombs

INTRODUCTION

The Psalter, like any hymnbook, has no continuity of thought. A running commentary on its content is impossible. In order to deal with the many repetitions of words, ideas, and situations in psalm after psalm numerous cross references are necessary. To minimize the confusion which the welter of references is likely to cause, the reader is advised first to read a particular psalm without the commentary. Next, study the commentary and skip the parenthetical references. Finally, read psalm and commentary side by side, checking all references and biblical quotations. [Because the authors and editors of the Psalms were more than likely male, the publisher has let stand those references to the Psalmist as "he."]

Authorship and Date

The titles of many of the psalms reflect the view which prevailed for centuries that David was their author. It is now clear that this view cannot be maintained. Many scholars have even insisted that the majority of the psalms were written after the Babylonian exile and that a large number date from the Maccabean period (second century B.C.).

Within the last half century, however, archaeological discoveries in the Near East have placed at our disposal the literatures of Israel's neighbors—the Babylonians, Assyrians, Egyptians, and Canaanites. This new knowledge makes clear that Israel originated neither the poetic form of the psalms nor their use in worship. Poetic technique and vocabulary were borrowed from peoples who had attained a high degree of culture before Israel emerged as a nation.

In the light of this ancient Near Eastern literature it is probable that the original version of almost every psalm was composed in preexilic times for use in public worship during the period of the monarchy. Once introduced into worship, however, a psalm would naturally be adapted and revised to make it appropriate to changing circumstances. Psalms originally spoken by the king at a time of national stress came to be used by individuals for crises in their personal lives. An ancient prisoner-of-war song might be sung by the exiles in Babylon to express their homesickness for Jerusalem and the temple.

The Psalter is thus the product of centuries of Israelite worship. It grew, changed, and shifted in emphasis in a changing political and religious environment. For most of the psalms, therefore, a search for clues to date and author does not repay the effort.

A more fruitful approach is to investigate the literary type to which each psalm belongs and the worship setting in which it was used. In this way the psalm ceases to be a sentimental lyric or a relic from a lifeless past. It can be seen as a vital part of dynamic and meaningful worship, affirming the faith of living men and women in the face of the triumphs and disasters of real life. Accordingly this commentary does not attempt to date individual psalms except in the rare cases where a specific historical allusion gives a substantial clue to the date. Unless otherwise noted, the psalms are assumed to belong to the period of the monarchy before the exile of 586 B.C. They are assumed to be of unknown, and often of composite, authorship.

Poetic Form

Judged by any standard the psalms are poetic compositions of the highest order. Unfortunately the full beauty of the poetry does not appear in the translation. The most obvious loss is the *rhythm* of the original. Hebrew meter did not take account of all the syllables in the sentence, but counted only those which carried an accent. Thus a Hebrew metrical foot consists of one accented syllable and an indefinite number of unaccented syllables associated with it. The result is a rhythm which has, not the mathematical regularity of a ticking clock, but the irregular beat of waves upon a shore.

English translations do, however, preserve the most conspicuous characteristic of Hebrew poetry—its *parallelism.* This literary device consists of a repetition of the same idea, or a balancing contrast to it, in two or more successive statements. In its simplest form the members of the parallelism correspond word for word to one another:

> No man who practices deceit
>   shall dwell in my house;
> no man who utters lies
>   shall continue in my presence (101:7).

A skillful poet could weave these threads of parallelism into a brilliant tapestry of words. The changing patterns capture the attention of the reader and lead the mind effortlessly from one idea to the next—now lingering on a significant thought, now leaping boldly forward to a new insight.

The literary principles by which the psalms were divided into longer units are unknown. Occasionally there is a built-in guide to the place where the stanza division should fall—a refrain (Psalms 42–43), the occurrence of "selah" (see below) at the end of a stanza, or a change in speaker indicated by a shift in the pronouns (85:7-8). Usually, however, the division into stanzas must be made conjecturally on the basis of major breaks in the sense.

The acrostic poem is an outstanding exception to this general uncertainty about stanzas, or strophes. Several psalms, usually of late date, were composed using the artificial technique of beginning each successive unit with the letters of the alphabet in sequence. The acrostic poems in the Psalter are Psalms 9–10; 25; 34; 37; 111; 112; 119; 145. Psalm 119 is the most complex acrostic. It has a stanza for each letter of the Hebrew alphabet, and each line of the stanza begins with the appropriate letter.

A large body of Canaanite poetic literature has been discovered at the site of the ancient city of Ugarit. This shows clearly that the Hebrews did not originate their poetic technique. Although they learned from the Canaanites in poetic matters, the Israelites outstripped their teachers. Nothing in Canaanite literature approaches the majestic style and elevated religious thought of the Psalter.

Ancient Near Eastern Background

Lyric poetry and sacred dance are ancient aspects of the human approach to God in worship, probably reaching back to prehistoric times. The great centers of culture in the Near East refined the primitive poetic expression and gave it artistic forms. Except for the Hymn to the Sun God, attributed to Pharaoh Akh-en-Aton (1369-1353 B.C.), Egyptian religious poetry had little direct influence on Israel.

The sacred literature of the Tigris-Euphrates Valley, however, contributed strongly to Hebrew poetic tradition. Mesopotamian poetic forms began in remote antiquity with the sensitive and artistic Sumerians. They developed in a straight line through the Assyrians and Babylonians. A wealth of hymns, songs of penitence and thanksgiving, prayers, odes, and wisdom poems were produced. These were used in the daily service of the temples and at the state festivals as well as in the private worship of individuals.

The state festivals were the occasions which called forth the richest expression of ancient poetic art. At these times the entire community gathered to affirm its faith and to draw from its religious resources. At the high points of the festival epic poems were recited. King, priests, and people dramatically enacted the events which the poems described.

Throughout the Near East in Sumerian, Assyrian, Babylonian, Hurrian, Hittite, and Canaanite cultures the crucial festival was that of the new year. Human society was not regarded as autonomous or self-determining. Mysterious but potent forces controlled the destiny of individuals and states, and no society could prosper unless it brought itself into harmony with those invisible powers.

The turn of the year, when a new cycle of existence began, was fraught with potentialities for good or evil. Society therefore brought all its resources to bear on insuring that in the new cycle of days the human world would be favorably related to the superhuman order.

In Babylon the new year festival lasted eleven days. Most of its ritual took place in the forecourt of the temple, where it could be viewed by the people. On each of the first seven days of the feast the images of the god and his consort were carried from the temple to their pleasure house. These gay and colorful processions were accompanied by joyful hymns of praise.

The next phase of the ceremonial was a period of mourning for the dead god. The ancients interpreted their cycle of two seasons as a struggle, between the rain-bearing god of fertility and the sinister lord of death and drought. During the dry season the fertility god was in the underworld and the earth was under the rule of the god of death.

During the period of mourning the king assumed the role of a penitent; he was struck and humiliated by the priests in the temple. The city and its sacred places were purified by ritual means from all uncleanness in preparation for the return of the god. When the god reappeared, the people greeted the god with joy and carried the god's idol in triumph to the temple.

But the evil powers which threatened the community were not yet overcome. Accordingly the worshipers recited and enacted an epic poem describing the combat between the high god and the monster of chaos. The monster was destroyed and the ordered universe established. Recitation of this myth brought the creative powers which had operated at the beginning into renewed activity against the destructive forces which threatened society. The god was then formally enthroned in the temple for another year. The god's first act was to fix the "destinies" of nature and society for the days ahead.

This pagan ritual, in which poetry and song played so spectacular a part, has direct relevance for the study of the psalms. The religious procession, the lamentation, the sorrow and penitence, the central role of the king, the emphasis on creation, and the determination by the deity of human destiny, society, and nature are all strongly present in the Psalter. Through the Canaanites, Israel inherited from Mesopotamia the themes and vocabulary, the technique and cultic use of poetry. They put this borrowed apparatus into the service of their distinctive faith. Out of old material they created a new thing—a body of religious poetry of unparalleled beauty and insight.

Covenant Renewal and Holy War

In the days before the monarchy Israel was a loosely organized association of tribes. Each tribe conducted its own affairs and lived in almost complete independence of the other members of the league. Annually, however, the tribes came together to renew their common allegiance to the LORD and to the covenant made at Sinai (Exodus 19). The ritual of covenant renewal has not come down to us, but it may be tentatively reconstructed as follows:

The tribes assembled at the designated place, probably the sacred area of the city of Shechem. As they came, they identified themselves as authentic members of the covenant league. The leader served as a kind of mediator of the covenant. He recounted God's mighty acts in delivering Israel from Egypt and giving it a homeland in Canaan (cf. Joshua 24:1-15). The assembly responded to God's deed by hearing the covenant law and by pledging allegiance to it. The ceremony concluded with blessings for those who obeyed and curses on those who violated the covenant. God's mighty acts in the formation of Israel are the starting point of all distinctively Israelite theological thought.

Many psalms reflect one or more portions of the covenant renewal ritual.

The tribes came together also to fight the wars of the LORD. If any member of the tribal league was threatened, messengers sped to all the tribes to sound the ram's horn (see below on 81:1-5*b*) and gather the warriors together. Once assembled, the soldiers sought a sign that God would approve the battle. When this had been obtained, perhaps through a prophet (cf. I Kings 22), the army was consecrated as a band of sacred persons. They awaited the coming of the LORD's heavenly hosts to lead the troops into battle (cf. II Samuel 5:24). Trust in the LORD was essential to success in the holy war (see below on 14:5; 20:6-9). God's theophany, or appearance to the people (see below on 11:4-7*a*; 18:7-19), are only two of the many influences of the battle assembly upon the structure and thought of the Psalter.

Agricultural Festivals

As Israel settled in Canaan and became increasingly a farming community, it adopted and adapted the agricultural feasts of the Canaanites. These in turn reflected the ritual patterns and ideas of general Near Eastern culture. The earliest Hebrew calendars indicate three principal festivals:

unleavened bread, to which passover was attached;

weeks at the beginning of the grain harvest;

ingathering at the end of the fruit harvest. Ingathering was later called tabernacles, or booths, from the practice of living in temporary shelters erected in the fields (Deuteronomy 16:13-16). These were pilgrimage festivals at which every male Israelite was expected to present himself. The sacred places must at these times have overflowed with pilgrims, joyful or sad depending on the state of the crops for that year.

The biblical descriptions of ancient festivals are so sketchy that we can form no precise idea of the ritual by which they were celebrated. Combining knowledge gained from Near Eastern studies with indications in the biblical text, scholars have reconstructed a new year festival and a feast of the enthronement of the LORD. It is impossible to demonstrate conclusively the ritual, or even the existence, of these festivals. But they provide a theoretical setting in which the psalms have living meaning, and undoubtedly in some respects at least they correspond to the facts.

An Israelite Festival

In earliest times the Hebrew new year began in autumn at the feast of ingathering. When the southern kingdom of Judah became a vassal of Babylon in 609 B.C. it adopted the Babylonian year, which began in the spring. Let us assume that during the monarchy Israel observed an autumnal new year festival and attempt to reconstruct a tentative outline of its ritual.

This would be a pilgrimage festival, and throngs of pilgrims would crowd into the sacred place. As they came they would sing of their adventures along the road and of God's guiding power which had brought them safely to their journey's end. The priests would meet the procession at the steps leading to the temple and welcome them with songs of praise and calls to worship. Those about to enter the sanctuary would question the priests as to the qualifications for admission. The priests would reply with appropriate answers. This question-and-answer ritual before the gates gave rise to such "entrance liturgies" as Psalms 15 and 24:1-6.

The assembled congregation would then expose itself to the purifying judgment and justice of God. Prophetic spokesmen declared God's verdict concerning the nation's loyalty to, or violation of, the covenant. Then the people confessed their national and personal sin. Now the ritual of covenant renewal (see above) would be conducted. It would bind every Israelite to wholehearted allegiance to the covenant God for the year which lay ahead. In this part of the ritual God's dealings with Israel from the time of the patriarchs to the conquest of Canaan were recalled in dramatic recitation—for example, in Psalm 105.

The festival then passed into a mood of rejoicing. The people, newly pledged to the covenant, welcomed the LORD as king. This was not an enthronement ritual in the strict sense of the word, since, unlike the dying-and-rising gods of paganism, the

LORD had never relinquished rule. It was rather the nation's recognition of the kingly majesty of God and acknowledgment of God's rule over Israel. At this point in the ceremony the ark of the covenant, the symbolic throne of the LORD, was carried in procession up the slope of Mt. Zion to its resting place in the temple. The glad crowds sang the praise of God the King, mighty ruler of the universe and of human history.

The Jerusalem Cult

This theoretical description of the Israelite new year festival combines motifs of the premonarchical covenant renewal ceremony with themes similar to those of the Babylonian and Canaanite new year feasts. Where would such a ceremony take place? The most reasonable answer is, in Jerusalem. The city belonged to the Jebusites and was not conquered until the reign of David. But soon after it was added to his possessions it became the religious center of his realm. The change in status was signalized by the bringing of the ark to the city.

Before its capture by David, Jerusalem was already an important religious center. Hebrew tradition concedes that its priest-king was an authentic minister of Abraham's God (Genesis 14:17-24). The deity worshiped there was "God most High," who was revered as the king of the gods, the God above the gods, and whose sovereignty expressed itself particularly in creative activity. Faith in God as creator was not a crucial part of Israel's covenant religion. This was focused instead on God's saving acts in history, particularly in the events of the Exodus. In the Jerusalem temple the Jebusite creation faith and Israel's historically oriented religion were brought into a splendid unity.

The theological basis of this unity was incorporated in the formula, repeatedly used in the psalms, the LORD's "steadfast love and faithfulness." The first term refers properly to God's mighty acts of deliverance in Israel's history by which God created and sustained the people. But under the influence of the Jerusalem cult the concept was broadened to include every aspect of God's government of the world (cf. Psalm 136). God's faithfulness is the absolute reliability of God's word and deed. God will never abandon or deceive the people.

This formula may be rendered by a single word, "righteousness," or "justice." The divine justice is the unalterable and perfect decree by which the LORD enforces order in nature and human nature. In the natural world God's righteousness is shown by the conquest of the unruly powers of chaos and disorder, often symbolized by the sea. In the human world divine justice characteristically takes the side of the downtrodden and oppressed. Exploitation in any form was to the Hebrew mind a violation of the ordering and harmonizing purpose of God. Thus Israel's national enemies will be destroyed because they interpose their will against God's purpose for the people. The Israelite who oppresses a fellow citizen stands in the path of God's destructive judgment.

The creation faith of the Jerusalem cult looked forward to the time when the LORD's enemies would be destroyed or converted. Creation would then be complete, and the divine order established and recognized universally. Before that consummation the nations would gather against Jerusalem. But, invulnerable under God's protection, the city would survive and her enemies perish.

The combination of Israelite and Jebusite themes which went on so vigorously in the temple can be seen in the way the Zion psalms (discussed below) play on and combine a variety of divine names. Yahweh is "the LORD," the personal name of Israel's God, to be distinguished from occasional occurrences of the title Adonai, "Lord," meaning "master" or "ruler." He is also called El, the generic Semitic name for the father and king of the gods, translated "God." He is also called Elohim—a plural form of El, also translated "God"—and El elohim—"God of gods."

Yahweh is given the title "LORD of hosts" (i.e. armies), a name stemming from the holy war tradition. On occasion the names given connect Yahweh with the traditions of the patriarchs and of the twelve-tribe league—"God of Abraham" and "God of Jacob." In addition, and often in the same psalm, titles which suggest Yahweh's creative and world-ruling power are used—for example, "God Most High" and "God Almighty."

A striking aspect of Jebusite religious practice was the priest-king who was head of both the state and the cult, the leader in war and in worship. The kings of the Davidic line took up the traditions of the priest-kings of Jerusalem. They frequently appear in the psalms as mediators between God and human beings. The special status of the king accounts for the presence in the Psalter of a number of songs in praise of the Davidic monarchy (the "royal psalms" discussed below).

The ancient traditions of holy war were attached to the temple worship through the figure of the king, who replaced the judge as the leader of the LORD's armies. This transfer was made easier by the fact that in both the Jerusalem cult and the holy war ideology the expectation of God's theophany—God's self-revelation to the people—played a large part. The consciousness of God's willingness to draw near to the people arises from this expectation. It is one of the most pervasive theological assumptions of the psalms.

Psalm Types

Modern research on the psalms begins with Hermann Gunkel's attempt in 1926 to classify the psalms according to literary type. This effort employs literary criteria and uses content and idea only as minor and supporting evidence. The scheme presented here follows that of Gunkel with only minor modifications.

Hymns

This category includes Psalms 8; 19:1-6; 33; 65; 100; 103–105; 111; 113; 114; 115; 117; 134–136; and 145–150. The hymn consists of three elements:

(1) a call to praise,
(2) a statement of the motive or reason for praise,
(3) a renewed summons to praise.

The hymn is the fundamental expression of Israel's approach to God. It is almost startlingly God-centered. It lifts the eyes and heart of worshipers from their own crises and problems to the God whom the congregation has assembled to honor. It follows, therefore, that God is praised, not so much for what is given to the people, as for what God is and does. Praise is most frequently directed to the "name" and the "glory" of God. The first of these words refers to God's active, mighty, saving presence with the people. The second refers to God's absolute authority as ruler of the world and of human events.

It is not possible to specify a single cultic setting for the hymns. They were used in the daily service and in connection with sacrifices of all kinds. They were frequently used during every festival, and probably also by individuals in their private worship. Ideally praise, publicly offered in the temple, was merely the climax of a national and individual life which was in every part an act of praise, being lived in the presence and under the authority of God.

Hymns of Zion

These hymns include Psalms 46; 48; 76; and 87. In them the worship of the congregation seems to be directed, not to God, but to the temple on Mt. Zion. Closer examination shows, however, that the temple is valued, not for its own sake or for any power intrinsic to it, but as the earthly "dwelling place" of the LORD. God chose this site to be the point of contact with the people. God's saving presence (God's "name") dwells in the temple. There God appears to the people in judgment and deliverance. Within the courts of the temple they find protection and draw near to God in worship. The hymns of Zion are therefore in reality praises of the presence of the God of Zion.

Enthronement Psalms

These are Psalms 29; 47; 93; and 95–99. The cultic setting of these specialized hymns has been described above in connection with the new year festival. As the procession bearing the ark approaches the temple, the people pour out their praise of God's sovereignty. God's triumph over chaos in every form rings through the poems. Majestic in holiness and power, God is the supreme warrior-king who will overcome all who oppose God's universal rule. This group of psalms provides the classic statement of the Old Testament doctrine of the sovereignty of God.

Lament Psalms

These poems form the largest group in the Psalter. They are constructed in four sections:

(1) a brief invocation of God, often no more than the divine name;
(2) a cry for hearing and help;
(3) a statement of the nature and causes of the misfortune;
(4) a prayer for deliverance.

The pathos of these psalms is due largely to the pendulumlike swings of the poetry from despair to confidence, from the psalmist's personal misery to the greatness and love of God. A single psalm may have several such changes of mood.

Suffering or disaster of any kind may provide the occasion for a lament. But the underlying motive for the prayer is not the disaster itself but the alienation from God which it produces. Disease, poverty, abuse, sin, oppression—all break the mood of praise and cut one off from God in radical loneliness. This was especially true for the Israelite, who regarded suffering as punishment for sin. Anyone under affliction was likely to be mocked by enemies and shunned by friends as a sinner under the wrath of God. Israelites could not sweep aside their sense of guilt as something unreal or unworthy. They had to deal with it in the context of worship, and consequently they were frequently in the mood of lamentation.

The prayer for deliverance often includes a "vow." Sufferers pledged that if they obtained relief from anguish they would make such and such an offering or perform some specified service. The vow was not an attempt to bribe God but evidence of the seriousness of the desire for deliverance and the reality of confidence in God. Laments were sung both by individuals during personal crises and by the community in times of national disaster.

Individual Laments

This literary type includes Psalms 3–7; 13; 17; 22; 25; 26; 28; 31; 35; 38; 39; 42–43; 51; 54–57; 59; 61; 63; 64; 69–71; 86; 88; 102; 109; 120; 130; and 140–143. The lament form probably originated in the ancient function of the temple as a place of asylum or sanctuary. Ordinary legal cases were dealt with by the elders of the village courts or the judges of the royal courts in the principal cities. When a case was too difficult for these bodies, it could be brought to the temple for adjudication by God.

The problem might be one which did not lend itself to a purely legal solution, such as malicious gossip or a whispering campaign against a prominent citizen. Or the contention might be directly between God and the sufferer. If one felt oneself to be afflicted with disease because of sin, no human court could offer acquittal. The only recourse was to the LORD's tribunal in the temple.

The ritual for the presentation of a legal case in the temple is unknown, but indications in the psalms permit us to attempt a reconstruction. In the presence of the priests those who had sought sanctuary stated their case. They did so in conventional language which portrayed them in the grip of death, drowning in the sea, slipping into the underworld, entangled in the hunter's net, mired in a bog, or torn to pieces by savage beasts. They declared their innocence of the specific charges, inviting the searching scrutiny of God to determine their guilt or innocence.

During the defense the victim often denounced the enemies in vigorous terms and heaped terrible curses upon them. These passages are couched in the traditional language of Near Eastern denunciations. The violence of the words is due to the fact that in the pagan cultures in which this literary form originated the enemies were often sorcerers attempting to destroy the sufferer by magical means. The victim sought to turn the evil back upon its perpetrators. In early times the innocence of the suppliant may have been tested by means of an ordeal, but only faint traces of this practice remain in the lament psalms.

After the case was presented in the correct ritual form, the suppliant spent the night in the temple precincts awaiting a sign of divine favor. This might be given in a dream or orally by a priest or cult prophet. Some of the psalms contain examples of the "oracles of salvation" spoken for the comfort and encouragement of the sufferer—for example, 55:22. Since the assurance of salvation came after a night's vigil in the temple, the morning was regarded as the time when God revealed salvation. Assured of deliverance, suppliants paid their vows—usually a thank offering and a public testimony to the goodness of God and departed.

When the ritual of sanctuary was no longer practiced, the various elements of the pattern broke apart. These often appear in isolation in the later psalms. The language of the suppliant's appeal became the accepted language of lamentation. It was used in poems of suffering and sorrow quite apart from the ritual of sanctuary.

Although the broken relationship with God results most frequently from the attack of enemies or the onset of disease, alienation caused by sin is occasionally the focus of attention. More rarely still the psalmist feels separated from God by geographical remoteness from the temple. Psalms with this emphasis may have originated as prisoner-of-war songs. In ancient thought, to be held captive in a foreign land was to be denied access to the god of one's own country. The Babylonian exiles used ancient prisoner songs as particularly appropriate means of describing their own plight. In the spiritual isolation of sin or the physical isolation of captivity the sufferer has no defense except confidence in the saving love of the LORD.

In the laments the psalmist seems always to be "poor," "needy," "afflicted," "meek," and "righteous." The enemies inevitably are "wicked," "proud," "arrogant," "liars." These two sets of terms should not be taken too literally. They are conventional designations for two groups opposed in spirit and often in fact: those who adhered loyally to the covenant, obeyed its laws, and honored its God; and those who rejected the covenant law and held the power of its God in contempt.

Community Laments

These are Psalms 12; 44; 58; 60; 74; 79; 80; 83; 90; 106; 123; 126; and 137. In these laments the whole community seeks the sanctuary of the temple and the protection of its mighty God. Expressions of national sorrow were called forth by a sense of the nation's sin and of the decay of the covenant community, by crop failure, by the threat of military attack, by defeat in war, or by the mockery of victorious enemies.

Songs of Confidence

These songs include Psalms 11; 16; 23; 62; 125; 129; and 131. Complete and unrelieved alienation from God would make prayer impossible. The sufferer would be able only to "curse God, and die" (Job 2:9). But in the Psalter the deepest anguish is lighted by faint rays of confidence. God has saved, and will save again. Thus a note of assurance, often muted, sounds in the bitterest laments.

Sometimes, however, the assurance of salvation becomes so strong that it pushes suffering and despair almost out of the picture. This mood gives rise to the song of confidence—a halfway house, as it were, between lamentation and thanksgiving. The psalms of this group have no definite literary pattern. They are recognized mainly by their use of words and images suggesting trust and assurance. All except Psalms 125 and 129 are sung by individuals. Taken together, this group of psalms is a splendid study of those qualities of the divine nature upon which one may anchor hope.

Thanksgiving Psalms

The individual thanksgiving psalms are: 30; 32; 34; 41; 66; 92; 116; and 138. There are three community thanksgiving psalms: 65 and 67—both connected with the agricultural feasts—and 124, for victory in war. These poems are in effect extensions of the lament form. They look back on distress and sorrow from the calm and security of deliverance. The period of alienation is still vividly remembered, but its bitterness has been removed by the restoration of communion with God. As the fourfold structure indicates, the thanksgiving psalm is a complete act of worship, beginning and ending with praise:

(1) An introductory passage blesses God for saving power.

(2) This is followed by a poetic narrative, patterned closely on the lament form. Here is recalled how in a period of deep distress the psalmist cried out to God for help. The suffering is described in detail. But, unlike the laments, the thanksgiving psalms weave an account of the deliverance into the description of trouble.

(3) This leads to a specific acknowledgment that the source of the psalmist's restoration and joy is the saving love of God.

(4) The psalm concludes with thanksgiving and praise.

Psalms of this category were probably used in the temple ritual just before the sacrifice of the thank offering. They were the public testimony of individuals or the community to the goodness of God which had touched and transformed their lives.

Royal Psalms

These include Psalms 2; 18; 20; 21; 45; 72; 89; 101; 110; 132; and 144. Solomon's temple stood side by side with the palace, and the king had direct access to the sacred building from his chambers. In many respects the temple was the chapel of the palace. The close proximity of palace and temple suggests the intimate relationship which was believed to exist between the Davidic monarchy and the God of Israel.

The line of David had been chosen by and was bound to God by a perpetual covenant (I Samuel 16:1-13; II Samuel 7:4-17). The reigning king was the adopted son of God. The king was God's representative, and almost vicegerent, on earth. Through the king's person the divine blessing was channeled to the nation. What happened to him happened to all his subjects. His two principal functions reflect attributes of God. First, he was to maintain the covenant law, the revelation of God's will, and justice. Second, he defended Israel against its enemies. It is not surprising, therefore, that the Psalter contains poems dealing with the person and office of the earthly king.

The monarch's status was conferred on him when the sacred oil of anointing was poured on his head during his coronation. It is not unlikely that when the king died, his successor was not formally crowned until the new year. His coronation formed part of the great feast and was seen in close conjunction with the enthronement of the LORD, as described above. Thus every new year was an anniversary of the coronation, and appropriate rituals undoubtedly marked this fact. Six of the royal psalms (2; 21; 72; 101; 110; 132) have their cultic setting in the coronation ceremony. Psalm 101 gives the king's response to the prayers made in his behalf.

The king's function as leader in war gave rise to two prayers for victory (Psalms 20 and 144) and a thanksgiving after victory (Psalm 18). The royal marriage, a significant event for king and nation, is celebrated in the most secular of the psalms (45). In addition to these specifically royal psalms the king appears as speaker in several laments and thanksgivings.

Wisdom Psalms

Included in this category are Psalms 1; 37; 49; 73; 112; 127; 128; and 133. The priests were teachers of the religious traditions of which they were custodians and guardians. The festivals to which people came from all parts of the realm provided the priests with a unique opportunity for instruction. Many of the psalms contain instructional passages. A small number bear the marks of the formal teacher and are closely related to the wisdom literature of Israel and the ancient Near East (see the Introduction to Job).

The principal aim of the wisdom psalms is to teach the doctrine that faithful obedience to the will of God brings material and spiritual prosperity. Rejection of God's will means destruction, no less complete because sometimes long delayed. Psalm 73 deals with the problem of the prosperity of the wicked at a deeper level than the other wisdom psalms and reminds one of Job. Psalms 127 and 133 deal with family problems, a favorite topic of the writers of proverbs.

Liturgies

These are Psalms 15; 24; 50; 75; 85; 118; and 121. Ancient Near Eastern literature contains several detailed accounts of rituals conducted in pagan temples. The most important of these is the Babylonian description of the new year festival. By contrast the Old Testament never outlines precisely the ritual setting in which the psalms were used.

Some psalms, however, display such abrupt changes of thought and mood that they appear to be composed of disconnected fragments. In certain psalms it is possible to detect changes of speaker corresponding to the changes in sense. We can probably assume that the psalms of this group were the spoken parts of now-unknown rituals. For the sake of convenience we may classify them as liturgies. When the following commentary speaks of three- or five-part liturgies, it refers to the number of changes in speaker or mood which can be identified with reasonable certainty.

The cultic setting of the liturgies is by no means always clear. Psalms 15 and 24 are entrance liturgies used at the gates of the temple. Psalms 50; 75; and 85 appear to belong to the new year festival and to express God's judgment on the nation, Israel's penitence, and God's final judgment on world history. Many consider Psalm 121 a pilgrim psalm (see below) sung during the dangerous journey to Jerusalem. But it is more likely for the dismissal of pilgrims leaving the temple on their homeward journey. Psalm 118, which gives thanks for victory in war, is closely related to the community thanksgiving psalms. Liturgical elements are present in many psalms not classified as liturgies.

Pilgrim Psalms

The pilgrims who gathered for the great annual festivals came singing. Most of their hymns are included in other psalm categories, but Psalms 84 and 122 belong so distinctively to the pilgrims as to form a separate group. The keynote of these psalms is joy. Psalm 84 expresses a delight at a safe arrival among the splendors of the Holy City and gratitude to God for guidance and protection during the dangerous journey. Psalm 122 is a song of the departing pilgims, radiant with their love for Zion, God's earthly dwelling place.

Psalms of Mixed Type

Under this heading fall Psalms 9–10; 14; 27; 36; 40; 77; 94; and 107. Poems of this category appear to consist of two or more psalms of different literary type loosely joined together. Their apparent disunity may be the result of their use in rituals the details of which are now unknown. The movement of the psalm would then correspond to the various phases of the ritual. For discussion of these psalms see the commentary on each. Because of their free composition the following psalms have not been classified: 19:7-14; 52; 68; 78; 81; 82; 91; 108; 119; and 139.

The "I" of the Psalms

In most of the Old Testament the religious unit is the nation, but the Psalter appears to be an exception to this general rule. Many readers turn to it as the richest expression of the personal piety of the individual Israelite. Recent scholarship has called this evaluation into question on the basis of the ancient Semitic concept of "corporate personality." Groups of any size, from family to nation, were regarded as possessing unity and solidarity, a common mind and will. This gave them a personality as real and definite as that of an individual. The group could speak and be spoken to as if it were a single person. Therefore the "I" of the psalms may in most cases be the worshiping community speaking with one voice out of its unified corporate life.

"Corporate personality," however, does not exclude individual piety, but fosters and deepens it. The ancient individual was not lost in the crowd. Individual personality was not submerged and obliterated by that of the group. The individual person was a living representative of society, carrying the history, ideals, and qualities of the total community. When the psalms were sung in corporate worship, the consciousness that they described as a personal condition, was not lessened, but enhanced. One realized that one's condition was shared with all who stood in the temple.

In several psalms where the corporate interest is clear the pronouns suddenly shift from the plural "we" to the singular "I"—in Psalm 85, for example. In these cases we must assume that an individual has stepped forward as the representative of the congregation. Because of his office the king was the most significant representative figure in the nation—for example 44:4, 6, 15. But in war psalms the single voice which spoke for the nation might be the commanding general or other high-ranking officer. The priests, and in particular the high priest, could represent the entire congregation (85:1-3), calling them to worship and pronouncing "oracles of salvation" and blessings.

The representative function cannot, however, be limited to these officials. Any person of status or authority in the community could speak for the whole group—for example, Psalms 30 and 94. The "I" of the psalms is sometimes clearly a prophetic figure. The personnel of the ancient temple included prophets whose duty it was to announce the decisions of the deity. The "cultic prophets" of the Jerusalem temple took part in the worship whenever the ritual contained a direct word of God (81:5*b*-15). Sometimes they pronounced oracles handed down in set traditional form from ancient times (60:6-8). On other occasions their words sound the notes of judgment and direct personal inspiration characteristic of the great prophets of Israel—for example 50:7-15 and 75:2-5.

Superscriptions

Most of the psalms—all except thirty-four untitled "orphans"—carry a superscription, or title, added at some time during the process of collecting and editing. These titles bristle with difficulties. We can do no more here than indicate the elements which make up the superscriptions and a possible interpretation of their meaning.

Authorship

In some cases the editors evidently intended to indicate whom they believed to be the author of the psalm. The majority are attributed to David. The editors tended to assign any psalm which dealt directly or indirectly with the monarchy to his authorship. Psalms are also attributed to Moses (90), Solomon (72; 127), Ethan the Ezrahite (89), and Heman the Ezrahite (88).

The last two "authors" were leaders of temple choirs and men renowned for their musical skill (I Kings 4:31: I Chronicles 15:16-19). The temple choirs, composed of Levites and named after their founder, had collections of psalms which formed their special repertoire and were sung in their distinctive style. Contributions have come from the hymnbooks of Asaph (Psalms 50; 73–83; cf. I Chronicles 6:39; 15:17) and the Sons of Korah (Psalms 42; 44–49; 84; 85; 87; 88; cf. Numbers 16 and I Chronicles 9:19). Jeduthun was the founder of a third choir (I Chronicles 25:1-7). The psalms which show his name in the title (39; 62; 77) were either attributed to his authorship or, more probably, sung in the style which he originated.

Type of Composition

A "Song" (Psalms 30; 46 etc.) is a sacred musical composition for use in worship. "Psalm" (Psalms 3–6 etc.) has much the same meaning. A "Prayer" (Psalms 17; 86 etc.) is a poem of lamentation and petition. "Love song" (Psalm 45) and "Song of Praise" (Psalm 145) are self-explanatory. Several enigmatic words may belong to this category. A "Maskil" (Psalms 32; 42–45 etc.) is probably a psalm of instruction, designed to teach wisdom. "Miktam" (Psalms 16; 56–60) may refer to a psalm which commemorates an event of permanent significance. Or, if it relates to a root meaning "to cover," a psalm for atonement rituals.

Cultic Occasion

Certain psalms are said to be used:

"for the memorial offering" (Psalms 38; 70; cf. Leviticus 2:1-3),

"for the thank offering" (Psalm 100; cf. Leviticus 7:11-15),
"for the Sabbath" (Psalm 92),
"for instruction" (Psalm 60),
"of one afflicted, when he . . . pours out his complaint before the LORD" (Psalm 102).

"At the dedication of the Temple" (Psalm 30) may refer to a ritual conducted annually as part of the New Year festival. It probably does not apply to any historic dedication of a new temple building.

The title "A Song of Ascents" (Psalms 120–134) probably belongs to this category. "Ascents" (literally "goings up") relates to both "staircase" and "pilgrimage." These psalms were probably sung during the pilgrimage feasts on the stairway leading up to the temple at the times when the pilgrims were arriving or departing. "Mahalath" (Psalms 53; 88) and "Leannoth" (Psalm 88) may mean respectively "in time of sadness" and "for affliction." But the first term may equally well refer to the sad mood of the music or the accompaniment of flutes—in which case "Mahalath Leannoth" would be a flute song rendered in a melancholy mood.

Musical Direction

The ambiguities of the last two terms point to this fourth element in the superscriptions. "To the choirmaster," which occurs in fifty-five psalms, tells us that the musical directions are intended for him, but does not tell us the significance of the directions. Some scholars believe that the Hebrew expression should rather be interpreted in the light of a root meaning "to shine." This would indicate a psalm for propitiation rituals—that is, for making God's face shine.

Certain phrases are clearly catch words identifying the popular tune to which the psalm was sung:
"Muth-labben" (possibly "Die for the Son," Psalm 9),
"The Hind of the Dawn" (Psalm 22),
"Lilies" (Psalms 45; 69; 80) or "Shushan Eduth" ("Lily of Witness," Psalm 60),
"The Dove on Far-off Terebinths" (Psalm 56). "Do Not

Destroy" (Psalms 57–59; 75) was evidently the song for the grape harvest from which a line is quoted in Isaiah 65:8. "For the flutes" (Psalm 5), a word not found elsewhere, may actually mean to the tune "Inheritances."

"According to The Gittith" (Psalms 8; 81; 84) may mean to the tune "The Wine Presses." It may refer to a musical instrument or style of music imported from the Philistine city of Gath.

"According to The Sheminith" (literally "eighth," Psalms 6:12) is puzzling and has been interpreted as a particularly deep tone or an eight-stringed instrument.

"According to Alamoth" (Psalm 46) seems to mean "in the style of the women," hence a high-pitched melody.

"Shiggaion" (root meaning "to wander," Psalm 7) possibly describes a fast-paced melody, but the word is quite obscure.

References to David's Life

Several superscriptions refer to an episode in the career of David as the occasion on which the psalm was composed. But these are guesses of late editors and have no historical value. The psalms in which these notes appear and the passages in the historical books on which they most closely depend are:

3—II Samuel 15
7—II Samuel 18:31-33
18—II Samuel 7:13-16
34—I Samuel 21:10-15
36—I Samuel 23:10-11
51—II Samuel 11–12
52—I Samuel 22:9
54—I Samuel 23:19-23
56—I Samuel 21:10-11 or 27:1-4
57—I Samuel 22:1 or 24:1
59—I Samuel 19:11
60—II Samuel 8:3-14
63—I Samuel 24:1-4
142—I Samuel 22:1 or 24:1

Selah and Higgaion

These obscure terms occur in the body of psalms. "Higgaion" (9:16) has the root meaning "sigh" or "meditate." It probably refers to a pause in the singing for meditation or for a musical interlude. "Selah" is one of the greatest puzzles of the Old Testament. Its meaning seems to be connected with rising or lifting. But it is not clear whether the congregation rises or lifts up its hands, head, or eyes, or whether the voices or the music rise at the indicated points. The word probably indicates that the singing should stop to allow the congregation an interlude for presenting its homage to God by some gesture or act of worship.

The Compilation of the Psalter

As it lies before us the Psalter consists of five books (Psalms 1–41; 42–72; 73–89; 90–106; 107–150). Each is clearly marked off by a closing doxology (41:13; 72:18-19; 89:52; 106:48). Psalm 1 is a prologue to the Psalter, giving a brief summary of its theology and religious significance. Psalm 150 is an extended doxology, a fitting conclusion to the whole collection. This arrangement is an artificial division made late in the history of the Psalter in order to produce five books of psalms parallel to the five books of the Law (Genesis–Deuteronomy).

Examination of the superscriptions shows that Psalms 2–41 and 51–72 generally bear the title "A Psalm of David." The intervening group, 42–50, are almost all psalms of the Sons of Korah, and 73–83 are psalms of Asaph. The first and second Davidic collections show noteworthy repetitions. Psalm 14 appears again as 53, and 40:13-17 is repeated as 70. The first Davidic collection prefers "the LORD" (Yahweh) as its principal divine name, whereas the second favors "God" (Elohim).

These observations indicate that at one stage in the history of the Psalter four small hymnbooks were in circulation—two Davidic, one Korahite, and one Asaphite collection. The first major compilation probably consisted of bringing together these four collections of psalms into a single book, roughly corresponding to our Psalms 2–83. Since this first edition left out many familiar and well-loved hymns, an appendix was added consisting of Psalms 84–89 (four Korahite psalms, one attributed to David, and one to Ethan the Ezrahite). This second edition closed with a doxology and a twofold "Amen."

At a still later date, and perhaps in several stages, another appendix of miscellaneous psalms (90–150) was added to the growing Psalter. Of these seventeen are ascribed to David and one each to Moses and Solomon. Many are without superscription. This appendix incorporated several smaller, originally independent collections. One of these is the block of fifteen "Songs of Ascents" (120–134) already mentioned. There are two "Hallel" collections (111–113 and 146–150) in which each psalm begins with "Praise the LORD" (Hebrew *hallelujah*). There are three "Give thanks" (Hebrew *hodu*) psalms (105–107).

It is possible, therefore, to outline the literary history of the Psalter in six stages.

(1) The psalms existed as independent poems, preserved in the Jerusalem temple and other Israelite shrines for use in the festival rituals and other acts of worship.

(2) Small collections of psalms were made. This was done in order to facilitate the preservation of accurate texts, because they were used in the same ritual setting, because they belonged to the repertoire of a particular guild of singers, or for some other reason.

(3) Four of these collections were combined to produce the first edition of the Psalter (Psalms 2–83).

(4) This work was subsequently enlarged by the addition of Psalms 84–89 with a closing doxology.

(5) The process of growth continued with the addition of Psalms 90–149.

(6) A prologue (Psalm 1) and a closing doxology (Psalm 150) were provided, and the completed work was divided into five books. This development, which began in very early times, reached its conclusion sometime between 400 and 200 B.C.

Religious Teaching

The psalms have no unified theological viewpoint. They represent all shades and varieties of religious thought which could exist in the context of Israel's covenant faith. The main themes of this collection of theological thinking have been indicated above. Readers who wish to pursue them further must turn to the individual psalms. A good concordance is an invaluable aid in following the use of a particular word or concept through the Psalter. The cross references included in the commentaries on specific psalms will guide the reader to companion statements of the same theme.

PSALM 1. THE ONE WHOM GOD APPROVES

This titleless psalm was added at a late date as an introduction to the Psalter as a whole. Its emphasis on the reward of virtue and the punishment of godlessness connects it with Israel's wisdom teachers, the compilers of Proverbs, Job, and Ecclesiastes. The "beatitude" with which it begins, **Blessed is** (Oh the manifold happiness of) **the man,** is a wisdom formula. However, the psalm is late in the history of the wisdom movement, dating from a time when wisdom and the law were virtually identified. God's guidance, not human instruction, is the source of wisdom. This suggests a date after the reform of Ezra, around 400 B.C.. The psalm is artistically constructed of two carefully balanced strophes: verses 1-3 and 4-6.

1:1-3. The first strophe describes the character of the one who wins God's approval (**the righteous,** verse 6) negatively, positively, and by means of a metaphor. Negatively, such a one shuns evildoers, refusing to follow the advice of those whom God condemns (**the wicked**). Such a one will not conform to the example of those who wander from the road (**sinners**), or join company with the arrogant who sneer at God (**scoffers**).

Positively, such a life is pervaded and ruled by **law**—not a written legal code, but the guidance and instruction of God (the original meaning of *torah,* "law"). This obedience is not a yoke or burden but a **delight,** for in the divine guidance the psalmist finds a stable foundation for life. The metaphor of the **tree** suggests prosperity, productivity, usefulness, and ability to endure the hardships of life—all made possible by the nourishing **streams** of God's guidance.

1:4-6. The second strophe shows the impermanence, worthlessness, and meaninglessness which by contrast characterize the wicked. Like **chaff** tossed in the air by a winnower the wicked are blown away, destroyed—not by natural weakness but by divine action. Tried and found guilty, they are barred from the community (**congregation**) of those with whom God is pleased. This present condemnation will be confirmed at the final judgment.

1:6. The metaphor changes to that of a **way**—literally "trodden path." The path followed by the **righteous** is broad and safe, because the LORD **knows** it—it is under God's protection. In contrast the path of the **wicked**, like a desert trail, leads nowhere and will soon peter out (**perish**)—perhaps beside a dry water hole marked by the skeletons of those who followed it.

PSALM 2. UNIVERSAL GOD AND UNIVERSAL KING

This untitled royal psalm (on the category see Introduction) was composed by a court poet for use at the coronation of a king or at the annual enthronement festival. It was inspired by the hope that the geographical limits and political glory of the kingdom of David would be restored to his successors. But it goes beyond this to assert the *worldwide* sovereignty of the Davidic king. However, the psalm is more than an example of the inflated "court style" of an oriental monarch. It rests on the theological premises of the universal creativity and sovereignty of God over world history. Because God rules all peoples in all ages, the Davidic king will enjoy worldwide dominion.

The psalm dates from a time after the reign of Solomon and before the fall of Jerusalem (931-586 B.C.). The New Testament gives it a messianic interpretation (Acts 4:25-26; Hebrews 1:5; 5:5), but in its original intention it did not refer to a future ruler. The four strophes (verses 1-3, 4-6, 7-9, 10-12) were spoken by the reigning king in reference to himself.

2:1-3. ***World Rebellion.*** In the ancient world the accession of a king was the opportunity for his vassal states to assert their independence. In accents of shocked wonder the Israelite king pictures this happening on a world scale. The **kings of the earth** plot revolt against the LORD and against the one who, by the sacred oil of anointing, was set apart as the Lord's earthly representative.

2:4-6. ***God's Decision.*** Their scheming is **in vain** and makes the occupant of the heavenly throne laugh. To plot the destruction of the king whom the ruler of the universe has established is ludicrous. God's calm, self-assured words in verse 6 sound to the plotters like the crack of doom. They know that by their scheming they have exposed themselves to the destructive judgment of God, **his wrath**. The Hebrew poets spoke of God in human terms (God laughs and is angry) in order to reinforce their conviction that the LORD was actively and personally involved in human history.

2:7-9. ***A Promise of Dominion.*** The LORD's decree in verse 7 means that the Israelite king is God's **son** by adoption. He is brought into that intimate relationship **today**—that is, at the time of his coronation. A similar theory of kingship was held by Babylonian rulers. Since his Father is lord of the universe, the king can have worldwide authority for the asking. His scepter, the symbol of his royal power, will **break** the rebels as easily as a **rod of iron** shatters an earthen **vessel**.

2:10-12. ***God's Ultimatum.*** The king warns the rebels that they must recognize and do homage to the LORD as ruler of the universe—figuratively **kiss his feet**, as the subjects of an oriental ruler did to their king. The alternative is destruction, for only those who acknowledge their dependence on the LORD can hope for the blessings of prosperity and peace. The Hebrew of verses 11*b*-12*a* is obscure, but the interpretation given is more in keeping with the context than either alternative: "rejoice with trembling, kiss with purity," or "kiss the son."

PSALM 3. A GOD OF DELIVERANCE

This psalm is an individual lament (on this category, the title, and **selah** see Introduction). It is based on one of the fundamental tenets of Israel's exodus faith: the God who saved Israel from Egypt is a God of **deliverance.** The root word means "make wide" or "give room to" (see below on 18:19). It is particularly appropriate to the psalmist's condition, hemmed in by enemies. The military metaphors in verses 3 and 6 suggest that the speaker is the king. But many psalms which originally belonged to the setting of the court were "democratized" and used by the people. The royal language was understood as only figurative.

3:1-4. Oppressed by enemies who scornfully declare that God cannot help, the psalmist does not lose confidence in the LORD. Recognizing that protection (**shield**) and worth (**glory**) are owed to the LORD, the psalmist recalls how in the past the psalmist bowed before God like a subject. The LORD answered the psalmist favorably. The psalmist feels assurance that the LORD will hear the servant and answer by action.

3:5-8. In this confidence the psalmist can **sleep** peacefully in the midst of **ten thousands** of armed enemies. Some have assumed from verse 5 that the psalm is a morning prayer, offered after a night spent in the sacred place, but the language hardly forces this conclusion. The psalmist calls on the LORD to **arise** from the throne and act. This is based on the psalmist's belief that God gives tit for tat to those who insult the Lord—striking their cheeks and smashing their scornful mouths.

PSALM 4. THE ONLY SECURITY

At first reading this individual lament appears to be a haphazard collection of disconnected verses (on this category, the title, and **selah** see Introduction). Scholars vary widely in their interpretations. With considerable emendation the psalm may be read as a pious person's reproof of those who have been led to apostasy by a succession of bad harvests. Other commentators understand the poem as the defense of a high official (king or high priest) against charges that an office has been abused. Still others regard it as the exhortation of a person of faith to those who have been disheartened by hard times.

The speaker, however, seems to be a poor person who faces

the lying accusations of the wealthy (verse 7). The designation translated as **men** (verse 2) is used in Egyptian and Babylonian literature to refer to persons of standing or wealth. These facts suggest that the psalm belongs to a legal context. In Israel, as throughout the ancient Near East, legal cases which could not be resolved by direct evidence were taken to the temple. There the accused swore an oath of innocence in the presence of the god. This psalm was probably originally a liturgy for use in a temple trial. Subsequently it was slightly modified to make it generally serviceable as a hymn of confidence.

4:1-5. The psalm begins, as usual in a lament, with a cry to God for aid. Significantly it addresses the **God of my right**—that is, the God who declares me innocent. By lying words the psalmist's accusers have attacked the psalmist's dignity. But the psalmist remains confident that the LORD will respond again (verse 3). Calmly it is urged that the prosecutors keep their anger and their plots to themselves, and so avoid the sin of lying publicly (verse 4). The psalmist enjoins them to true worship and to trust in the LORD (verse 5).

4:6-8. The psalmist's many accusers display their lack of trust by complaining about their lot. Piously they use words reminiscent of the priestly benediction (verse 6; cf. Numbers 6:26; in ancient thought the rejection of the worshiper was signified by the aversion of the god's eyes). But the psalmist's consciousness of innocence and fellowship with God give more inner joy than enemies derive from the material possessions which they covet (verse 7). Confident in the LORD's protection, the psalmist sleeps peacefully—possibly in the temple itself during the ordeal of the trial (verse 8; cf. 3:5).

PSALM 5. ALIENATION AND ACCEPTANCE

This beautifully constructed individual lament unfolds in four stages (on this category and the title see Introduction). It begins with a repeated appeal to God for hearing and help. God is addressed with the cultic formula **my King and my God**. The psalm goes on to describe the alienation from God of the psalmist's enemies and the psalmist's own acceptance by the LORD. This leads to a prayer for guidance and justification, to a condemnation of the enemies and a cry for vengeance, and finally to a meditation on the joy and blessing of the righteous.

5:1-7. The setting is the **morning** service of the temple, to which the psalmist brings offering and waits expectantly for an answer from the LORD (verse 3). Two qualities of the divine nature assure the worshiper that prayers will be heard. The first is God's hatred of **evil** in any form (verses 4-6). The second is God's **steadfast** love—that is, God's nature as one who acts to save—toward the weak and helpless. Because of the first, the proud, violent, deceitful who oppose the psalmist are denied entrance to the temple—that is, they are cut off from fellowship with God (verses 4-5; cf. verse 10). By virtue of the second the psalmist has free access to the sanctuary, which is entered with **fear** (i.e. reverential awe).

5:8-12. The psalmist's prayer is threefold:

(1) that he may be guided in God's **way**, from which his **enemies** try to divert him (verse 8);

(2) against those who plot violence even while they speak flattering words (verses 9-10);

(3) on behalf of all who trust in the LORD for their defense, that they may receive **joy** and blessing (verses 11-12). The vengeance called down on the enemies will be both the judgment of God and the consequence of their crimes—just as the joy of the righteous is both the natural outpouring of their gratitude and the direct gift of God.

PSALM 6. IN THE FACE OF DEATH

This typical individual lament (on this category and the title see Introduction), is a patchwork of traditional cultic phraseology. Implicitly the psalmist acknowledges that suffering is the result of sin—that is, it has been visited on him by the wrath of God. Thus this psalm is traditionally regarded as the first of the seven penitential psalms (along with 32; 38; 51; 102; 130; and 143), although it contains no word of confession.

6:1-3. The psalmist pleads for relief from the divine **wrath**. He complains of sickness (verse 2) and mental anguish (verse 3). His **bones**, the most stable part of the physical frame, and his **soul**—not the immortal spiritual part but the total personality as a living being—are in disorder.

6:4-5. On the basis of the LORD's **steadfast** (delivering) **love** (see above on 5:1-7) he begs for his life. He is in terror because **death** will plunge him into **Sheol,** the underworld, where his existence will be reduced to just short of the vanishing point. The LORD's presence does not reach this dark and cheerless place far beneath the surface of the earth (see below on 18:7-18). The shades even lack **remembrance** of their God (cf. 30:9; 88:10-11; 115:17). Verse 5 is a fair representation of the hopelessness with which the Hebrews of the classical period faced death as the end of meaningful human experience, including fellowship with God.

6:6-7. With characteristic oriental exaggeration the psalmist describes his **bed** as soaking wet from his **tears** and his **eye** as worn out with weeping. His distress is due also to human **foes.**

6:8-10. So confident is the psalmist of God's willingness to answer his **prayer** for the thwarting of his **enemies** that he regards it as already accomplished.

PSALM 7. AN OATH OF INNOCENCE

This is an individual lament (on this category and the title see Introduction). On the basis of changes in style and mood some have viewed verses 6-11 as a separate poem inserted in the middle. Such a division is unnecessary, for the psalm can be read as the unified utterance of one person.

7:1-5. Pursued by savage enemies the psalmist has fled to the temple for sanctuary (verse 1-2; cf. I Kings 2:28). In the sacred place he swears an oath of purgation (verses 3-5; cf. I Kings 8:31-32), in which he declares his innocence—not of all sin but only of the crimes with which he is falsely accused. He asks that, if he is guilty, his enemies be allowed to **trample** him to death.

7:6-11. The scene in the divine court, where the LORD sits enthroned among the courtiers and messengers, is a common motif in the Old Testament (see below on 58:1-5; 82:1-5). The psalmist prays that the court be convened and the LORD, who judges the nations, sit in **judgment** between himself and his **enemies.** He wishes not only that he be found not guilty but also that his enemies be utterly destroyed. His plea for vengeance is based on the belief that the judge of the earth is a **righteous God**—that is, a God of moral perfection—and is therefore always moved to anger by evil or injustice (verses 9-11; on **minds and hearts** see below on 16:7-8; 26:1-3). In his concentration on the judgmental character of God he does not entertain the possibility that the LORD may love the evildoer.

7:12-16. These verses are a meditation on the nature of the righteousness of God. They involve a Semitic ideal of justice found in many Near Eastern law codes. In the code of Hammurabi of Babylon (around 1750 B.C.) the perjurer receives the punishment which he tried to bring on his victim. In this psalm the **wicked** are trapped in their own plots and tumble into the **pit** which they prepared for the psalmist. This "poetic justice" of God is swift as war **arrows** and deadly as the cut of a **sword.**

7:17. The psalmist is certain of vindication by the righteous God. He concludes with a vow to acknowledge his gratitude publicly in the temple by means of a thank offering and songs of **praise**. The vow is a common feature of psalms of lament or thanksgiving.

PSALM 8. THE DIGNITY OF HUMAN BEINGS

This familiar hymn (on this category and the title see Introduction) belongs to the evening service of the temple, when the night sky was visible above the open courts of the building. It was sung antiphonally.

8:1-2. ***Ascription of Glory.*** This part was sung by the people (note **our Lord**). In Hebrew a **name** is more than a title by which a person or thing is designated. It summarizes and *contains* the nature and character of its bearer. The key to the LORD's character is **glory**. This means "weight" as measured by a scale or—figuratively—"honor," "dignity," or "reputation." When applied to God, it means God's authoritative presence in creation, salvation, or judgment. This authoritative presence of God fills the whole **earth**, and is the object of Israel's praise.

8:1*c*-2. The Hebrew of this passage is difficult. Punctuated as in the Revised Standard Version, it may contain a mythological reference. That is, angelic hosts, innocent as **babes,** who surround the throne of the LORD **above the heavens,** overcome the dark demonic powers of the universe by the harmony of their praise to the King of kings. It is probably better, however, to put a semicolon after verse 1 and read the passage as meaning that the stars in the sky (verse 1*c*) and children on earth (verse 2) both proclaim the divine glory. Another possibility is to regard **above the heavens** as an adjectival phrase defining **glory** and thus confine the whole scene to earth. In the latter sense the passage contains the familiar Old Testament idea that the LORD uses the humble and weak to carry out great designs. The Lord can make the songs of **infants** a fortress strong enough to hold back the wicked and reduce them to silence.

8:3-8. *The Glory and Insignificance of Humanity.* This part was sung by a solo voice (note I). Contemplation of the night sky makes one acutely aware of one's humanity. We seem too insignificant to merit the attention, much less the loving care, of the Creator, who shaped the heavenly bodies one by one and fastened them in the vast dome of the sky. But size is not everything. For all our earthbound littleness we humans have a crown of kingly authority and a dignity which places us just below the level of God.

In the phrase **little less than God** the Hebrew word *elohim* may be translated "judges," "heavenly beings," "gods," or "God." The Septuagint took it to mean "angels," but since it is a normal Old Testament word for "God" this seems the best translation here. We are Godlike in our ability to control the rest of the created order. This mastery over the world is the "image of God" of which Genesis 1:26 speaks. But it does not belong to us as a possession. The **crown** of dignity and **dominion** are bestowed as a gracious gift by the Creator of earth and heaven.

8:9. ***Ascription of Glory Repeated.*** The refrain was sung again by the people. Contemplation of dignity, understood in the terms of the psalm, lead, not to pride, but to renewed praise of the **majestic** nature of God—an observation not without value in a technologically oriented society.

PSALMS 9–10. THANKSGIVING AND LAMENTATION

In the Greek Septuagint these psalms appear as one. That this tradition is correct is indicated by two facts. First, Psalm 9 ends with **selah** (on this word and **higgaion** see Introduction), which rarely concludes a psalm (only Psalms 24 and 46). Second, Psalm 10 has no title (on the title to Psalm 9 see Introduction). Similar in subject matter, the two psalms taken together once formed a single poem in which the strophes began with successive letters of the Hebrew alphabet (an alphabetic acrostic; see Introduction). The pattern is now much disturbed. In form 9:1-12 is a thanksgiving hymn, and 9:13–10:18 is an individual lament (on these categories see Introduction).

9:1-12. ***Praise for God's Justice.*** The hymn, an extended invocation introducing the lament, begins with praise of the wonderful deeds of the **Most High**. This is an ancient divine name going back to the days before Moses (cf. Genesis 14:19). The wonderful deeds are the LORD's acts of judgment (verses 3-10). The Lord turned back the psalmist's **enemies** at the gates of the temple and overthrew them. The Lord **destroyed** the turbulent **nations** of the earth, blotting out their **name** and **memory**—a Hebrew idiom for total annihilation.

The heavenly court of the divine King-Judge figures prominently in these verses (see comment on 7:6-11; 58:1-5;

82:1-5). To those whom God finds guilty God is a ruthless destroyer (verse 12), but to those who trust God and know God's true nature (**name**) God is a sure defense (verses 9-10). God's every decision is scrupulously correct (verses 7-8). The thanksgiving hymn closes with praise of this perfect justice.

9:13-17. ***Former Blessings from God.*** Appropriately the lament begins with remembrance of past blessings (verses 13*b*-18). The LORD restored the psalmist to his people after his enemies had pushed him to the point **of death** (see above on 6:4-5). **Daughter of Zion** is a poetic personification of Jerusalem. The **I** of the psalm may be the king, speaking as the representative of the nation. God's treatment of the enemy nations is marked by poetic justice (see above on 7:14-16). God sends them to **Sheol** (the underworld; see above on 6:4-5), whither they have tried to dispatch the psalmist. The **net** (9:15; 10:9) is an animal trap triggered when the victim steps on a release mechanism.

9:18–10:18. ***The Question of Theodicy.*** This portion deals with the thorny question of the apparent reversal of God's justice in actual life. The wicked prosper (10:5*a*) and the poor are afflicted (9:18). This obvious inequity makes even the persecuted righteous doubt that God is at all concerned over their plight (10:10-11). **The wicked** are atheists in practice (10:4). They deny, not God's existence, but God's effective control over the world (10:6, 13), contending that god cannot, or will not, take action against them. The psalmist recognizes that their attitude is in fact self-deification. Forgetting their humanity, they behave as if they were God (9:20).

In characteristic Hebrew fashion the psalmist does not try to settle the problem of the prosperity of the wicked by logical argument. Instead he reaffirms his faith. It is the basic Old Testament conviction, derived from the exodus, that the eternal **king** will oppose the powerful and aid the helpless and **oppressed. Poor, afflicted,** and **meek** are alternative translations of the same Hebrew word.

Psalm 11. Sanctuary in the Temple

This is a song of confidence (on this category and the title see Introduction). It is the work of an unknown refugee who sought sanctuary in the temple (see above on Psalm 7).

11:1-3. The wicked are on the warpath and his friends advise him to **flee . . . to the mountains.** Justice and right dealing, **the foundations** of stable society, **are destroyed** (cf. Amos 5:7). The persecuted **righteous,** of which he is perhaps a leader, are helpless.

11:4-7*a*. The psalmist views flight as a denial of his trust in the LORD. He comes instead to the **temple,** to await the theophany—the manifestation or revelation of the deity (see Introduction). He hopes that the "coming" of the LORD celebrated in the cult will now be actualized. He bases his expectation on his understanding of the nature of God. The LORD, who is present in the temple with the people, is at the same time enthroned as judge above the earth (see above on 7:6-11). The LORD's unhindered vision **tests** everyone's deeds. The LORD reacts to what is seen with a vigor which can be described only by analogy with the most intense of human emotions, hate and love (verses 5*b*, 7*a*).

The LORD's appearance in judgment is described in traditional metaphors of theophany (cf. 18:7-19; 29:3-9)—the volcanic **fire** which destroyed Sodom and Gomorrah (cf. Genesis 19:24) and the east **wind** from the desert which can kill the spring grass in a day (cf. 90:5-6; Isaiah 40:6-7). **Cup** in verse 6 probably alludes to the practice of trial by ordeal. The accused was given a cup of sacred liquid to drink; if guilty its contents destroyed the accused (Numbers 5:23-28).

11:7*b*. The reward of the **upright** at the coming of the LORD will be fellowship with God—to **behold his face.** In paganism to "behold the face" of a god was to enter the inner shrine where the idol stood. In the Old Testament it is a technical term for entrance to the sanctuary—but with the wider connotation of communion with God and the consciousness of being accepted by God.

Psalm 12. Vileness Exalted

This is a community lament (on this category and the title see Introduction). The God-fearing congregation cries for **help** and prays for vengeance against its enemies (verses 1*b*-4). Lying and boasting are symptoms of the decay and disintegration of society. A prophetic voice interrupts the congregational prayer to assure the people that God's long-awaited response is at hand (verses 5-6). In answer the congregation renews its petition for protection (verses 7-8).

The psalm displays an extreme pessimism concerning the condition of society. The reason for this emphasis is that the complete triumph of evil is a feature of eschatological thought, which was concerned with the end times. It is the signal for the Lord to break into history in the final act of salvation and judgment (verse 5; see Introduction).

12:6. The **promises of the Lord** are literally "words," and the reference is to passages such as Deuteronomy 27–28 in which curses are directed against the wicked and blessings promised to the righteous. Such passages were recited in the temple cult as part of the ritual of the covenant renewal festival (see Introduction). By contrast with the lying speech of **the wicked** the Lord's words are true, pure as molten **silver** fresh from the refiner. **In a furnace on the ground** presents difficulties. Some commentators emend it to read "in a crucible" or "in a workshop." It is probably a metal workers' technical term, perhaps referring to the pouring of the melted silver into an earthen mold.

Psalm 13. An Appeal for Deliverance

This individual lament (on this category and the title see Introduction) conforms perfectly to the pattern. There is an appeal to the Lord, the reason for the lamentation, and a hymnic expression of confidence.

13:1-4. The meaning can best be seen by following the

thought backward from verse 4 to verse 1. For a long time his enemies have oppressed the psalmist and brought him near death (see above on 6:4-5). But his bitter anguish and inner turmoil (verse 2) are caused, not so much by the triumph of his foes, as by his belief that the LORD rewards the righteous with prosperity. In the light of that conviction his suffering is evidence that the Lord has forgotten him—hidden his face (cf. 6:1-3). The cry **how long?** is a cultic formula of lamentation. It appears in the Babylonian Lament of Nebuchadnezzar and frequently in the Old Testament.

13:5-6. The psalmist bases his confidence in the Lord's saving action toward the weak (**steadfast love**) and the Lord's readiness to save. Both qualities of the divine nature are derived from Israel's historic exodus faith.

PSALM 14. THE REIGN OF FOLLY

This psalm is of mixed type and basically a community lament (on this category and the title see Introduction). It incorporates prophetic (verses 1, 5-6) and wisdom (verses 1, 2*b*) characteristics. Like Psalm 12 this poem is a prayer that the heavenly Judge will enter history in the final act of judgment against the wicked and salvation for Israel. The total corruption of society indicates that the divine action will soon take place (see above on Psalm 12).

14:1-4. The portrait of the wicked is sharply drawn. The Hebrew word for **fool** refers, not to simpleminded people, but to coarse, brutal, self-centered rogues. They deny God, not by intellectual arguments, but by a **corrupt** life (see above on 9:18–10:18). They lack **knowledge**—that is, an intimate, personal experience of the LORD's nature and will. They refuse to seek or to **call upon** God, a radical assertion of their independence (verses 2-4). All this issues in violence toward the true **people** of God (verse 4) and in **abominable deeds,** actions hateful to the LORD.

14:5-7. The term **terror** is drawn from the ancient tradition of the holy war (see Introduction and on 20:6-9). At the crucial moment of the battle dread of the LORD seized the enemies and brought them to ruin (cf. Exodus 23:27; Deuteronomy 11:25; Joshua 11:8). For the descendants of Jacob-Israel the appearance of the LORD means salvation. The **deliverance . . . out of Zion** is brought by the LORD, coming forth from God's temple. The congregation prays that the LORD may soon appear. On **restore the fortunes** see below on 85:1.

PSALM 15. DEMAND FOR MORAL PURITY

This is an entrance liturgy (on this category and the title see Introduction). It reflects the ancient Near Eastern insistence that certain conditions be fulfilled before admission to the sacred place (cf. 24:3-5; Isaiah 33:14-16). Egyptian and Mesopotamian stipulations for entrance to the sanctuary were usually of a ritual nature. By contrast this psalm demands moral purity. The pilgrims approach the temple during the great festivals (see Introduction). They formally ask the priests who meet them at the gates what the requirements for admission are (verse 1). The priests reply with a poetic description of the character pleasing to God (verses 2-5), ending with a promise of blessing for those who conform to their instructions. Entrance liturgies of this kind (cf. Psalm 24) are adaptations to community use of the practice of settling disputes or solving problems by asking the priest for a "directive" from the LORD (cf. Haggai 2:10-14).

15:1. The use of **tent** for the Jerusalem temple on the **holy hill** preserves the memory of the tabernacle or tent of meeting during the era of Moses. Its use in verse 1 shows how the Sinai covenant dominates the thought of the psalms from beginning to end.

15:2-5. Verse 2 gives a general description of the person whose whole being and every act accords with the requirements of the covenant. Verses 3-5 show how this character expresses itself in specific social situations. Blameless people avoid

slander or the passing on of malicious gossip. They value their fellow citizens on the basis of their relationship to the God of the covenant, not the size of their bankroll (verse 4*ab*). They keep their word even if to do so puts them at a disadvantage (verse 4*c*). They will not exploit their wealth by exacting **interest** from a fellow Israelite (among Israel's pagan contemporaries the going interest rate was 33⅓ to 50 percent). Neither will they exploit their influence in the community by accepting a **bribe**. This kind of loyalty to the covenant is rewarded by permanent prosperity within the covenant community (verse 5*c*).

Psalm 16. The Decisive Choice

This psalm is a song of confidence (on this category see Introduction). It is a classic example of the doctrine that virtue and reward go hand in hand.

16:1-2. The psalmist begins in the mood of lamentation. But he declares that good fortune came because he submitted his life voluntarily and unreservedly to the LORD.

16:3-4. This is a digression from the main theme, and its meaning is obscure because of difficulties in the text. As the Revised Standard Version translates it, verse 3 expresses the psalmist's **delight** in the nobility of the **saints,** the true members of the covenant community. Perhaps, however, we should follow the Septuagint: "The Lord deals gloriously with the saints in the land." Numerous other emendations have been suggested. Verse 4 contrasts the depravity of the idolater with the nobility of the saints. It specifically rejects two pagan practices—pouring out offerings of blood to the gods and using their names in magical incantations.

16:5-6. The psalmist expands on the consequences of his decisive choice in verse 2. **Cup** is a cultic metaphor for "destiny." The rest of the vocabulary—**portion . . . lot . . . lines** (a measured plot of ground) . . . **heritage**—recalls the division of the Holy Land among the twelve tribes after the conquest of Canaan. As the LORD gave the people an inheritance in Canaan, so the LORD gave the psalmist a goodly and pleasant place in the covenant community.

16:7-8. The psalmist moves to the less tangible results of his choice—guidance and inspiration. The LORD is like a guide before him and a companion at his side. God's will is revealed to the psalmist, and **in the night** the psalmist's inner being responds to the revelation. **Heart** is literally "kidneys." In Old Testament the vital organs were regarded as the seat of one's private inner life.

16:9-12. In verses 9-10 we learn the source of the psalmist's confidence. He was near death and the LORD rescued him from **Sheol** and **the Pit** (the underworld; see above on 6:4-5). No doctrine of resurrection is involved. After a close brush with death the poet rejoices in a sound **heart** and **soul** and **body** (on **soul** see above on 6:1-3). He exults because the LORD has given him **life,** showed him how to live it, and crowned it with **joy** and endless delight.

PSALM 17. SAVAGE INNOCENCE

This is an individual lament (on this category and the title see Introduction), in which a fugitive comes to the temple to present a case before the divine Judge. The fugitive spends the night in the sacred place awaiting the verdict (see above on Psalms 3; 4; and 7). The psalm follows the pattern of a legal argument:

17:1-2. *Address to the judge,* stressing the justice of the psalmist's **cause,** his sincerity in setting it forth, and his demand for **vindication.** This word means not only the recognition of innocence but also the reward which innocence deserves.

17:3-5. *Oath of purgation* (see above on 7:1-5). The psalmist swears that he is guiltless of deceit and violence, which are the specific charges against him. He claims complete innocence in thought and word by whatever test the LORD wishes to apply.

17:6-9. *Prayer for deliverance,* based on his proved innocence. He appeals to the LORD's concern for and willingness to save the weak, **those who seek refuge** in the temple (cf. 13:5-6). **Apple of the eye** is an obsolete English idiom for "eyeball." The Hebrew here is literally "the little man in the eye"—the pupil which reflects the image of anyone who looks into it, and which its owner carefully protects from injury. **The shadow of** God's **wings** may be a reference, not to the mother bird's care for her young, but to the Persian and Egyptian practice of representing the deity as a winged solar disc. Or it may refer to the outspread wings of the cherubim on the ark of the covenant (see below on 99:1-5).

17:10-12. *Countercharges*, declaring that the psalmist's enemies are corrupt outwardly and inwardly (**mouths** and **hearts**) and fierce as a hunting **lion** (cf. 7:2; 10:9).

17:13-14. *Prayer for vengeance*, based on the countercharges, and blending two motifs of Old Testament religion. The God who cuts down enemies with the sword comes from the holy war tradition (see Introduction and below on 20:6-9). The sacred food or drink which swells the **belly** of the guilty and kills him is derived from the trial by ordeal (see above on 11:5-6). The demand for vengeance is as extreme as the protestation of innocence, "Let the family of the wicked suffer to the third generation."

17:15. The closing *expression of confidence* corresponds to the opening cry for justice. When morning comes the psalmist will receive a vision of God—**behold . . . thy form,** as Moses did in the tabernacle (Numbers 12:5-8). The divine revelation will satisfy him by establishing his innocence (see Introduction).

This psalm shows the dangers inherent in a sense of innocence. It breeds intolerance, spiritual superiority, and the tendency to equate one's own enemies with the enemies of God. The cry for vengeance is then inevitable (cf. Matthew 5:43-48).

Psalm 18. The Lord at War

Although the title has little historical significance, it is correct in connecting the psalm with the monarchy, for it is a royal hymn of thanksgiving (on this category see Introduction). It is a liturgy spoken in the temple by the king after a military triumph and possibly repeated annually in the enthronement festival. Its archaic language indicates that it may be as old as the tenth century B.C. A somewhat later version of it appears in II Samuel 22.

Some commentators regard this as two psalms. Verses 1-30 are considered the lament of one beset by enemies, and verses 31-50, a royal thanksgiving hymn. However, the poem is a tightly knit artistic unit. It has a hymnic passage at the beginning (verses 1-3) and at the end (verses 46-50). The body of the psalm contains two accounts of the king's victory. In the first (verses 4-19) God is the chief actor, breaking into the human scene to rescue the king from certain defeat. In the second (verses 31-45) the king plays the leading role, but the victory is still the LORD's. Verses 20-30 are a meditative interlude on the relationship between the LORD and the David king. The imagery of the psalm reflects the holy war tradition (see Introduction and on 14:5-7; 20:6-9).

18:1-3. The metaphors here are all military. The **rock** is a promontory on which a fortress is built, and the **horn** (of a bull) is the symbol of strength. **Salvation** in this context means "victory."

18:4-6. The king is portrayed as driven to the edge of disaster. **Sheol** (see above on 6:4-5) is compared to a bird net made of **cords** which has almost entrapped him (verse 4*a*) and to a flash flood rushing toward him (verse 4*b*). In this extremity he prayed in the **temple** and the LORD heard his **cry** for deliverance.

18:7-18. The wonder of God's delivering action transcends ordinary speech. It is described as a battle between heaven and Sheol for the life of the king. It involves upheavals of nature traditionally associated with a theophany—the manifestation of a god (see above on 11:4-7*a*). Attended by earthquake and volcanic **fire**, the LORD thrusts through the dome of the sky (verse 9*a*). The LORD is surrounded and supported by storm **clouds** and carried along by the **wind.** Hail and thunder precede the LORD and with **arrows** of lightning the LORD strikes down the enemies, the LORD cleaves through the **sea . . . and the foundations of the world** to Sheol itself and lifts the king to safety through the subterranean **waters.**

The cosmology involved in this description is the ancient Mesopotamian conception of the three-storied universe. Heaven, the abode of God, is above the dome of the sky (the firmament). The inhabited world is a flat disk, anchored over the subterranean waters. Sheol, the realm of the dead, is within the waters and far below the earth.

18:19. The metaphor **brought me forth into a broad place** (cf. verse 36) is based on the root meaning, "make wide," of the Hebrew word for "save" (see above on Psalm 3).

18:20-30. The meditation turns on the fact that the Israelite king was not an absolute monarch. Like the other members of the covenant community he was obligated to obey the covenant law (**ways of the LORD . . . ordinances . . . statutes**). The LORD, whose every action is above reproach (verses 25*b*, 30), rewards such **humble** loyalty with steadfast support (verses 25*a*, 26*a*, 27*a*). The LORD guides the king, and renews his life and strength (verses 28-29).

18:31-45. The second account of the victory is introduced by general statements of the LORD's saving and strengthening power (verses 31-33). It quickly moves into the military sphere and describes in violent poetry the overthrow of the king's enemies. Emphasis falls on the superhuman speed, agility, and **strength** which the LORD gives to the king (verses 33-34, 39). But it is the LORD, not the king, who wins the victory (verses 39-40). The ensuing peace is a complete triumph for the Davidic monarch and inaugurates his worldwide rule (verses 43-45; see above on Psalm 2).

18:46-50. The conclusion is a hymn of praise to God for goodness to the king. The last line refers to the fact that the LORD's covenant with the house of David was to last forever (cf. II Samuel 7:16).

PSALM 19. WITNESSES TO GOD'S AUTHORITY

Two poems, different in age, meter, and subject matter, have been combined in this psalm. One is a pre-exilic nature psalm (verses 1-6). The other is a late poem in praise of the law (verses 7-14). The two have been forged into a single hymn (on these categories and the titles see Introduction). The second reflects an age when the written law was the object of religious veneration and is therefore probably later than the reform of Ezra (around 400 B.C.; cf. Nehemiah 8:1-8). The concept of the **glory of God** (authoritative presence; see above on 8:1-2) gives these poems a theological unity. The **firmament** (the dome of the sky; see above on 18:7-18) bears witness to God's creative power in nature. The law declares God's authoritative presence in history, in particular in the history of the covenant people, of which also God is the creator.

19:1-6. *The Testimony of Nature.* The stars have no audible voice and speak no intelligible language (verse 3). Yet they are custodians of a mysterious **knowledge** which day after day they proclaim to **all the earth.** They know and declare that they were created and are kept in their places by the authoritative word of God.

These verses reflect the world view of the ancient Near East. This is particularly true of the hymn to the **sun** (verses 4*c*-6), which is closely related to similar poems in Babylonian and Egyptian literature. The sun waits the night in its **tent** at the extremity of the earth—or, by a slight emendation of the word translated **in them,** "in the sea" (verse 4*c*). At the time appointed the sun emerges, glowing with the radiance of a **bridegroom** and the strength of an athlete, to follow its path across the sky and sink in the evening into the western sea. The sun completes the **circuit** by returning to its tent at night through the waters of the underworld (see above on 18:7-18). The psalmist, like the pagan poets, personifies the heavenly bodies, but he does not give them the status of gods. To him they are examples of God's craftsmanship and witnesses to God's glory.

19:7-14. *Hymn to the Law.* This hymn consists of six beautifully balanced statements of the nature of the law and its effect on human life (verses 7-9). These are followed by a prayer for aid in keeping the law (verses 10-14). Verse 7 is the basic statement, and the rest is commentary on this. The law is no mass of lifeless ordinances, but a living expression of the totality of God's will. To obey it is to have one's life renewed. It is God's self-witness to the divine will (**testimony**), and standing orders to and detailed demands upon the people (**commandment** and **precepts**), the justice by which God rules history (**ordinances**). It is the speech by which God makes the divine purpose known to Israel (emending **fear** to "word" in the interest of the parallelism). **Perfect** and **enduring,** the law is the fountain from which flows everything of supreme value to men and women. The connection with wisdom in verse 7*b* recalls Psalm 1.

19:11-13. The **reward** is not material prosperity but the kind of life which the law promotes and produces. But our inadequate self-understanding keeps us from this life-giving obedience. We cannot recognize our own **errors.** We unknowingly violate God's will (**hidden faults**). We flout it consciously because of cocky self-confidence (**presumptuous sins**). The law can be obeyed only by relying on God's sustaining power.

19:14. This is a dedicatory formula (cf. 104:34; 119:108) of the type spoken at the presentation of a sacrifice. Here the offering is not an animal sacrifice but a hymn expressing the total dedication (**mouth** and **heart**) of the worshiper to God.

Psalm 20. A Prayer for Victory

This is a royal psalm (on this category, the title, and **selah** see Introduction). It is a prayer for **victory** offered on behalf of the king by a choir of priests on the eve of battle.

20:1-5. The **name** of the Lord is the divine presence residing in the temple (cf. I Kings 8:17). The identification of the Lord's dwelling as both the temple and heaven (verse 6) may be noted in other psalms (see above on 11:4-7*a*). In the temple the king presents a grain offering and a whole burnt offering (verse 3). Sacrifice and prayer belonged together in the temple ritual. To set up the standards on a battlefield (verse 5) may be a sign of victory. But in the interest of parallelism it may be better to emend the word translated **set up our banners** to "delight."

20:6-9. A solo voice among the choir sings 6-8, or at least verse 6. The ideology of the holy war (see Introduction) which underlies verses 7-8 goes back to the period of the tribal confederacy, around 1250-1000 B.C. The size and equipment of the army has no bearing on the outcome of the battle, since the LORD, the real commander of the host, *gives* the victory. Absolute trust in the LORD's power to overthrow the enemy is all that is required of Israel (see above on 14:5-7). Calculating relative strength indicates a failure of trust and invites disaster. The Revised Standard Version translation of verse 9 is taken from the Septuagint and other versions as fitting the sense of the psalm much better than the Hebrew text translated in the footnote.

PSALM 21. A CORONATION LITURGY

Analysis of this royal psalm shows that it is appropriate to a variety of cultic occasions (on this category, the title, and **selah** see Introduction). Verses 1-7 are a thanksgiving hymn sung by the priests in acknowledgment that the king's prayer has been answered. In verses 8-12 a priest or cultic prophet pronounces an oracle assuring the king of victory over his enemies. Verse 13 is a doxology offered by the congregation. The psalm would fit the coronation of the king or the annual festival commemorating the king's enthronement (verse 3), the eve of a battle (verses 8-12), or the festival of the enthronement of the LORD (verse 13; see Introduction).

21:1-7. This hymn expresses the Israelite theory of kingship. The monarch's well-being (**blessings**) and authority to rule (**glory**) are derived from his relationship to God, from the divine **strength** and **presence.** The king's trust in the LORD is answered by God's **steadfast** (helping and delivering) **love.** The supreme blessing which the king receives in consequence of this relationship is a long and successful reign. **For ever** in verse 4 does not signify immortality (see above on 6:4-5). It means the inviolable sanctity and complete fulfillment of life which the LORD bestows on the king.

21:8-12. In the tradition of the holy war this oracle declares that the king's victories are due to the LORD's intervention on behalf of Israel (see above on 20:6-9). The extravagant language of the psalm, the oriental "court" style, emphasizes the irresistible power of the covenant God and of God's chosen king.

PSALM 22. DERELICTION AND DELIVERANCE

This is an individual lament (on this category and the title see Introduction). It begins with radical despair (verses 1-21) and ends in thanksgiving and praise (verses 22-31). Its setting is any cultic occasion marked by the mood of rejoicing after sorrow.

22:1-21. *Despair*. Three times the psalmist struggles through sorrow toward confidence, only to be overwhelmed again by despair:

22:1-5. To the tormented mind of the psalmist his suffering is proof that the LORD has **forsaken** him. His passionate and continuous prayer falls into an unhearing void. In this overpowering sense of alienation, shared by Jesus on the cross (Matthew 27:46; Mark 15:34), the psalmist draws comfort from reflection on the history of his people. This sacred history witnesses to a God who is **holy**—that is, other than and different from human beings. But he is always present with the people, **enthroned** on their hymns of praise as on the cherubim above the ark (cf. 99:1-5; Isaiah 37:16). The LORD has never disappointed those who trust.

22:6-11. The psalmist's enemies mock his confidence with gestures of derision. Their cruel taunts confirm his belief that God has abandoned him. He is stripped of his humanity and reduced to the lowest form of animal existence. He obtains temporary relief from this agony by remembering his personal history. From his first stirrings in **the womb** God has protected him.

22:12-21. His enemies tear at his legs like a pack of **dogs** and charge him with the fierceness of wild **bulls of Bashsan** (the grasslands of northern Transjordan). The thought wears him down like a wasting disease, strips the flesh from his **bones,** and leaves him dry, brittle, and useless as a broken pot. Some commentators believe that the animal imagery refers to the demonic creatures who, according to pagan mythology, brought disease to humans (see below on 91:5-10). They point out that verses 14-15 describe the effects of fever. Crowding around his emaciated body, the psalmist's enemies treat him as if he were already dead. They confiscate his **garments** and divide the plunder by casting **lots** (cf. John 19:24). This time the psalmist can find no ground for confidence and simply utters a naked appeal for **help.**

22:22-31. ***Rejoicing.*** The psalmist looks back on his torment from the tranquility following deliverance.

22:22-24. The psalmist offers public testimony before the worshiping **congregation** in the temple. He testifies to the salvation which God has brought to him and exhorts all true worshipers and genuine Israelites to praise the LORD for delivering power (the LORD's **name**).

22:25-26. The psalmist acknowledges that his ability to praise is the consequence of his deliverance. In payment of his **vows** (see Introduction) he provides a sacrificial meal to which his friends are invited. **The afflicted** are the God-fearing Israelites, not the materially poor or downtrodden (see Introduction). **Live for ever** is an oriental exaggeration meaning "live long" (cf. I Kings 1:31; Nehemiah 2:3). It does not refer to immortality (see above on 6:4-5).

22:27-31. The Hebrew text of these verses is difficult, and numerous emendations have been suggested. The readings accepted by the Revised Standard Version seem best—except that in verse 29*a* "those who sleep in the earth" is preferable to **the proud of the earth.** Under the inspiration of his deliverance the poet's vision broadens to include all time and space. The whole **earth,** the **generation** yet to be born, and the dead in the underworld will accept the rule of the LORD and proclaim the LORD's saving acts. The conviction that God's power extends beyond death and reaches even to Sheol is the first theological step toward a doctrine of resurrection (see above on 6:4-5).

Psalm 23. Shepherd and Host

This poetic gem is a song of confidence (on this category and the title see Introduction). A worshiper, grateful for deliverance from human **enemies** (verse 5) and unnamed perils (verse 4), presents a thank offering in the temple. Some interpreters hold that the psalm involves only the metaphor of the shepherd. Others see in it an interweaving of three images: shepherd (verses 1-3*a*), guide (verses 3*b*-4), and host (verses 5-6). But **rod** and **staff** tie verse 4 to the shepherd metaphor, whereas verses 5-6 clearly describe a sacred meal. Therefore, it seems best to regard the psalm as based on the double imagery of shepherd (verses 1-4) and host (verses 5-6).

23:1-4. The poet's choice of metaphors is determined by the structural and theological center of his psalm—the triumphant affirmation of faith, **Thou art with me.** In ancient Near Eastern literature kings are called shepherds of their people. In the Old Testament this language is applied primarily to the LORD's relationship to Israel (cf. 80:1; 95:7; 100:3). Because of his place in the covenant community the psalmist lacks nothing. The Shepherd-God leads him by the right paths to nourishment and rest. If the way leads through a dark, precipitous defile (**the valley of the shadow of death,** i.e. death shade), the sheep fears neither pitfalls nor enemies, for the shepherd with club and staff is near at hand to defend them. **For his name's sake** may mean "in order that his name may be exalted"—or, more probably, "because that is the kind of God he is."

23:5-6. Verse 5 probably refers to the sacrificial meal associated with the presentation of thank offerings (Leviticus 7:11-17). In the thought of the psalm, however, the LORD, not the worshiper, is the host, and the LORD provides for the guests with lavish generosity. Ancient laws of hospitality required that the host take the guests under protection. The psalmist has come to the temple followed by enemies. Now he will be followed by God's saving **goodness and mercy** ("steadfast love," as the Hebrew word is usually translated elsewhere in the Revised Standard Version). Verse 6 is probably a confession of the Levite priesthood, originally expressing the priest's joy because of his permanent residence in the temple. But to the psalmist, God's presence *is* the holy place, and in that protecting presence he will live the rest of his life. **For ever** here is literally "for length of days" (cf. the Revised Standard Version footnote; see above on 6:4-5).

PSALM 24. AT THE GATES OF THE TEMPLE

This liturgy is in three parts (on this category, the title, and **selah** see Introduction). It consists of a hymn (verses 1-2), an entrance liturgy for the people (verses 3-6), and an entrance liturgy for the LORD's coming to the temple as king (verses 7-10).

24:1-2. During the festival of the enthronement of the LORD (see Introduction) a cultic procession bears the ark, the LORD's throne (Exodus 25:10-22). The procession moves up **the hill of the LORD** toward the great gates of the temple and sings in praise of the world-embracing sovereignty and creative power of God (verses 1-2). For the concept of the world anchored in the ocean and above the subterranean waters see above on 18:7-18 and 19:1-6.

24:3-6. The procession asks the priests for the conditions of entrance to the temple. The answer is a general requirement and two concrete illustrations (see above on Psalm 15). One who would worship in the temple must be **clean** not only ritually but also morally in both outer and inner life (**hands** and **heart**). He must **not lift up his soul to what is false** (worship idols) and must be honest in social relationships. Perjury is a violation of the integrity which makes possible a stable society. On verse 6 see above on 11:7*b*.

24:7-10. Twice the procession calls on the temple **gates** to open and admit the LORD, symbolized by the ark. The Egyptians believed that when the **doors** of the earthly temple opened, the portals of heaven (eternal gates) swung wide as well. This psalm may reflect a similar concept. The Hebrew word translated **ancient** may mean either "everlasting" or "very old." The God who seeks entrance is the **King of glory**—the ruler whose power and authority are unlimited. From within the temple the priests demand further identification of the deity. The procession answers that the LORD is the God of the old holy war tradition, the **mighty** warrior and commander of Israel's **hosts** (army; see Introduction and on 20:6-9). This tradition was originally associated with the ark at Shiloh (I Samuel 4:1-9). It was transferred to Jerusalem when the ark was brought there at the order of David (II Samuel 6:12-15).

PSALM 25. GUIDANCE AND FORGIVENESS

This individual lament is interspersed with expressions of confidence (verses 8-10, 15). In places it is reminiscent of the wisdom psalms (on these terms and the title see Introduction). The psalm is an alphabetic acrostic (see Introduction), and the form has taken precedence over logical development of the thought. It can therefore best be discussed topically rather than verse by verse.

The immediate cause of the psalmist's lamentation is the violent attack of treacherous **enemies** (verses 2, 19). They have isolated him and plunged him into loneliness and despair (**troubles,** literally "narrowness," **of my heart;** verses 16-17). He wonders if he is being punished for his present sins and those of his youth (verses 7, 18; cf. Job 13:26). He is able to approach God, however, because the LORD has been revealed in Israel's history in the covenant. The LORD is a God who pardons **sinners,** saves the afflicted, and removes the barriers which restrict the lives of the people (verses 5, 8, 10, 11). **Salvation** comes from a root meaning "make wide"; see above on 18:19.

The psalmist bases his prayer on his own character as well as on the name (nature) of God (verse 11*a*). He will **lift up** his **soul to** (worship) and **trust** only the LORD (verses 1-2*a*). Eagerly and expectantly he will **wait** (hope) for divine aid (verses 5, 21). He will **fear** the LORD—that is, worship humbly and with reverential awe (verses 12, 14). Strengthened by these considerations he prays that God will **deliver** him from his enemies (verses 2, 15, 19-20; on the **net** of verse 15 see above on 9:13-17). As well as physical deliverance he prays that God will **forgive all** his **sins** which have caused his distress (verses 7, 11, 18). He asks that God **teach** and **lead** him in the true meaning of the **covenant**, which will keep him from further offenses (verses 4-5, 8-10).

Above all other gifts the psalmist craves admission into God's **friendship** (a weak translation of *sodh*, which means a circle of intimate companions, verse 14). If he is granted this relationship, **integrity and uprightness** will be like guardian angels, preserving his life (verse 21). Verse 22 was added outside the acrostic pattern to make this highly personal psalm suitable for congregational use.

Psalm 26. A Plea of Innocence

This is another individual lament (on this category and the title see Introduction). The psalmist asks that God declare him not guilty of charges made against him by his enemies (verses 1-2). He takes an oath of innocence (verses 3-5). He then performs an appropriate ritual (verses 6-7) and renews his prayer for vindication (verses 8-11), and affirms his confidence (verse 12). On the setting and theology of this type of psalm see above on Psalms 7 and 17.

26:1-2. The psalmist prays for vindication on the ground that his inner life will pass the test of the LORD's searching examination. **Heart** and **mind** are literally "kidneys" and "heart" (see above on 16:7-8).

26:3-5. Inspired by God's **steadfast** (saving) **love,** he is always loyal to the LORD. He has nothing to do with those who conceal their real thoughts in order to deceive others. He hates the society of the wicked and godless.

26:6-7. In confirmation of his oath he washes his **hands**—an ancient means of declaring one's innocence (cf. Deuteronomy 21:6; Matthew 27:24). Then he joins in a solemn procession around the **altar, . . . singing** of God's mighty acts in Israel's history (or perhaps of the wonderful deliverance which God will perform for him).

26:8-12. The psalmist professes his love for the temple, the place where Israel confronts the majestic, authoritative presence of the LORD—God's **glory.** This moves him to renew his prayer for vindication. He prays that his **integrity** be recognized, and that he not receive the penalty merited by the violence, sexual immorality (**evil devices**), and graft of which his enemies accuse him. In view of his exemplary life he is confident that God will deliver him and establish his position in the community. The **foot** that slips is a frequent Old Testament metaphor for destruction.

PSALM 27. THE CONQUEST OF FEAR

Most scholars believe this to be two separate psalms. It combines a song of confidence (verses 1-6; cf. Psalm 23) and individual lament (verses 7-14; cf. Psalm 13; on these categories and the title see Introduction). It is possible, however, to view the psalm as a unity describing the experience of a fugitive who seeks refuge in the temple (see above on Psalms 7 and 11). While still at a distance and beset by enemies he sings of his confidence in the LORD. Arrived at the temple he pours out his distress in the traditional lament form and receives an encouraging answer from a priest or cult prophet (verse 14).

27:1-6. ***Song of Confidence.*** The psalmist has reason to be afraid. His enemies rip at his flesh like a pack of wild beasts (verse 2; see the Revised Standard Version footnote). They come against him like a hostile army (verse 3). **Uttering slanders against me** in verse 2 is a questionable translation. It is based on evidence that in later times "to eat up my flesh"—the literal translation—was a common metaphor for malicious accusation (cf. Daniel 3:8). The psalmist's complete trust in the LORD as his **light**, his deliverer, and his fortress casts out his **fear**. His **one** prayer and desire is to reach the **temple**. There he will find permanent refuge and will contemplate the beauty of the sacred place which is the beauty of the LORD. **To inquire** may be a technical term for offering a sacrifice in the expectation of receiving an oracle from God. **Behold the beauty of the LORD** in pagan religion meant viewing the idol. Here it perhaps signifies looking at the ark.

27:5-6. These verses reflect the function of the temple as a place of refuge for fugitives. They describe it in archaic terms reminiscent of the tent of meeting of the wilderness period (see above on 15:1). **In the day of trouble,** when his enemies come forward to condemn him, the psalmist will be exalted over them—as the **rock** on which the temple stood was exalted over Jerusalem. In gratitude he will present the thanksgiving offering with singing and rejoicing.

27:7-14. *Individual Lament.* Verses 7-13 are a prayer for hearing (7-9*a*), acceptance (9*b*-10), guidance (11), and deliverance (12). A brief cry of confidence follows in verse 13. To **seek** the **face** of the LORD is a technical term for entering the temple (see above on 11:7*b*). **Servant** is a common Near Eastern word for "worshiper." The psalmist has been rejected by all human society, even his parents. But he will be adopted by the LORD (verse 10). The metaphor may have been suggested by the royal psalms in which the king is the LORD's adopted son. As in many lament psalms the enemies are those who bring false charges against the psalmist (cf. 7:3-4; 35:11). **I believe** is a powerful word signifying "I have anchored my life on the conviction that I will live and receive good from the God in whom I trust."

27:14. This closing oracle responds to the psalmist's lament. It urges him to show strength and inner **courage,** and to **wait** (hope) expectantly and eagerly for the saving power of the LORD (cf. 25:5, 21).

PSALM 28. IF GOD BE SILENT

This individual lament has a cultic setting (cf. Psalms 7 and 17; on this category and the title see Introduction).

28:1-2. These verses are a prayer for hearing. If the psalmist receives no answer, he is as good as dead and in the lowest part of Sheol (**the Pit;** see above on 6:4-5). Lifting up the **hands** is an ancient gesture of supplication and appeal. In this case it is directed toward the innermost room (Holy of Holies) of the temple, where the LORD was enthroned above the ark (cf. I Kings 8:6-7). On **rock** see above on 18:1-3.

28:3-5. The psalmist appeals against enemies who greet him as friends while plotting his ruin. They have disqualified themselves from membership in Israel by their unconcern for God's mighty acts in the nation's history. **Peace** (*shalom*), meaning total well-being rather than mere absence of conflict, is still the common word of greeting among Semitic peoples. On God's "poetic justice" see above on 7:12-16.

28:6-9. After hearing an oracle of assurance from a priest or cult prophet (cf. 27:14) the psalmist expresses his thanksgiving and joy (verses 6-7). To bless God is to acknowledge the LORD's might and saving power. Unlike his enemies the psalmist is an authentic Israelite. He cannot rejoice in his own salvation without recognizing his involvement with the nation and its anointed king (verses 8-9). On **shepherd** see above on 23:1.

PSALM 29. PRAISE IN HEAVEN

This is a hymn for the enthronement of the LORD (on this category and the title see Introduction). The background is the ancient Near Eastern concept of the council of the gods (see below on 58:1-5; 82:1-5).

29:1-2. The **heavenly beings,**—literally "sons of God" or "sons of gods"—are lesser deities. In monotheistic Israel they have only the status of servants and choir boys. They are exhorted to praise the **glory** of the LORD's **name** (see above on 8:1-2) and to fall down before God "when he appears in his holiness"—a translation which seems more probable than the Revised Standard Version's **in holy array** (clad in holy garments) or "in the beauty of holiness" (King James Version).

29:3-8. The song of the heavenly beings is modeled on Canaanite hymns to the weather god, Baal-hadad. **The voice of the LORD** is thunder (cf. 18:13). It sounds above the celestial ocean (verse 3; cf. Genesis 1:7), heralding the approach of the storm. The tallest trees are broken, and the land is shaken from end to end—from the northern mountains (**Lebanon** and **Sirion,** the Phoenician name for Mt. Hermon) to the desert of **Kadesh,** fifty miles south of Beer-sheba.

29:9. The Hebrew text of verse 9*a* with vowels added says that the thunder makes the does writhe—that is, in the throes of giving birth (cf. the Revised Standard Version footnote). But consonants alone, as written during biblical times, spell either "does" or **oaks**. With slight emendation verse 9*b* can be read "and causes the goats to give birth." The irresistible power of the LORD moves those assembled in the heavenly palace (in Hebrew the same word as **temple**) to shouts of acclamation.

29:10-11. The congregation prays to the God who rules **for ever** from the throne above the celestial ocean for **strength** and **peace**—that is, well-being (see above on 28:3-5).

PSALM 30. JOY IN THE MORNING

This is a thanksgiving psalm (on this category and the title see Introduction). The occasion is the presentation of a thank offering in the temple.

30:1-3. The psalmist says he will **extol** (literally "lift up") the LORD, because his God has raised him from a deadly sickness (verse 3) and from the rejoicing of his enemies over his misfortune (verse 1*b*). For **Sheol** and **the Pit** as synonyms for death see above on 6:4-5.

30:4-5. The psalmist invites the worshipers gathered in the temple (**saints**) to join his songs of praise. God's wrath is a secondary and transient aspect of the divine nature. God's true and permanent purpose is gracious and favorable.

30:6-10. From the vantage point of deliverance the psalmist looks back on his trouble. In good times he had been proud and self-satisfied. Perhaps to teach him humility the protecting presence of God was withdrawn (verse 7*b*) and he fell desperately ill. He appealed to God on the ground that since the dead cannot **praise** God (see above on 6:4-5) his passing into **the Pit** (Sheol) would be all loss and no gain for the Lord.

30:11-12. He acknowledges that this prayer was abundantly answered. God completely reversed his condition of misery, giving him a festal robe instead of the **sackcloth** garment of the mourner. He is sure that his new estate will be permanent. On **soul** and **for ever** see above on 6:1-3 and 22:25-26 respectively.

Psalm 31. In the Hand of the Lord

Basically an individual lament, this psalm incorporates features of the hymns and thanksgiving psalms (on these categories and the title see Introduction; for the cultic setting see above on Psalms 7; 17; and 22).

31:1-8. After a typical opening prayer (verses 1-2) the lament appeals to God to act in accordance with the Lord's revealed character (**for thy name's sake,** verse 3; see above on 23:1-4). In describing the divine character the psalmist emphasizes protection, guidance, justice, hatred of idolatry, and **steadfast** (delivering) **love.** Into the hands of this reliable and **faithful** (consistent) **God** he commits his life (**spirit** means "wind" or "breath" and hence life power; cf. Luke 23:46). He has complete confidence that the Lord, whose saving power he has already experienced, will save him once more. The hunter's **net** in verse 4 (see above on 9:13-17) is a metaphor for hidden peril which strikes without warning. Salvation is appropriately symbolized by **a broad place** (see above on 18:19).

31:9-13. Despair temporarily overcomes the psalmist's confidence. He is ridden with disease (verses 9-10; cf. Psalm 22), mocked and falsely accused by enemies who are openly plotting to do away with him (verses 11, 13). Isolated from his fellow citizens and from God (verse 22), he is as much forgotten as if he were in his grave (verse 12). This acute sorrow has been with him for a long time (verse 10).

31:14-18. These verses begin with the congregational confession of faith, **Thou art my God.** They represent a return of confidence. At all stages (**times**) of the psalmist's life the LORD has kept him (verse 15). He prays that the LORD's **face** will **shine**—that is, be gracious and favorable—and will bring deliverance to him and total destruction to his enemies (verses 17-18; on **Sheol** see above on 6:4-5).

31:19-24. Verses 19-22 are a final confession of faith. The mood is that of a thanksgiving psalm sung by one who has already experienced deliverance. The clump of bushes and the hut which shelter the wayfarer from the desert storm (verse 20) are powerful metaphors for the protecting power of the LORD. The didactic note of verse 23 is a common feature of thanksgiving psalms. Verse 24 may be an addition, perhaps reflecting the oracle of assurance spoken by a priest or cult prophet (see above on 27:14).

PSALM 32. REPENTANCE AND FORGIVENESS

This psalm is an individual thanksgiving (on this category, the title, and **selah** see Introduction). It is one of the seven penitential psalms (see above on Psalm 6). It was probably sung in the temple in connection with the presentation of a guilt offering (Leviticus 6:1-8). After two beatitudes (verses 1-2) the psalmist tells of his experience of alienation and forgiveness (verses 3-5). He confesses his indebtedness to the grace of God (verses 6-7). He then instructs his fellow worshipers in the style of a wisdom teacher (verses 8-10) and invites them to join him in praise (verse 11).

32:1-5. Three words are used to describe alienation from God: **transgression,** literally rebellion; **sin,** literally wandering from the road or missing the mark; and **iniquity,** literally distortion or perversion. By concealing his true condition from himself and God, the psalmist incurred a heavy weight of guilt which **wasted**

his **body** and sapped his **strength** like a disease. But when he acknowledged his guilt to God and figuratively cast it upon God (**confess**), God **covered** his **sin** and thought no more of his **iniquity**. The broken relationship was healed, and the psalmist was received back into fellowship without prejudice and without reservation (**forgive**). This forgiveness brought healing, blessing, and purification of the vital power of his life (**spirit**; see above on 31:1-8). He no longer misled or dealt treacherously with his fellows (**deceit**).

32:6-7. In verse 6*b* **distress**—literally "evil"—is a translation of two Hebrew words meaning "finding" and "merely" or "at the least" (cf. the Revised Standard Version footnote). The King James Version reads ". . . in a time when thou mayest be found: surely in the flood . . ." The text can be interpreted as meaning that one who calls on the LORD at the appropriate times will not be overwhelmed when trouble overcomes like a flash flood (cf. 124:4) or like an outbreak of the chaotic waters of the underworld (see above on 6:4-5; 18:7-18). Suffering may lead not only to prayer (verse 6) but also to confidence in God's saving power (verse 7).

32:8-9. Opinions differ as to whether the speaker here is the psalmist or God. The warning against brutish indifference to religion (verse 9) would have more weight as a divine word mediated through a priest or a cult prophet (see above on 27:14). The eye of God on the worshiper would then be an assurance of God's saving presence, not an expression of the psalmist's interest in the welfare of his hearers.

32:10-11. Verse 10 restates the psalmist's experience. When, like **the wicked**, he withheld his confession of guilt, he suffered. When he opened his life to God, he felt the **steadfast** (saving) **love** of the LORD surrounding him.

PSALM 33. GOD'S WORD AND WORK

This typical hymn (on this category see Introduction), was suitable for any cultic occasion where the predominant theme was praise. It was especially appropriate to the new year festival (see Introduction), which throughout the ancient Near East centered in the motif of creation (cf. verses 6-9).

33:1-3. The call to **praise** summons the congregation, who are conventionally called the **righteous** and **upright**. They are called to join in the hymn to the accompaniment of stringed instruments and cries of joy. **New song** does not necessarily mean a recent one. It could be a familiar hymn, renewed in the present experience of God's majesty and the present impulse to praise. On the musical instruments see below on 92:1-4 and 150:3. **On the strings** is not in the Hebrew text; it is one of several proposed emendations to fill out the meter of the line.

33:4-5. A generalized summary introduces the reasons for praise—not what God gives but what God is and does. The LORD's creative **word** is above reproach. God's **work** is absolutely trustworthy. God loves **justice,** displaying it in actions and demanding it of God's servants. The LORD fills **the earth** with acts of **steadfast** (saving) **love.**

33:6-9. The general statements of verses 4-5 are illustrated first by the LORD's control of nature. Creation by the word of God is not unknown in ancient mythology. The official theology of Old Kingdom Egypt taught that the natural order came into being by the command of Thoth. But in these theologies creation by the word is one concept among many. In Israel it was the ruling, if not the only, doctrine of creation (verse 9; cf. Genesis 1). Verse 7 has a mythological ring. God collected as if in a **bottle** (waterskin) the great ocean above the sky (cf. Genesis 1:7; see above on 18:7-18). God stored the water to pour out as rains (cf. Genesis 7:11).

33:10-15. The summary of verses 4-5 is further illustrated by the LORD's control of history. **Counsel** is a considered decision of plan of action. When God's plans collide with those of humans, the human schemes come to nothing. In the Old Testament the **heart,** rather than the brain, is considered to be the organ of thought. On God's judgment throne in heaven see above on Psalm 7. The decisions of that judge are the determining force in history (verses 13-15).

33:16-19. The summary of verses 4-5 is again illustrated by the LORD's saving power. On the holy war ideology which underlies verses 16-17 see Introduction and on 20:6-9. Not human power, calculated in military terms, but humility and reverence (**fear**) are the prerequisites of deliverance.

33:20-22. As the plural pronouns indicate, the conclusion is a congregational response to God's **holy name** (the divine nature) and **steadfast** (delivering) **love.** The response consists of expectant **hope** (cf. **waits,** verse 20) and **trust.**

PSALM 34. THE FEAR OF THE LORD

This individual thanksgiving has the form of an alphabetic acrostic (on the terms and the title, which has no historical value, see Introduction). It shows how the temple service could combine instruction and worship. After a hymnic introduction (verses 1-3) and a narrative of deliverance (verses 4, 6), the psalm teaches the meaning and saving value of the **fear** of the LORD. Hence it has strong affinities with the wisdom literature (cf. Psalm 1; Proverbs 1:7; 9:10).

34:1-3. The introduction provides an epitome of the Old Testament language of praise. To **bless the LORD** is to acknowledge God's preeminence and authority over every aspect of life. To **exalt his name** is to extol the divine nature by reciting God's saving acts.

34:4-10. The psalmist has recently experienced the LORD's saving power. He was delivered from an unnamed anxiety which had set his life in turmoil (verses 4, 6). This experience is available to all who come into the LORD's presence as humble suppliants. This meaning underlies the rich vocabulary of the approach to God found in this passage—especially the metaphor of tasting in verse 8. This may have been suggested by the sacrificial meals in the temple. The **angel** (literally "messenger") is probably the commander of the LORD's heavenly army (cf. Joshua 5:13-15), who includes those who fear God within the protective circle of his camp (cf. II Kings 6:17).

34:11-22. Despite the impression created by verses 10, 12, and 17, the fear of the LORD is not naïvely presented as a means to prosperity and long life. The overall impact of this passage shows that to fear the LORD is to be humble in God's presence. Such a life is marked by an orientation toward what God approves (**good**) and what makes for well-being (**peace**; see above on 28:3-5). Outwardly it manifests itself in honesty of speech (verse 13).

But it gives no guarantee against trouble. **Many . . . afflictions** may shatter the inner being of the **righteous** and crush the vital power (**spirit**; see above on 31:1-8). But real existence and security are at a depth that suffering cannot reach, and at that level God's presence restores and preserves. **The wicked** lack this depth. They are destroyed by the physical appearance of **evil,** which is suffering. God's absence from their lives, which is the real cause of their destruction, thus takes on the appearance of divine wrath (verse 16).

PSALM 35. A PLEA FOR VINDICATION

The background of this individual lament (on this category and the title see Introduction) is like that of Psalms 7 and 22. It is the prayer of the hunted for the vindication and destruction of enemies.

35:1-18. The word **contend** is a technical term meaning to enter a legal controversy. The standard imagery and language of the lament dominate the psalm: the **pursuers** (cf. 7:1), the hunter's metaphors of **net** and **pit** (see above on 9:13-17), the outcry for poetic justice (cf. 7:12-16), the false **witnesses** (cf. 27:12), the comparison of the enemy with wild beasts (cf. 22:12-13, 16), the mockery in word and gesture (cf. 22:7). Verses 5-6 ask that a warrior **angel** from the LORD's heavenly army be sent to drive the enemies **like chaff** from the threshing floor.

35:19-28. The psalmist's anger against his enemies (verses 15-17, 20-21) and the intensity of his prayer (verses 13-14, 22-24) increase. Finally he is demanding that God **awake** and do something (verse 23). Like all sufferers he sees the world through the narrow window of his own agony. He prays for the destruction of his enemies (verse 26) and for the happiness of those who side with him (verses 27-28).

PSALM 36. HUMAN EVIL AND GOD'S LOVE

This psalm has features of both the hymn (verses 7-9) and the lament (verses 10-12; on these categories and the title see Introduction). There are three sections. The first two (verses 1-4, 5-9) contrast the wickedness of the psalmist's enemies with the love of God. The third (verses 10-12) prays for the blessing of God's love on those who live in fellowship with God and divine judgment on those who reject God.

36:1-4. The wicked person, having neither reverence for God nor **fear** of judgment, is devoted to **mischief and deceit**. Evil has captured the **heart**.

36:5-9. The **steadfast love** of God rules the universe. The psalmist makes skillful use of ancient cosmology (see above on 18:7-18) to show the universality of divine love, which is also God's steadfastness and justice (verses 5-6). It reaches from the **heavens** to the clouds that brood over the earth and from the highest **mountains** to the **great deep** of the underworld. The **children of men**—that is, all humanity—may shelter in that love and enjoy its bounty (verses 7-9). The imagery of these verses was suggested by the temple—the outspread **wings** of the cherubim over the ark and the abundant food and drink of the sacrificial meals. From the living God all life flows, like water from a **fountain** (a natural spring). In the light of God's presence the people of God **see light** (live). The psalm shows clearly that God's steadfast love is delivering love.

PSALM 37. TRUST VERSUS ENVY

This is a repetitious acrostic poem (on this term and title see Introduction). By means of a series of proverbs it reinforces the main thrust of Israel's wisdom teachers (cf. Psalm 1).

Though temporarily shaken and distressed, **the righteous** will be rewarded with long life and prosperity. But **the wicked,** though they may live well and lord it over the righteous, will be destroyed as the spring grass perishes before the first hot wind of summer (verses 2, 20). In the experience of a long life the psalmist has never seen an exception to this rule (verse 25).

The terms **righteous, meek, poor, needy, upright, blameless,** and **saints** mean the same thing. They refer to the faithful adherents to Israel's covenant faith whose chief characteristic is unshakable confidence in the God of the covenant (they **trust in** and **wait for the LORD**). As a result of this attitude they are **generous** (verses 21, 26), speak with **wisdom** and **justice** (verse 30), and obey the **law** (verse 31).

The repeated warning **fret not yourself** shows why the psalm was included in the temple service. The prosperity of the wicked might arouse the envy of the faithful and tempt them away from the trust which was the foundation of their lives.

PSALM 38. UNDER GOD'S WRATH

This individual lament (on this category and the title see Introduction) is one of the seven penitential psalms (see above on Psalm 6). The background is given in the comment on Psalms 7 and 22.

The lament begins and ends with a cry to God for help. The body of the psalm is an extended account of the psalmist's plight, brought about by deadly sickness (verses 1-11) and the attack of enemies (verses 12-20). Expressions of confidence appear in the midst of the lamentation at verses 9 and 15-16. The festering **wounds** (verse 5), the wasted **flesh** (verse 7), and the fact that the sufferer is able to move about (verse 6) indicate leprosy.

The Babylonian prototype of this kind of psalm was used as a magical incantation to remove a spell cast by one's enemies. But in the theology of the psalmist illness and persecution were evidence of the **anger** of God and proof of the sufferer's guilt.

Like Apollo in Greek mythology, the LORD shoots **arrows** of sickness (verse 2; cf. 91:5).

Convinced his suffering is caused by his **sin** and **foolishness** (rejection of God's discipline), the psalmist is alienated from himself (verse 8) and from his **friends** (verse 11). He is like a **deaf** mute before his enemies. All he can do is **confess** the sin he cannot name and cast himself on the mercy of the God of **salvation.**

PSALM 39. FORCED TO PAY

This is the cry of one who attributes suffering to the wrath of God, brought on by sin (verses 10-11). Like Psalm 38, it is an individual lament (on this category, the title, and **selah** see Introduction).

39:1-6. Verses 1-3 are an unusual biographical note. In order not to compound his **sin** or to hearten his enemies the psalmist resolved to keep **silent** (cf. verse 9). But the unspoken complaint **burned** within him and forced its way to utterance (cf. Jeremiah 20:9). The words thus wrung from him (verses 4-6) are as darkly pessimistic as Ecclesiastes. **Life** is short, one's strength a **shadow**, and all efforts futile.

39:7-11. From his own hopelessness the psalmist turns to the one ground of **hope** left to him. But he sees God only as wrath, as a deity who **like a moth** consumes the sinner's dearest possession, his life. He therefore prays only to be delivered from the consequences of his sin and from the derision of those who mock his faith (**the fool**; see above on 14:1-4).

39:12-13. The concluding prayer returns to the transience of human life. The psalmist is a **guest** in God's tent and a **sojourner** (resident alien) in God's land. He could claim hospitality and protection. But whereas other psalmists pray for the presence of God, he asks only that God withdraw and leave him a brief period of happiness before he is finally cut off by death (see above on 6:4-5).

PSALM 40. OUT OF THE PIT

This psalm of mixed type begins with thanksgiving (verses 1-10) and ends with lamentation (verses 11-17; on these terms and the title see Introduction).

40:1-3. In deep distress the psalmist remembers the LORD's goodness in the past. The **pit** "of tumult" (Revised Standard Version footnote) and **the miry bog** are common Near Eastern metaphors for the underworld (see above on 6:4-5). When the psalmist was at the point of slipping into the realm of the dead, the LORD entered into his misery and delivered him. His ability to praise is thus the gift *of* God, and not a gift *to* God (verse 3*a*; on **new song** see above on 33:1-3). His deliverance obligates him to testify to others (verse 3*b*; cf. verses 9-10).

40:4-5. The "new song," his testimony to the congregation, may be quoted in these verses. Unshakable confidence in God implies not only blessing but also rejection of arrogant self-confidence and idolatry. Prideful self-assurance necessarily involves rejection of the LORD. Recitation of the LORD's saving **deeds** was the chief feature of the covenant renewal ceremony (see Introduction).

40:6-8. The offering acceptable to the God of the covenant is the worshiper himself (**Lo, I come**). The sacrificial system is secondary and unessential—the **sacrifice** of an animal killed for the common meal, the cereal **offering** of homage to the LORD as King, the **burnt offering** consumed on the altar, and the **sin offering.** What is required is **an open ear,** itself a gift of God, and conformity of the whole personality to God's **will** as it is recorded in the sacred scrolls (verse 7).

40:9-10. The **law** is not a burden but **glad news of deliverance.** It reveals a God who acts consistently in **saving . . . love.**

40:11-12. Remembering the divine **mercy,** the psalmist asks a renewal of that mercy in his present plight. He is acutely conscious that his **iniquities** have distorted his mind. He has been robbed of his power of discernment and left helpless.

40:13-17. The psalmist here quotes a traditional supplication—almost identical with Psalm 70. It does not continue the theme of sin but reverts to a motif familiar in lament psalms—the attack of enemies (cf. Psalms 7; 22; 38; 39). The plea of verses 13-15 is that these foes—who are to be equated with the proud idolaters of verse 4—be stripped of their honors and struck with terror. **Shame** is a common Old Testament expression for idol worship. **Aha** expresses an unpleasant combination of mockery and delight. The psalmist prays that joy may reside where it properly belongs, in the community of the faithful worshipers of the LORD (verses 16-17). The cultic cry **Great is the LORD** suggests the amazing condescension of God, whose majesty does not prevent God from bending toward **needy** servants. This emphasis conforms the traditional lament to the trustful spirit of verses 1-10.

PSALM 41. INTEGRITY SUSTAINED

This is an individual thanksgiving (on this category and the title see Introduction). It praises God for deliverance from malicious enemies (cf. Psalms 7; 22; 38; 39).

41:1-3. The opening beatitude indirectly provides the reason for the psalmist's deliverance—his concern for the helpless and needy. This kind of action results in salvation, the providential care of God, a good reputation, and protection from **illness** and **enemies.**

41:4-10. Because he **sinned** the psalmist fell ill. He was tormented by malicious enemies who desired his death and the extinction of his **name**—that is, his family. Hypocritically they visited him with **empty words** of comfort, only to go away and spread rumors of what a thoroughgoing sinner he was (verses 5-7). **"A deadly thing** (literally "thing of Belial") **has fastened upon him"** has the ring of a sorcerer's formula. It reflects the original connection of this type of psalm with Babylonian incantation texts (see above on Psalm 38). Thinking that the psalmist is cursed by God, his closest **friend** joined ranks with his tormentors. The psalmist prayed for recovery in order that he might revenge himself on his enemies and turncoat friends (see above on Psalm 17).

41:11-12. The LORD has been **pleased** with his endurance under trial and granted his prayer. He is able again to enter the temple. He can look forward to a life of continuous fellowship with God (on **for ever** see above on 22:25-26).

41:13. An added benediction closes Book I of the Psalter (see Introduction).

PSALMS 42–43. A PSALMIST'S DIALOGUE WITH HIMSELF

Psalms 42–43 were originally a single individual lament (on this category and the title see Introduction). This was divided into three strophes by a refrain of haunting melancholy and soaring hope (42:5, 11; 43:5). Thrice the psalmist sinks into depression and rises again to faith.

42:1-2*a*. The psalmist begins abruptly with the memorable metaphor of a thirst-crazed deer frantically searching the desert for a stream of water. With the same intensity as the animal seeks the "living water" the psalmist seeks the **living God,** from whom life and hope come. **My soul** (see above on 6:1-3) is an emphatic equivalent for "me."

42:2*b*-4. The psalmist's sorrow arises from his inability to get to Jerusalem, the only place where the living God may properly be worshiped. **Behold the face of God** is a technical term for ceremonial entrance into the temple (see above on 11:7*b*). The psalmist's depression is aggravated by the taunts of his neighbors, who question the existence of his God. He is rescued from this despair by memories of the temple service. In former days he attended the festival with joyous pilgrims singing psalms. The Hebrew of verse 4*b* is corrupt and should be emended to read:

> how I went into the tent of the Glorious One,
> in procession to the house of God.

On the use of "tent" for the temple see above on 15:1.

42:5. Under the inspiration of these memories the psalmist in his refrain gently chides his soul for its restlessness. He expresses the confident **hope** that he will again sing the LORD's **praise** in the temple.

42:6-11. Despair returns and the psalmist's vital power (**soul**) is at a low ebb. He is an exile, or more likely a prisoner of war (cf. 43:1-2), far to the north of Jerusalem near the source of the **Jordan** River on the slopes of Mt. **Hermon. Mount Mizar** is one of the peaks in the Hermon range. Lonely and isolated among enemies, he feels his homesickness beat in his ears. It is like the noise of the chaotic underworld ocean rushing to carry him down to the realm of death (verse 7; see above on 6:4-5; 18:7-18). He seems to be forsaken by God (verse 9). The pagans around him wound him like a fatal sword thrust by their mocking denial of the reality of his God (verse 10). **Hope** comes from memory of the hymns of the temple and from prayer, but especially from meditation on the **steadfast** (saving) **love** of God. This is his **rock**—solid ground amid the shifting sands of his loneliness.

43:1-5. The last strophe is a prayer for vindication before his pagan tormentors. This will take the form of a return to the temple. The psalmist prays that the LORD's **light** (guiding power) and **truth** (the certainty of his salvation) will stream across the intervening miles to bring him home to the **holy hill** in Jerusalem. Restored to the temple, he will place the thank offering on the **altar** and join the congregation in joyfully singing the psalms of thanksgiving. On **lyre** see below on 150:3.

PSALM 44. WAKE UP, O LORD!

This psalm is a community lament over military defeat (on the category, the title, and **selah** see Introduction). The "I" of verses 4, 6, and 15 is the leader of worship—possibly the king—speaking as representative of the nation.

44:1-8. Verses 1-3 refer to the recitation of God's saving acts during the exodus period. This recital was the chief feature of the ritual of covenant renewal (see Introduction). The ideology of the holy war (see Introduction and on 14:5-7; 20:6-9) fills the psalm. **Victory** is won by the LORD (verses 3-5), who leads the army to battle (verse 9). The LORD's **countenance** brings terror on the enemy (verses 3*c*, 7*b*). Absolute **trust** is required of Isarel's army and king (verses 6-8).

44:9-16. The LORD has granted past deliverances (verses 1-3) and more recent victories (verses 4-8). But the LORD has been absent from the battle just concluded (verse 9). Fighting in an unholy war the people have been slaughtered **like sheep,** plundered, and taken prisoner (verses 10-11). Like every defeated nation of antiquity they must face **taunt** songs of the enemy (verses 13-16; cf. Judges 5:28-31). The LORD has **sold** out the **people** and gained no profit.

44:17-22. The LORD's action is inexplicable. Israel has rejected idolatry, kept the terms of the **covenant**, and preserved the purity of worship. The defeat has figuratively thrust the nation into the underworld, the realm of death (verse 19; see above on 6:4-5). **Place of jackals** (*tannim*), if correct, refers to wasteland abandoned to wild animals. But parallelism with the following line makes more likely "place of the dragon" (*tannin;* cf. 74:13; Isaiah 27:1; 51:9). God must be asleep rather than arbitrarily opposed to the people. Hence the *demand* that God **rouse** and behave like a God of saving love. **Soul** in verse 25 has its physical meaning "upper chest."

PSALM 45. A ROYAL MARRIAGE

This is a royal psalm in the flamboyant oriental court style (on this category and the title see Introduction). It was probably composed for the wedding of Ahab to the Tyrian princess Jezebel (see below on verse 12*a*; cf. I Kings 16:31). The poem gained such popularity that it was used at later royal weddings and probably also at the festival of the enthronement of the king (see Introduction).

45:1-9. After a vainglorious introduction in verse 1 the poet addresses the royal bridegroom, stressing the two principal functions of the king—to lead in war (verses 2-5) and to maintain justice (verses 6-7). Verse 6*a* begins literally "Your throne, O god." Although the Israelite monarch was never regarded as an incarnate god, as were the pharaohs of Egypt, he could be given a divine title because at his coronation he became the son of God by adoption (see above on 2:7-9). His adoption, symbolized by **the oil** of anointing, and the attendant blessing of God were the sources of his majesty (verses 2*a*, 7*b*). The catalogue of his royal splendors climaxes in the gold-decked figure of the new **queen** standing in the place of honor beside him. **Ivory palaces** refers to ivory inlays used in furniture and decorated paneling (cf. I Kings 22:39). **Ophir** was probably in southeastern Arabia (cf. I Kings 9:28; 10:11; 22:48).

45:10-17. The latter half of the poem is addressed to the bride. She is admonished to **forget** her foreign origin and to devote herself to her new master. If she does so, she will receive the homage of her Israelite subjects (verses 10-13*a*). In verse 12*a* the text probably should read, "The people, O daughter of Tyre." The poet then reminds the queen of her glorious entrance into **the palace.** He assures her that her permanent fame will rest, not with her pagan ancestry, but with her children who will occupy the Israelite throne **for ever and ever** (verses 16-17).

PSALM 46. A MIGHTY FORTRESS

This hymn of Zion consists of three balanced strophes (on this category, the title, the divine names, and **selah** see Introduction). Each ends with a majestic refrain (verses 7, 11, but missing after verse 3). The God who dwells on Mt. Zion is a sure defense for the people, even in the catastrophic events of the end of the world. The theme of the end of the age (eschatology) is rare in the Psalter, but common in prophecy.

46:1-3. The imagery of the first strophe has mythological origins. The chaotic **waters** of the underworld break forth, shaking and submerging **the mountains** and overwhelming **the**

earth, so that it reverts to the chaos from which God created it (Genesis 1:2; see above on 18:7-18).

46:4-7. In Jerusalem, where **a river** of life and health flows from the temple, all is quietness and security (verses 4-5). At the end of the age the heathen will **rage** against the Holy City, but the sight of its God-given majesty makes them reel. At the sound of the LORD's **voice, the earth melts.**

46:8-11. The last strophe invites Israel to **behold** the result of these cataclysmic events. The earth is covered with broken and burned weapons of war. God's eternal reign of peace has begun. The goal to which history moves is universal knowledge of God and the submission of all to him. The direct word of God in verse 10 was probably spoken by a cult prophet.

PSALM 47. THE ENTHRONEMENT OF THE LORD

This hymn is for the enthronement festival, celebrated along with covenant renewal rituals at the new year feast (on this category, the title, the divine names, and **selah** see Introduction). The theme is God's sovereignty over world history. The repeated claim that the LORD rules **all the earth** is not political wishful thinking. It is the result of the faith that, since God's authority governs the whole sweep of history, it will eventually be recognized by all peoples of the world.

47:1-4. The people are invited to raise the festal cry as they remember how their **terrible** (awe-inspiring; see above on 14:5-7) God overcame the Canaanites and gave them the land which was promised to their ancestor **Jacob.**

47:5-7. These mighty acts of God were recited during the covenant renewal ritual. The people then formed a procession to bear the ark, the throne of the LORD, into the temple (see above on 24:1-2). The procession was probably accompanied by the singing of these verses and the blowing of the ram's-horn **trumpet** (see below on 81:1-5*b*).

47:8-9. As the ark entered the Holy of Holies the congregation sang the concluding verses. Here the universalism of the hymn is magnificently expressed. History moves toward the time when the rulers of foreign **nations** and the covenant **people,** the heirs of **Abraham,** will form a single congregation. All will pay homage to the king of the earth, to whom all world power (**shields**) belongs.

Psalm 48. The Strength of Zion

This hymn of Zion praises both **Mount Zion** and the **great King** who dwells there (on this category, the title, and **selah** see Introduction). The two themes are combined in a single shout of praise. Jerusalem is surrounded by precipices on three sides. The heights were crowned by massive stone walls and numerous defense towers. The palace and the temple were formidable fortresses (verses 3, 13). The visible fortifications symbolized Jerusalem's unseen defense—the protecting presence of its God, which set it apart from other cities and made it **holy.** Canaanite mythology placed the home of the gods on a mountain **in the far north.** Sacrificing geographical accuracy, the psalmist took over this traditional phrase to describe the home of the one God **of all the earth.**

48:4-8. These verses reflect on the cultic recitation of God's saving acts in which the worshiper could "see" and "hear" (verse 8) the defeat of Israel's enemies on land and sea. **Ships of Tarshish** were deep-water vessels capable of sailing to Tarshish, which was probably on the southwest coast of Spain. The terror inspired by God is a feature of the holy war ideology (see above on 14:5-7; 44:1-8).

48:9-14. Verses 9-11 express the universal rule of Zion's king, whose fame and **praise** have spread from the temple throughout the earth. In holy war contexts God's **steadfast love** is the power to bestow **victory.** Verses 12-14 emphasize the community's responsibility to educate its children in the traditions of God's guiding and protecting actions (cf. Deuteronomy 6:20-25).

Psalm 49. The Delusions of Wealth

This wisdom psalm exposes the futility of trust in wealth (on this category and the title see Introduction and on Psalms 1; 37).

49:1-6. The wisdom teacher calls for a universal audience to consider a universal problem (**riddle**). His personal experience (verse 5) forced him to ask, "How can one maintain trust in God when the wicked prosper and use their power to exploit the weak?" (cf. Psalm 73). By meditation and as a revelation from God (verses 3-4) he has obtained an answer. He has cast this in the form of a poem and recites it to the accompaniment of a **lyre** (see below on 150:3).

49:7-19. Equanimity, says the teacher, can be preserved by contemplation of the common human **fate.** A multimillionaire cannot buy escape from death (verses 7-9). Death, the great leveler, makes all equal—**wise,** godless (**the fool**), boors, and kings. It brings them all to the same permanent **homes**. Led by **Death** like **sheep** by a **shepherd,** stripped of their possessions, their shades troop to the dark underworld (see above on 6:4-5) while their bodies rot in the family **grave.**

49:15. This verse is a faintly sounded intimation of immortality (cf. 73:23-24). Money cannot **ransom** one from **Sheol**, but God may. The teacher does not know how God will buy him back from the power of death. But even beyond the grave he will be in communion with God, and that suffices him.

Psalm 50. God Judges the People

This prophetic liturgy belongs to the new year festival (on these terms, the title, the divine names, and **selah** see Introduction).

50:1-6. The theophany of the Lord from the temple is accompanied by light and storm (verses 2-3; see above on 11:4-7*a*; 18:7-18). The Lord comes as **judge** to bring the people to trial before they enter into the ritual of **covenant** renewal. The

LORD's mighty voice calls the whole universe to witness judgment (verses 1, 4).

50:7-15. These verses were probably spoken by a cult prophet. They give the verdict against the whole congregation. The covenant making at Sinai was accompanied **by sacrifice** (cf. Exodus 24:3-8). But now the people have developed a false faith in their sacrifices. They believe that the sacrificial meals and **burnt offerings** bind God to them and minister to God's needs. To think that the creator and ruler of the world needs gifts or feeds on animal flesh is ridiculous (verses 9-13). What God requires is grateful acknowledgment of total dependence (verses 14-15). To **pay . . . vows**—pledges made **in the day of trouble**—is to acknowledge publicly one's debt to God. The psalmist's insight is still too easily forgotten: Sacrifices which bind the worshiper to God are valid, but those which attempt to bind the deity to the worshiper are not.

50:16-23. The Judge's second verdict is again probably spoken by a cult prophet. This denies the right of **the wicked** to participate in the covenant renewal. They have rejected the terms of the covenant by word and deed. They have mistaken God's patience for approval (verse 21). God makes a last attempt to reform them by showing the deadly peril in which their conduct has placed them.

PSALM 51. REPENTANCE AND CLEANSING

This individual lament is one of the seven penitential psalms (on this category and the title, which has no historical value, see Introduction; also see above on Psalm 6). For the vocabulary of sin and forgiveness see on Psalm 32.

51:1-2. God's **mercy** and **steadfast** (saving) **love** create the *possibility* of forgiveness.

51:3-5. The four aspects of repentance are given:

(1) recognition that **sin** has obtained control over one's life (verse 3);

(2) understanding that sin is directed, not against self or others, but against God (verse 4*a*);
(3) willingness to assume full responsibility (verse 4*b*);
(4) abandonment of all claim to merit (verse 5).

Verse 5 does not condemn the sexual act or reflect on the chastity of the psalmist's *mother*. It recognizes that life is lived in an environment of temptation. At no time from the moment of conception can one claim innocence.

51:6-9. It is God's nature to desire sincerity in one's inner life. God alone can implant **truth** there and **purge** (literally "unsin") the sinner. The deeply ground-in stain of sin can be removed only by vigorous scrubbing (cf. verse 2). A cleansing agent as potent as the herb **hyssop**—used in the purification of lepers (Leviticus 14:4)—is needed.

51:10-12. The new life is a creation as miraculous as the formation of the universe. It brings a new inner life (**clean heart**) and a new life power (**right spirit**; see above on 31:1-8). It is characterized by a marvelous **joy** (cf. verse 8).

51:13-17. The one valid missionary motive is desire to share the experience of God's saving love with others. The psalmist does so by teaching, by public testimony, and by participation in the temple services. Verses 16-17 make the same point concerning sacrifice as 50:7-15. **A broken spirit** is one in which selfishness and willfulness have been shattered and replaced by conformity to God's will.

51:18-19. This ending was added during the exile by an enthusiastic advocate of sacrifice, who longed for the day when the ruined temple and its sacrificial system would be restored.

Psalm 52. The Final Condemnation

This psalm is an announcement in the prophetic style of God's judgment on the wicked (cf. Isaiah 22:15-25). Possibly it is a formula for the expulsion of an offender from the covenant community (the **godly** or **righteous**). On the title, which has no historical value, and **selah** see Introduction).

52:1-7. The **mighty man** is a Hebrew term for a hero. Here it is used sarcastically. This person is described as so steeped in **evil** that all values are reversed. This person takes pride in oppression (verse 1), loves vicious deeds and **lying** words (verses 2-4). This person trusts completely in possessions (verse 7). Rather vindictively verses 5-7 predict the total destruction and pleasure this will give to this person's victims. **Tent** in verse 5 may mean "temple" (see above on 15:1) and may refer to expulsion from the religious community. Or it may signify simply "household."

52:8-9. The conclusion sounds the theme of the power of trust in God's **steadfast** (saving) **love.** But the psalmist is too sure of his own innocence (see above on Psalm 17 and contrast Psalm 51). Trees, symbols of the goddess of fertility, often grew in pagan sacred places. In the temple the worshiper, secure in God's **presence,** is the symbol of power, the **green olive tree.**

Psalm 53. The Fate of the Wicked

This psalm is almost identical with Psalm 14. It uses **God** instead of "the Lord" (see Introduction). Verse 5 has major differences from 14:5-6, drawing more directly on the holy war concept of the terror of the Lord (see above on 14:5-7). To **scatter the bones,** the most permanent part of the body, signifies complete destruction.

Psalm 54. Ringed by Foes

This is an individual lament (on this category, the title, and **selah** see Introduction; on the cultic setting see on Psalms 4 and 7).

54:1-3. The cry for help is based on the **name** (the saving nature) of God, here equated with **might.** The psalmist is under attack by foreign enemies who do not reverence Israel's God. Perhaps, therefore, the original suppliant was the king. In verse

3 most Hebrew manuscripts read "strangers" rather than **insolent men** (cf. 86:14).

54:4-5. The expression of confidence presents a textual difficulty in verse 4*b*. The Hebrew text reads "The Lord is with those who uphold my life"—that is, the armies of Israel. If the speaker is the king, we should probably follow this reading. **Requite** means pay the reward due for their deeds.

54:6-7. These verses are a vow, a pledge made in time of **trouble.** To **give thanks** means in this context to offer a thank offering. **A free-will offering** is one which is not prescribed by law but is presented voluntarily as an act of homage to God. The psalmist's memory of past deliverances makes him confident of God's present help.

Psalm 55. The Treacherous Friend

This individual lament may be two poems joined together (on this category, the title, and **selah** see Introduction; on its cultic setting see on Psalms 4 and 7). Many commentators regard it as such, but they rarely agree on the limits of each. However, it may be taken as a single composition, disjointed in structure because of the intense emotion of its author.

55:1-11. The appeal for hearing (verses 1-2) arises from the attack of vicious enemies (verses 3-11). **Horror** of the dread realm of **death** oppresses the psalmist's mind (see above on 6:4-5). He expresses his desire to escape in the splendid **dove** metaphor. **In the wilderness** he could find refuge from the violence of nature. **In the city** he can find none from the cruelty of his fellows. In prophetic disgust he condemns the total depravity of a community where rogues continually walk the **walls** and wait in the **market place** to cheat and defraud the citizens.

55:12-23. His enemies include one who was his best **friend** (verses 12-14, 20-21), but who has broken the mutual bond of friendship (**covenant**). To the Hebrew **fellowship** in worship is the most intimate of human relationships, the real seal of friendship. Going down **alive** to **Sheol** (see above on 6:4-5) was the punishment of Dathan and Abiram (Numbers 16:31-33). **Evening and morning and at noon** were the customary hours of prayer. Verse 22 is an "oracle of salvation," probably spoken by the priest for the comfort and encouragement of the sufferer.

PSALM 56. TRUST CASTS OUT FEAR

This individual lament has a refrain at verses 4 and 10-11 (on this category and the title see Introduction). Some interpreters believe the refrain originally appeared at the end of each strophe—that is, after verses 7 and 13 also. Others consider a refrain inappropriate and explain the inclusion of verse 4 as a copying error. Since the cry for help in verses 1-2 uses military language and verse 7 identifies the enemy as **the peoples,** the original speaker may have been the king.

56:1-4. The word translated **be gracious** is a specific term for a monarch's willingness to hear and act on the petition of one of his subjects. The expression of confidence in verses 3-4 voices the faith that complete **trust . . . in God** casts out **fear** (cf. verses 10-11). **Flesh** is humanity in its weakness in contrast to the majesty of God.

56:5-7. The reason for the lament is the lying charges and malicious plots of the psalmist's enemies. The fear of death is present, but in a muted form (verse 6; cf. verse 13).

56:8-11. The renewed expression of confidence is an impressive description of the depth of God's concern. God counts how many times the psalmist tosses on his bed. The sufferer's **tears** are not lost. God collects them in a **bottle** (waterskin) and enters each drop in a ledger.

56:12-13. The psalmist pledges a thank offering if his prayer is answered (see above on 54:6-7). The perfect tense in verse 13 indicates that the psalm was sung just before the presentation of the offering.

PSALM 57. PRAISE AFTER PERSECUTION

This is another individual lament (on this category, the title, which has no historical value, and **selah** see Introduction). It follows the usual lament pattern:

(1) cry for help (verse 1),
(2) description of the trouble (verses 4, 6, interrupted by a refrain in verse 5),
(3) expression of confidence and vow (verses 7-10, followed by the refrain in verse 11).

The normal elements of the lament are present:

(1) appeal to the divine mercy (verse 1),
(2) comparison of the enemy to wild beasts and of their schemes to a hunter's traps (verse 4, 6),
(3) God's poetic justice (verse 6*b*),
(4) oath of innocence (verse 7),
(5) and vow (verses 8-10).

On these features see above on Psalms 7; 17; 22; 31.

57:1-6. On **the shadow of thy wings** see above on 17:6-9. Verse 3, looking forward to the theophany (see above on 11:4-7*a*), personifies God's **steadfast** (saving) **love and his faithfulness** (self-consistency). These qualities are described as ministering angels (cf. verse 10, which marvels at the magnitude of these divine qualities that fill the universe). On **net** see above on 9:13-17.

57:7-10. The closing expression of confidence is especially fine. The psalmist declares that he has responded to God's faithfulness by consistent loyalty to his Lord. He then pictures the joy of the morning (cf. Psalm 30) when, after his night's vigil in the temple, he awakes to the assurance that he has been vindicated at the bar of God's justice. He greets the new day with music (see below on 150:3), song, and sacrifice which will be heard in foreign lands (verse 9)—or perhaps by Jews from other parts of the world gathered in the temple.

57:11. The psalmist's universal outlook appears in the refrain in the prayer that God's **glory** (authority) be recognized in **the heavens** and on **earth.**

Psalm 58. Demons in Heaven and Earth

This community lament is unusual in structure and rich in varied word pictures (on this category and the title see Introduction).

58:1-5. The question and answer of verses 1-2 are spoken by God to the members of the heavenly court (see above on 7:6-11; 29:1-2). In Babylonian mythology the council of the gods met annually to determine the fates and inscribe them upon the Tablets of Destiny. In Old Testament thought the divine council is an assembly, not of gods of roughly equal status, but of the Lord and angelic messengers and servants whose duty is to maintain the Lord's justice in the world (cf. 82:1-5). God charges these servants with rebellion and with corrupting his moral order. **The wicked** are the human agents of these demonic beings. They are like viper's **venom** in the bloodstream of society. They heed warnings and entreaties no more than a **deaf adder** responds to the **voice** of snake **charmers.**

58:6-9. The psalmist appeals to God to destroy the wicked in heaven and on earth as quickly as cooking **pots** heat up over a fast-burning fire of **thorns**. Dry thorn bushes are still gathered for fuel in the Holy Land. The slimy track of **the snail** suggested to the prescientific mind that the animal was dissolving as it crept along.

58:10-11. In the extinction of the wicked the faithful members of the covenant community (**the righteous**) will see their own **vengeance** and the operation of the perfect justice of God. The bloodbath is an ancient symbol of vengeance. In Canaanite mythology the goddess Anath walked knee-deep in the blood of her enemies.

Psalm 59. A Prayer Against the Nations

This is an individual lament (on this category, the title, which has no historical value, the divine names, and **selah** see Introduction). It alternates between prayers (verses 1-2, 4*b*-5,

8-13, 16-17) and descriptions of the psalmist's distress (verses 3-4*a*, 6-7, 14-15).

The psalm has many of the standard features of Hebrew lament poetry:

(1) fear of death (verse 3*a*; cf. 6:4-5),
(2) oath of innocence (verse 3*b*; cf. Psalm 4),
(3) appeal to God to **come** (verses 4*b*, 10; cf. 18:4-9),
(4) comparison of the enemy to wild beasts (verses 6-7, 14-15; cf. 22:12-21),
(5) cry for vengeance and the destruction of the enemy (verses 10*b*-13; cf. Psalm 17),
(6) pledge of songs of praise in the morning after God has made clear the divine intention to save (verse 16; cf. 4:7; 5:3).

Less usual are the references to the LORD as God of the covenant people (verses 5, 13) and as ruler of history who laughs at the would-be world powers (verse 8).

God is described in military terms (**strength . . . fortress, shield**). The psalmist identifies his enemies as **nations,** accusing them of bloodthirstiness, pride, and treachery (verse 2), and denial of the sovereignty of God (verse 7). He calls Israel **my people** (verse 11). These facts indicate that the king was the suppliant who originally offered this prayer in the temple.

PSALM 60. A NATION REJECTED

This psalm is a community lament in liturgical form (on this category, the title, which has no historical value, and **selah** see Introduction). Its date is uncertain, but since Shechem is in enemy hands (verse 6), it was perhaps composed after the Assyrian conquest of the northern kingdom of Israel in 722 B.C. On the holy war ideology see Introduction and on 14:5-7; 20:6-9.

60:1-3. After military defeat the nation, broken and reeling like a drunkard, gathers in the temple for a ceremony of national lamentation. The belief that disaster in war was caused by the anger of the national deity was widespread in antiquity. A commemorative stele of Mesha, king of Moab, attributes his defeat by the Israelites to the fact that the Moabite god "Chemosh was angry with his land."

60:4-5. Already God's **banner** has been raised to rally the scattered troops. The peasant soldiers of Israel, mostly spearmen, naturally feared **the bow,** the weapon of trained warriors. The people pray for victory in order that God's **beloved**—Israel—may be saved. They appeal to God for an answer.

60:6-8. The response comes in an oracle spoken by a priest or cult prophet. The central highlands around **Shechem** and the **Vale of Succoth** east of the Jordan will be reconquered and reapportioned as in the days of the original conquest (verse 6). All the land east of the Jordan (**Gilead** and **Manasseh**) belongs to Israel's God. On the west the two great tribes, **Ephraim** in the north and **Judah** in the south, are God's battle armor. Judah holds the supremacy since it is God's **scepter,** the symbol of God's royal power. God's rule extends to the vassal states of **Moab, Edom,** and **Philistia.** The Dead Sea (Moab's sea, since that nation occupied its eastern shore) is God's **washbasin.** God casts a **shoe** (an ancient symbol for claiming possession) over Edom.

60:9-12. Assured of God's sovereignty over the whole territory, the king or the commanding general seeks God's guidance for a campaign against Edom (verse 9) and reflects on the reason for the recent defeat (verses 10-11). God rejected the people and did not go with them to battle. If, however, God will accept the people's prayer and fight for them, defeat will be turned to victory.

Psalm 61. A Prisoner's Lament

This individual lament was sung by one far from the temple and surrounded by enemies (on this category, the title, and **selah** see Introduction). Since it assumes that a king is reigning in Jerusalem, it must date from before the exile. The singer is likely a prisoner of war.

61:1-4. Verses 1-2*a* are a cry for hearing. Then the psalmist, conscious that he cannot reach the temple (**the rock**) by his own power, prays for the guidance and protection of God. He longs to live the rest of his days in the environs of the sacred place. On **tent** and the **wings** of God see above on 15:1 and 17:6-9 respectively.

61:5. The psalmist is a true Israelite—one of those whose ancestors received the Holy Land as a heritage from God, and one who reverences God's mighty nature and saving deeds (God's **name**). He is therefore certain that God has heard his pledge of sacrifice and praise to be performed in the temple and will enable him to fulfill his **vows** (cf. verse 8; see above on 7:17).

61:6-8. Prayers for **the king** in language like that of verses 6-7 are frequent in ancient Near Eastern religious poetry.

PSALM 62. WHAT SUPPORTS TRUST?

This song of confidence has features of the lament and wisdom psalms (on these categories, the title, and **selah** see Introduction).

62:1-7. The psalm begins in a mood of serene confidence that God will deliver the psalmist from his trouble (verses 1-2). Virtually the same words reappear in verses 5-7. On **my soul** see above on 6:1-3 and 42:1-2*a*. The psalmist then castigates his enemies for taking advantage of his weakness and trying to topple him like a shaky stone **wall** (verses 3-4). He was evidently a person of authority whom political opponents tried to unseat by slander and lies.

62:8-10. The psalmist here speaks as a wisdom teacher. He exhorts the people to **trust** and prayer. Human nature, no weightier than a **breath**, cannot be trusted. Crime and confidence in **riches** delude but do not save.

62:11-12. The conclusion has the form of a numerical proverb (cf. Proverbs 6:16-17). God was revealed in the deliverance of Israel from Egypt and the psalmist has heard the message repeated in the temple worship. God is a God of justice (verse

12*b*). God's deeds of **steadfast** (saving) **love** are backed by unlimited **power.** *God* can be trusted to save.

PSALM 63. A THIRST FOR GOD

This individual lament weaves the customary phrases and ideas of lament poetry into a composition of uncommon beauty (on this category and the title, which has no historical value, see Introduction). It is spoken by one who has sought **sanctuary** in the temple (verses 1-3) and found refuge and a renewal of joy (verses 5-8). At the end his vision broadens beyond his own situation. He reaches the certainty that the king, who is lord of the temple, and the nation which he represents will prosper.

63:1-4. As a desert wanderer longs for water, the psalmist yearns with his whole being for the protective presence of God. **Looked upon thee** is a technical term for God's self-revelation to worshipers (theophany; see above on Psalm 11). To experience God's **steadfast** (saving) **love** and to witness to it in worship **is better than life.** Standing with **hands** extended, palms upward, was the traditional posture for prayers of petition.

63:5-11. During a night vigil the psalmist is given the certainty that he is safe under God's protection. This satisfies him as if it were the richest of foods (verses 5-6). On the **wings** of God see above on 17:6-9. Poetic justice will overtake his enemies (see above on 7:12-16). They seek his life but will themselves **go down** to the realm of death (see above on 6:4-5). The **sword** and the scavenging **jackals** are common Old Testament symbols of destruction. As in Babylon and Egypt, oaths were taken in Israel **by . . . the king.**

PSALM 64. THE DESTROYER DESTROYED

This psalm is an individual lament (on this category and the title see Introduction).

64:1-6. The prayer for hearing in verse 1 is followed by a bitter description of the enemies. Like archers **shooting from ambush** or hunters setting **snares,** they try to destroy the psalmist by **secret plots** and lying charges. They hold God's justice in contempt and trust the profundity of their own scheming minds (verses 5*b*-6).

64:7-10. God will destroy the destroyers (see above on 7:12-16). The **arrow** of God usually refers to sickness (cf. 38:2). Others will profit by the fate of the malicious liars, learning to reverence God and to meditate on God's mighty deeds (verse 9). The **righteous** and **upright**—the faithful members of the covenant community—will **rejoice.**

PSALM 65. CREATION, PROVIDENCE, AND SALVATION

This is a hymn of thanksgiving (on this category and the title see Introduction). In a time of drought the congregation pledged that if God would send rain, they would offer a sacrifice of praise. The psalm is the payment of that vow (see above on 7:17).

65:1-4. The drought was regarded as punishment for national sin. Strophe 1 appropriately praises God for God's willingness to hear **prayer** and to **forgive** sin. The **temple** on Mt. **Zion,** the dwelling of God, is the source of the prosperity of the land. Any member of the chosen people who enters its courtyards comes within the sphere of blessing (verse 4).

65:5-8. Strophe 2 draws a universal lesson from the deliverance from drought. Israel's God is the hope of the whole earth, for the LORD is its creator. Verse 7 refers to the Babylonian belief that before they created the ordered universe the gods had to subdue the raging sea of chaos, personified as the dragon-monster Tiamat (see below on 74:12-14). The psalm historicizes this mythological concept by equating the turbulent sea with the unruly nations, Israel's historic enemies (verse 7*c*). Dawn and sunset are visible signs of God's authority over the world from end to end. The pagans recognize that this is so, but wrongly attribute the movement of the heavenly bodies to the activity of their many gods (verse 8).

65:9-13. Strophe 3 pictures the rejoicing of nature at the coming of the rain. It streams from **the river of God**—that is, the ocean above the heavens (cf. Genesis 1:7; 7:11; see above on 18:7-18; 33:7-9). The Canaanites believed that their fertility God, Baal, the rider of the clouds, brought the rain. Verse 11 retains the pagan imagery but identifies the cloud **chariot**, in whose rain-soaked **tracks** the land springs to life, with the chariot of the LORD (cf. 104:3). The bountiful harvest is a crown on the head of the **year.**

PSALM 66. DELIVERANCE ACKNOWLEDGED

This psalm is an individual thanksgiving to accompany the payment of a vow (on this category, the title, and **selah** see Introduction).

66:1-4. The psalmist summons **all the earth** to praise the **glory** (authority) of God's **name** (nature), which are revealed in historic acts of salvation and triumph over God's **enemies.** Verse 4 might be better translated: "Let all the earth worship thee; let them sing praises. . . ."

66:5-7. The congregation is invited to dramatic recollection of God's greatest saving deed—the deliverance from Egypt. Especially remembered are the drying up of the **sea** (Exodus 14:21-29) and the **river** (Joshua 3:14-17) and the defeat of the **nations** who opposed Israel.

66:8-15. The hardships of the wilderness period were a test of Israel's loyalty to its God (verse 10). But in the end God brought the nation safely into the **spacious place** of Canaan (see above on 18:19). The psalmist regards these events as typical of all God's saving deeds, including the deliverance which he has personally experienced. While in distress he vowed to offer **burnt offerings** in the temple. Now he is ready to pay his vows with costly sacrifices (verses 13-15).

66:16-20. The psalmist gives his testimony to the congregation (verses 16-19). He claims, not that he was sinless, but that sin did not gain control of his inner life (verse 18). Even in his distress he did not lose the spirit of praise (verse 17). Therefore God heard him and delivered him by an act of **steadfast** (saving) **love.**

Psalm 67. A Harvest Thanksgiving

This is a community thanksgiving for the harvest festival (on this category, the title, and **selah** see Introduction). There are two principal themes: praise to God for bounty (verse 6) and a prayer that all nations will reverence Israel's God (verse 7 and the refrain, verses 3 and 5).

67:1-3. The congregation recalls the prayer for blessing which was offered at seedtime (verse 1). The words are reminiscent of the benediction of Aaron in Numbers 6:26. Israel sought prosperity as a visible sign to the whole world of the **power** of its God (verse 2).

67:4-5. In the same universal spirit the second strophe extols God's perfect justice. Although not universally recognized, this in fact rules and guides all history and all peoples.

67:6-7. The congregation gratefully acknowledges that its prayer for blessing has been answered by a good harvest. It renews its prayer for the conversion of the world.

Psalm 68. Themes from the Theophany

In both text and interpretation this psalm is the most difficult in the Psalter. Some regard it as a unified composition used in a procession (verse 24). Others see it as a mere index of first lines. It seems to be a collection of fragments united around the idea of the theophany—God's appearing to people (see Introduction and on 11:4-7*a*). The dominant motif is the warrior God leading the holy war (see above on 14:5-7; 20:6-9), found in five of the poems. On the title, divine names, and **selah** see Introduction.

69:13-18. The psalmist calls on God for help on the basis of divine **steadfast love** and abundant mercy.

69:19-29. The psalmist again laments that those from whom he expected comfort have given him heartbreaking insults and **poison for food** (verses 19-21). Then he voices a terrible prayer for vengeance (verses 22-29). His enemies have tried to poison him; may their hypocritical participation in the **sacrificial feasts** poison them, glazing **their eyes** and making their limbs shake (verses 22-23). May their families be destroyed (verse 25). May their **punishment** be endless, without hope of acquittal (verse 27). May their names be erased from God's ledger of **the living** and from the rolls of **the righteous** (the covenant community, verse 28).

69:30-33. If he is delivered from his enemies, the psalmist vows to **praise** God with a grateful heart—a more acceptable offering than costly sacrifices. Others in peril or need will **see** his deliverance and will have their faith renewed.

69:34-36. The concluding call for universal praise may have been added during the exile. A poet later saw in the psalmist's plight a parallel to the suffering of the exiles in Babylon and used the psalm to pray for the restoration of **Zion** (Jerusalem) and **Judah**.

Psalm 70. A Plea for Help

For comment see above on 40:13-17, where this psalm is quoted almost word for word. On the title see Introduction.

Psalm 71. Distress in Old Age

This individual lament is spoken by an old man (on this category and the divine names see Introduction). He is so hard pressed by the lying charges of **cruel . . . enemies** (verses 4, 10-11, 13) and by the sense of alienation from God (verses 11, 18) that he has become the symbol of what the wrath of God can do to a person (verse 7). In this extremity he seeks sanctuary in the temple and vindication from the God of justice—the **refuge** of every needy soul (verse 3). God has watched over his **birth,** supported him in his **youth** (verses 5-6), and educated him in the sacred traditions of the covenant people (verse 17).

The psalmist's single appeal for vengeance is comparatively mild (verse 13; cf. 69:22-29). His expressions of confidence are frequent (verses 3, 5, 19-21). In his trouble he makes two vows. The first is public testimony to God's **deeds of salvation** in Israel's history and in his personal experience (verses 15-19). The second is joyful songs of **praise** (verses 22-24).

For background and further details see above on Psalms 4; 7; 9–10; 22. On **harp** and **lyre** see below on 150:3.

Psalm 72. A Coronation Hymn

This is a royal psalm for the accession of a crown prince (on this category and the title see Introduction). It is composed in the exaggerated style of the court poets.

72:1-7. The new **king** is the human agent through whom God's **justice** reaches the nation (verses 1-4; cf. verses 12-14; on the concept of justice see above on 7:12-16; 68:5-6). The poet prays that the royal justice will fill both society and nature (verse 3). The king's intimate relationship to God makes him the bearer also of the blessings of prosperity and fertility to the land (verse 6; cf. verse 16). In his prosperity the nation flourishes, and the poet prays for his long life (verses 5, 7).

72:8-17. The poet further prays that the king may be blessed with victory, worldwide **dominion,** and wealth. According to ancient geography the inhabited earth was bounded by **sea** on all sides. **The River** in verse 8*b* is the Euphrates. The places mentioned in verse 10 stand for the remote, the foreign, and the exotic—**Tarshish,** probably on the southwestern Spanish coast, the **isles** of the Mediterranean, **Sheba** in southern Arabia, and **Seba**, probably in Ethiopia. On the theological implications of the claim to world domination see above on Psalm 2.

72:18-20. Verses 18-19 are the closing benediction to Book II of the Psalter. Verse 20 probably marks the end of an early compilation (see Introduction).

PSALM 73. THE PILGRIMAGE OF A SOUL

This wisdom psalm depicts a journey from the dark night of doubt to the dawn of faith (on this category and the title see Introduction).

73:1-3. The psalmist, a priest or leader of the religious community, **had well nigh slipped** from the belief that loyalty to God means prosperity (verse 1). In the world as he saw it arrogance and brutality paid dividends. To his horror, he found himself envying **the prosperity of the wicked.**

73:4-14. The social situation which created his doubts is described. Free from pain and **trouble,** the oppressors wear **pride** and **violence** as badges of distinction. Instead of shunning them **the people** rush to do them honor. They blaspheme God and exploit their neighbors (verse 11). Daily they grow fatter and more self-satisfied (verse 7). The psalmist has apparently been loyal and devout for no purpose (verses 13-14).

73:15-17. The psalmist's first reaction was to publicize his doubts before the congregation. But that would solve nothing and would merely injure the congregation of which he was leader (verse 15). He sought the solution of his problem by earnest thought, but only pain and bitterness filled his mind (verse 16). At the end of his resources, he entered the temple to lay his case before God. There he discovered the answer to his problem.

73:18-28. At one level the answer is simply that wealth is a precarious foundation for life. Standing on the **slippery** edge of an abyss, the wicked will suddenly disappear over the edge and be forgotten **like a dream.** At a deeper level the psalmist learned that material prosperity is irrelevant to true religion. In his envy of the wicked he was **like a beast** displaying exclusive concern for its own comfort.

The center of life must be God, not possessions. The one who possesses communion with God is richer than any plutocrat (verses 25-26, 28). Communion with God is permanent. It guides this life and endures into the mysterious **afterward** beyond death, where God's **glory** (authority) still rules (verses 23-24). This passage seems to be one of the rare exceptions to the usual view in the Psalter that death brings only a shadowy existence in Sheol (see above on 6:4-5 and 49:15).

Psalm 74. The Destruction of the Temple

This community lament bewails the destruction of the temple (on this category and the title see Introduction). This destruction was probably by the Babylonians in 586 B.C., though some have argued for the desecration by Antiochus IV in 168 B.C.

74:1-11. God is bluntly accused of abandoning the people in anger. God has forgotten the covenant and the divine dwelling place on **Mount Zion.** The **enemy** have set up their battle standards in the temple, **hacked** away the woodwork for its gold and ivory inlay, burned the **sanctuary,** and **destroyed** the places of assembly in the outlying towns. During this disaster God has kept the delivering **right hand** tucked in the divine robe (verse 11). No **signs** of deliverance or prophetic word of assurance have come from God to dispel the anxiety of the people.

74:12-14. In Babylonian mythology the god Marduk split in half the dragon monster Tiamat, symbolized by the chaotic ocean. From her carcass Marduk created the universe. The Canaanite Baal was said to have broken **the heads** of the unruly Judge River (Hebrew **Leviathan**) with a magic club. But it was the LORD, rather than the pagan deities, who in the beginning overcame all forces of disorder.

74:15-23. The LORD who controls the **springs** and rivers, **day** and **night,** the stars and the seasons can easily dispose of a puny human enemy. By the LORD's known merciful character (verse 21), by the promises of the **covenant** (verse 20), and by the shame to which inactivity exposes him (verses 22-23), the nation calls on God to act.

Psalm 75. God's Coming in Judgment

This is a liturgy for the ritual of covenant renewal (on this category, the title, and **selah** see Introduction). The congregation recited God's wonderful deeds of the past and looked for new manifestations of God's power.

75:1-5. After a congregational thanksgiving in the opening verse a cult prophet gives a direct word from God (verses 2-5). **At the . . . time** determined by the sovereign will God promises to come in final judgment of **the wicked.** Meanwhile when the foundations of society tremble, the creator of the world holds them **steady.** On the **pillars** of the world see above on 18:7-18 and 19:1-6. The **horn,** the armament of the powerful bull, is an ancient oriental symbol for might.

75:6-10. The congregation responds to the word of God (verses 6-8). They acknowledge that justice can be found nowhere in the world but in God alone. The concept of the **cup** of God's wrath which crazes and destroys the wicked probably originated in the ordeal in which a suspected criminal was made to drink a cup of sacred liquid (Numbers 5:16-32; see above on 11:4-7*a*). A solo voice leads the concluding thanksgiving to the God of justice.

Psalm 76. The Terrible God

This is a hymn of Zion (on this category, the title, and **selah** see Introduction). It celebrates the theophany of God in the temple (see above on 11:4-7*a*; 18:7-18).

76:1-6. Though God dwells in heaven (verse 8), the point of contact with the world is Mt. **Zion**. This is located in **Salem,** a pre-Israelite name for Jerusalem (cf. Genesis 14:18). There God's **name** (saving nature) is **known** and proclaimed. God's presence makes Zion **more majestic than the everlasting mountains.** God is a warrior God, and the terror of the divine presence makes enemies fall unconscious (verses 3, 5-6); on this terror in the holy war ideology see above on 14:5-7).

76:7-9. The God who appears on Mt. Zion is the heavenly God whose authority embraces the whole **earth.** The theophany is the revelation of **judgment,** which means peace for the world and deliverance for **the oppressed.**

76:10-12. God makes even the hostility of enemies a source of **praise,** and those who survive **the residue of wrath** (judgment) worship the LORD. To this kingly and victorious God it is appropriate to pay **vows** (see above on 7:17; 50:7-15) and offer homage. On **spirit** in verse 12 see above on 31:1-8.

PSALM 77. THE DEEDS OF THE LORD

This individual lament changes at verse 11 into a hymnic meditation on Israel's deliverance from Egypt (on these categories, the title, and **selah** see Introduction).

77:1-10. In an agony of body and mind the psalmist tosses sleepless on his bed. He searches his inner being for the reason God has deserted the covenant people, canceled **promises,** and apparently denied the divine **gracious** and saving nature (**steadfast love**). Instead of answering these desperate questions he turns to reflection on what it was like before God's **right hand** (delivering power) **changed.**

77:11-20. The deliverance from Egypt demonstrated the uniqueness of Israel's God. God's difference from all other deities—that is, God is **holy** (verse 13). Verses 15 and 20 are conventional statements, but the description of the miracle of the **sea** crossing in verses 16-19 is alive with poetic imagery (cf. Exodus 14:21-29). Verse 16 compares the event to God's victory over the primeval ocean of chaos (see above on 74:12-14). Verses 17-19 contain all the accompaniments of the theophany of the warrior God (see above on 11:4-7*a*; 18:7-18; 68:7-10). Being invisible, God cuts a **path through the great waters** for the people.

PSALM 78. THE RIDDLE OF REBELLION

This psalm belongs to none of the basic types. On the title and the divine name see Introduction.

and King. The Shepherd, angry at his flock, feeds it on **tears** (cf. 23:1-3). The national sorrow is caused by a military defeat in which God seems to be destroying the creation. On God **enthroned upon the cherubim** see below on 99:1-5. **Benjamin** and **Joseph** were the children of Jacob's favored wife, Rachel. **Ephraim** and **Manasseh** were Joseph's sons. Benjamin, Ephraim, and Manasseh were the principal tribes of the northern Kingdom, and their mention together in verse 2 indicates that the psalm had a northern origin.

80:8-19. Using the allegorical figure of the vine, strophes 3 and 4 describe God's mighty acts in Israel's history—the Exodus (verse 8); the conquest of Canaan (verse 9); and the empire of David and Solomon, extending from **the River** (the upper Euphrates) to **the sea** (the Mediterranean, verses 10-11). Now the stone **walls** of God's protecting presence are gone. Enemies crowd in to strip the vine of **its fruit** and to uproot it like wild pigs (verses 12-13). The psalmist prays for the return of God's saving presence (verses 14-16). In verse 17 he asks that the divine power come upon the king. Though a mere mortal (**son of man**) the king is **the man of thy right hand** (cf. 110:1), endowed by the LORD with more than human power. Because of the names in verse 2 some have dated this psalm before 722 B.C. and applied it to a northern king. More probably, however, it comes from a later time. Verses 17-18 are a prayer for the restoration of united Israel under the Davidic king in Jerusalem.

PSALM 81. A PROPHET AT A FEAST

This is an unclassified psalm. On the title, the divine names, and **selah** see Introduction.

81:1-5*b*. The hymnic beginning speaks to pilgrims approaching the temple with music, songs, and shouts of joy. It reminds them that the festival to which they come was specifically prescribed in the Sinai covenant. A fifteen-day feast, it begins **at the new moon** and ends **at the full moon.** It opens and closes to the sound of the ram's-horn **trumpet**—the *shophar*, still used in the synagogue in the autumn new year service and at other special times (cf. 47:5). On the instruments of verse 2 see below on 150:3, 4. The description suggests the new year festival (ingathering or booths; see Introduction).

81:5*c*-10. In the ancient Near East the new moon was considered a favorable time for prophecies. Here a prophet, inspired by the mysterious **voice** of God, recalls the nation's deliverance from **basket**-carrying slave labor in Egypt. God answered their cries for help in the wilderness and was revealed in **thunder** from Sinai. God also tested the nation at **Meribah** (cf. Exodus 17:1-7; Numbers 20:1-13). The covenant established by these events requires unswerving obedience to the first commandment (verses 8-9). This is vividly reinforced by reference to the ancient covenant formula (verse 10; cf. Exodus 20:2-3).

81:11-16. In its desire for self-determination the nation turned a deaf ear to God (verse 11). God allowed them their independence, and they were overrun by enemies (verse 12). If they would now obey God, their enemies would be permanently subdued. The nation would be satisfied by a miracle greater than those of the wilderness period—**honey**, not water, **from the rock** (verses 14-16).

Psalm 82. The Judgment of the Gods

This psalm is a prophetic vision of the heavenly **council** (see above on 7:6-11; 29:1-2; 58:1-5). It is meeting as a legal body to hear the case of the divine beings accused of dereliction of duty. On the title, the divine names, and **selah** see Introduction.

82:1-5. The high God, king of the gods (cf. 86:8; 97:7*c*; 135:5) has entered and **taken his place** of honor. God states the case against the rebels (verses 2-4). They have failed to be God's agents in the administration of **justice** in the world (see above on 7:12-16; 68:5-6). The accusation asserts that they have willfully preferred the **darkness** of their own ignorant and incapable minds. The resulting perversion of justice has shaken **the**

foundations of the earth. In Hebrew thought the justice of God maintains both the stability of nature and the order of society.

82:6-8. The divine beings are **sons of the Most High,** not by physical generation, but by sharing in divine qualities. The most decisive of these is freedom from death. Their sentence is that, their divinity taken away, they will **die like men.** The congregation responds to this vision by calling for a similar just and final judgment on **the earth** and its **nations.**

Psalm 83. A Covenant Against God

This is a community lament (on this category, the title, the divine names, and **selah** see Introduction). It was composed in the face of a threat from a coalition of nations against Israel. The description does not fit any known historical situation and probably involves poetic exaggeration of the actual crisis.

83:1-8. Surrounding **enemies** have conspired under solemn oath to destroy Israel. Throughout the ancient Near East the wiping out of a **name** from memory signified complete extinction. The league against Israel includes most of her neighboring states: **Edom . . . , Moab . . . , Ammon . . . , Philistia . . . , Tyre** (Phoenicia). Included also are various desert tribes: **the Ishmaelites . . . , the Hagrites** (probably meaning descendants of Ishmael's mother Hagar), **Gebal** (here not Byblos in Phoenicia but a bedouin tribe from south of the Dead Sea) **. . . , and Amalek.**

The Assyrian invasions of 732-722 B.C. gave these lesser powers the opportunity to plunder Israel. But since **Assyria** here seems to be a secondary menace, it may be a figurative name for some later Mesopotamian power. **Children of Lot** means specifically Moab and Ammon (cf. Genesis 19:36-38; Deuteronomy 2:9, 19). Here it is used as a slur on all who are in collusion with them.

83:9-18. The prayer for vengeance refers to two of the LORD's victories over those who tried to take possession of Israel's territory (verse 12) during the period of the judges. The

Canaanites, led by **Sisera and Jabin,** were defeated by means of a flash flood of **the river Kishon** (Judges 4–5). God also defeated the Midianite generals **Oreb and Jeeb** and their kings **Zebah and Zalmunna** (Judges 8). **En-dor** in verse 10 has been suspected by some as a scribal error because it is not mentioned in Judges 4–5. Probably it is used because it is near Mt. Tabor, where the Israelite army assembled before the battle against Sisera.

The congregation calls on God to come as victorious storm God and sweep away the enemies of the people like a tumbleweed (see the Revised Standard Version footnote) or **chaff.** As lightning sets forested **mountains** aflame God is asked to destroy the foe. This final victory will establish God's worldwide rule.

Psalm 84. The Pilgrim Way

This is one of the most popular of the pilgrim psalms (on this category, the title, divine names, and **selah** see Introduction).

84:1-4. The pilgrim cries out in admiration of the beauty of the temple. He vividly recalls how he has longed to see it (verse 2; on **my soul** see above on 6:1-3, 42:1-2*a*). The birds nesting among the beams remind him that to be in the presence of the God whose house shelters even the swallow's **young** is life's greatest good.

84:5-7. God's blessing is not confined to the temple. It radiates outward to those in remote places whose minds are set on the pilgrimage **to Zion.** The fall **rain** and **springs** of water convert an arid valley, fit only for balsam trees (the meaning of **Baca**), into an oasis before them. Defying fatigue, they get stronger as they approach Zion, where God is revealed.

84:8-9. The festival to which the pilgrim has come is the autumn new year feast, during which the enthronement of God as king was celebrated (cf. verse 3, and see Introduction). The **prayer** for the human king (**our shield**) is appropriate to this occasion.

84:10-12. This is a lyrical statement of the conventional Old Testament doctrine that trust in God means spiritual and material prosperity. A single **day** spent as a pilgrim before the temple gate **is better than a thousand** in the homes of those who reject God (verse 10). **Be a doorkeeper** is literally "stand at the threshold" (cf. I Chronicles 26:1-19). The **sun** was a common ancient symbol for divine lifegiving power. But nowhere else is it used of the LORD, perhaps because of pagan associations.

PSALM 85. A PLEA FOR RESTORATION

This liturgy is in five parts (on this category, the title, and **selah** see Introduction).

85:1-3. A solo voice praises God for mercy in forgiving Israel's **sin** and removing the destructive effects of divine **anger.** On the vocabulary of sin and forgiveness see above on 32:1-5. In verse 1*b* most recent translators have accepted **restore** (literally "turn") **the fortunes** rather than the traditional "turn the captivity" wherever this phrase appears in the Old Testament—for example, 14:7; 53:6; 126:1, 4. However, the two variant spellings of the Hebrew word for "fortune-captivity" may indicate that scribes confused two words which originally differed in different passages—for example, Jeremiah 29:14; 30:3 and Ezekiel 29:14; 39:25. If "turn the captivity" was original here, the psalm is postexilic, and the return from Babylon is the great example of God's forgiving love.

85:4-7. The congregation pleads for a new manifestation of God's **steadfast love.** God's wrath has placed the people in the realm of death; hence the prayer "Restore us to life again" (verse 6).

85:8-9. A priest or prophet will listen for God's answer to the nation's prayer. He is confident that God will assure the **saints** (faithful people) of **peace** (complete spiritual and physical well-being; see above on 28:3-5). God will bring them to **salvation,** and God's divine **glory** (authoritative presence) will be in their midst.

85:10-11. God's answer indicates that salvation is a joyous meeting, like that of friends long separated. God's saving love will meet the people's loyalty (verse 10*a*). God's justice meets the people's well-being (verse 10*b*). **Faithfulness** from the earth encounters **righteousness . . . from the sky.**

85:12-13. In response the congregation acknowledges that all its welfare is God's gift. It expresses confidence that God will come in justice and that the land will prosper. The Hebrew of verse 13*b* makes little sense. It probably should be emended to "and salvation in the way of his footsteps."

Psalm 86. From Self to God

This is an individual lament (on this category, the title, and the divine names see Introduction). One who is pursued by godless enemies has fled to the temple to seek help from God.

86:1-7. At first the psalmist concentrates on his need, his piety, and his trust (verses 1-3). But the act of exposing his life before the God of **forgiving . . . love** (verse 5) shifts his vision from himself to God.

86:8-13. Thinking about God changes the psalmist's mood to one of praise. Israel's unique God (verses 8*a*, 10*b*) has performed unparalleled deeds (verses 8*b*, 10*a*). To this creator God and Lord of history all people will eventually come (verse 9). To **glorify thy name** is to acknowledge the authority of God's nature as revealed in divine acts of saving love. Thoroughly humbled, the psalmist recognizes the need for divine instruction, so that his disturbed life may be unified by reverence for God (verse 11). He gratefully recalls that God's love has rescued him from death (verses 12-13; on **soul** and **Sheol** see above on 6:1-3, 4-5).

The psalmist thinks of his **ruthless** enemies (cf. 54:3). He prays for **a sign** which will rebuke them by showing God's **favor** to him. Here he has an ancient cultic description of the goodness of God in mind (verse 15; cf. Exodus 34:6). Just as the child of a female slave was the property of her master, the psalmist will remain God's **servant** as long as he lives (verse 16; cf. Exodus 21:4).

Psalm 87. Zion's Children

This is a hymn of Zion (on this category, the title, and **selah** see Introduction). It dates from the postexilic period when the Jews were scattered throughout the ancient world. The order of the lines has been disturbed in the transmission of the text, but scholars are not agreed on a reconstruction.

87:1-3. Standing on Mt. **Zion** the psalmist watches a procession of pilgrims approach the gates of the temple with singing and dancing (verse 7). He thinks of the **glorious** traditions of the Holy City (verse 3). God has favored this spot over all the cities and shrines of Israel. God's dwelling there has guaranteed the security of the city (verse 1; cf. verse 5*b*).

87:4-6. Among the pilgrims are Jews from many lands. Seeing them, the psalmist reflects that Jerusalem is the true home of every Jew. He hears God declare that in the book which contains the list of all the living (cf. 69:28) God is writing after the name of each pilgrim "A native Jerusalemite." **Rahab** (cf. 89:10) is a Hebrew name for the dragon monster of chaos, corresponding to the Babylonian Tiamat (see above on 74:12-14). Here it is applied metaphorically to Egypt (cf. Isaiah 30:7). Some interpreters believe that the names to be written in the book are not those of Jews, but of the foreign nations that will eventually acknowledge God's rule (cf. 86:9).

87:7. The pilgrims in their hymn speak of the river of blessing which flows from the temple (cf. 46:4).

Psalm 88. Unrelieved Sorrow

This individual lament contains no expression of confidence or hope (on this category, the title, and **selah** see Introduction).

After an intense plea for hearing and **help** (verses 1-2), the psalmist bitterly describes his plight (verses 3-18). A deadly disease which has plagued him **from my youth up** has now brought him to the point of death (verses 4, 15). God has turned away favor (verse 14). God's **wrath** attacks the psalmist (verse 16), floods over him like the sea (verses 7, 16-17), and pursues him with nameless horrors against which he has no defense (verse 15*b*). This incomprehensible anger of God (verse 14) has shut him in a narrow prison (verse 8*c*), the opposite condition to salvation (see above on 18:19). His friends, horrified at his loathsome condition, have abandoned him (verses 8, 18).

88:10-12. The psalmist's chief dread is that he will be plunged forever into the deepest part of **Sheol** (the underworld; see above on 6:4-5). In that dark realm, also called **the Pit** and **Abaddon** (literally "destruction"), **the shades** cannot remember God's saving love. Hence they cannot worship God (verse 10; cf. 30:9). They are beyond the reach of God's **steadfast love . . . , faithfulness . . . , and saving help** (verses 11-12). **The grave** terminates the human relationship with God.

Psalm 89. The King Rejected

To an ancient royal psalm (verses 1-37) has been added a later lament over the defeat and humiliation of the king (verses 38-51; on these categories, the title, the divine names, and **selah** see Introduction). The historical occasion for the lament is described in some detail. Though other possibilities have been suggested, none fits so well as the surrender and exile of Jehoiachin in 597 B.C. (cf. II Kings 24:8-15).

89:1-4. The introduction states the twofold theme to be developed in the royal psalm: God's permanent consistent **love** and the divine indissoluble **covenant** with the family of **David.**

89:5-18. The God of Israel is infinitely superior to the angelic beings of the heavenly council (verses 5-8; see above on 58:1-5; 82:1-5). God overcame the powers of chaos and created the universe (verses 9-11; see above on 74:12-14; 87:4-6). The entire land of Palestine, including its great mountains, is God's creation and is protected by might (verses 12-13). God's heavenly authority (**throne**; see above on 7:6-11) is founded on justice and saving love. These bring blessing and power (**horn**; see above on 75:1-5) to the worshiping people and establish the throne of the Davidic monarchy (verses 15-18).

89:19-37. These verses claim to repeat God's promise to David through Nathan (verse 19; cf. II Samuel 7). But in fact they are a compilation of several older oracles concerning the Davidic king. God chose David and adopted him as son (verse 26; cf. 2:7-9) by the sacred ritual of anointing (verse 20). Thus God gave him victory (verses 22-24), empire (verses 25-26), and the eldest son's preeminence over other kings (verse 27). The relationship thus described in the royal covenant will be inherited by David's descendants as long as the universe endures (verses 28-29, 35-37). Rebellion by the king will bring punishment, but will not cancel the promise to which God has pledged on oath (verses 30-34).

89:38-51. The Babylonian armies have devastated Jerusalem. The youthful Jehoiachin has surrendered the city and been taken prisoner to Babylon (verses 38-45). The impossible has happened. God has broken the divine word and stripped a descendant of David of **crown, scepter,** and **throne,** the symbols of his kingly office. The lament calls on God to withdraw **wrath** (verse 46) and to **remember** the human frailty and bondage to death (verses 47-48; cf. 6:4-5). Finally God is asked to reinstate the covenant with the family of David (verse 49).

89:52. This verse is not a part of the psalm but the benediction closing Book III of the Psalter (see Introduction).

Psalm 90. The Brevity of Life

This is a community lament (on this category, the title, and the divine names see Introduction). Praise for the creator of time and space (verses 1-12) leads up to a plea for pity and renewed favor (verses 13-17).

90:1-12. God is the true, eternal home of the people. From the remotest imaginable past to the furthest, conceivable future God remains the same (verses 1-2). God's independence of time and space exposes the dreariness of fleeting, dreamlike human existence (verses 4-6). God has decreed death for all people, commanding them to return **to the dust** from which they were made (verse 3; cf. Genesis 2:7; 3:19). Our brief miserable life is the result of our chronic sinfulness standing face to face with God's moral purity (verses 7-8). We cannot throw off our sin and therefore must live perpetually under its consequence—the **wrath** of God which brings us under the control of death (verses 9-10). Understanding this position and its causes is wisdom (verses 11-12).

90:13-17. Such wisdom leads us to recognize that our deepest need is for God's presence and **steadfast** (saving) **love.** In the lament proper the congregation now prays for this. God's love will not bring escape from death, but it makes possible joyful acceptance of the limitations of life (verses 14-15). Undergirded and supported by God's saving **work** (verse 16), the **work** of the nation will endure (verse 17), though the workers perish.

PSALM 91. SECURITY IN TRUST

This psalm of trust was spoken to instruct the congregation by a priest or by a worshiper who had experienced God's delivering power (see above on Psalm 34; on the divine names see Introduction).

91:1-4. To be in the temple is to be in God's **shadow** and under the protection of **his wings** (see above on 17:6-9). The worshiper whose confidence is complete is safe from enemies (**the snare of the fowler**) and from disease.

91:5-10. These verses reflect the ancient belief that **pestilence** is the work of demons, like the plague god Nergal, the night hag Lilith, and the seven Udugs (see above on 22:12-21). They prowl the earth at **noonday** and dark of **night**, shooting **the arrow** of sickness. Ancient people trusted for their protection against these evil powers to magical incantations and spells. But the psalmist believes that one who trusts in God is safe though **ten thousand** should **fall**. The plague is God's instrument for **the recompense of the wicked** and is under God's control (verses 7-8).

91:11-13. For protection God sends **angels**—that is, messengers from the heavenly council (see above on 58:1-5; 82:1-5). They keep the trusting person from stumbling on life's road. Snakes and wild beasts were regarded as agents or incarnations of the demonic powers.

91:14-16. God declares that the one who holds fast **in love** and is intimately acquainted with God's **name** (saving nature) will enjoy a threefold salvation—deliverance, **honor** and **long life**.

PSALM 92. RIGHTEOUSNESS REWARDED

This individual thanksgiving was probably used during the presentation of a thank offering (on these terms, the title, and the divine names see Introduction). It is a beautiful but naïve expression of the doctrine that righteousness brings prosperity and sin disaster (cf. Psalm 73).

92:1-4. The opening hymn gives the psalmist's reason for thanksgiving—the character of God as it is publicly declared in the morning and evening worship in the temple. This nature is invoked in four ways: God's **name** (authoritative presence), **steadfast** (saving) **love, faithfulness** (unalterable self-consistency), and **works** (historic acts through which God is made known). **Lute** (literally "ten"), may mean a ten-stringed instrument different from the usual **harp.** Or possibly the line should be emended to read with the Septuagint: "to the music of the ten-stringed harp" (cf. 33:2; 144:9; see below on 150:3).

92:5-9. The psalmist isolates one aspect of God's dealings in which divine wisdom is most evident. **The wicked** may prosper for a time, and their success may confuse and mislead **dull** (brutish) men. But their final fate is eternal **destruction.**

92:10-11. In strophe 3 the psalmist offers personal thanksgiving for the downfall of his **enemies** and his own present strength and joy. **Oil** is a symbol of rejoicing (cf. 45:7). The **horn . . . of the wild ox** signifies strength (see above on 75:1-5).

92:12-15. Strophe 4 takes a wide view. It describes the prosperity, long life, and productive vigor of all righteous people, of whom the psalmist himself is but one instance. Their well-being is not their own achievement, however. It is the gift of God's justice and the illustration of its perfection. On trees in the temple see above on 52:8-9.

Psalm 93. The Majestic King

This psalm is a hymn for the enthronement festival (on this category see Introduction and on Psalm 47).

93:1-2. Strophe 1 announces that the Lord, attired in kingly **majesty** as in a royal robe, has ascended the **throne.** Because God's authority, symbolized by the throne, is eternal, the order of nature and society which God has **established** will endure.

93:3-4. Strophe 2 depicts the struggle of the forces of chaos to disrupt the order and harmony of God's creation, a struggle which goes on even to the present (verse 3*c*). The **floods** represent these chaotic forces (see above on 74:12-14). God is **mightier than** chaos, and order stands fast. God's rule guarantees that the world will not be overwhelmed by cosmic or political catastrophe.

93:5. Strophe 3 insists once more on the security of what God has ordained. God's utter majesty adorns the temple, where the worshiping congregation continuously proclaims God's absolute power.

Psalm 94. Confidence in the Lord

This psalm combines lament (verses 1-11) and confidence (verses 12-23; on these categories see Introduction). It was spoken by an individual who felt his cause to be so closely allied with that of the people that he could come forward as their spokesman (verses 4-7, 14-15, 21).

94:1-3. The psalmist calls on God to appear as **judge** (see above on 7:6-11; 11:4-7*a*) and avenger (cf. Deuteronomy 32:35).

94:4-15. The **evildoers** who oppress Israel, exploit the helpless (see above on 7:12-16; 68:5-6), and mock God are evidently Israelites in positions of power. But they do not really belong to the people of God. They are gross, godless, and bestial (verse 8). They are incapable of understanding that their acts and motives cannot be hid from the creator of **ear, eye,** and mind (verses 9-11). The righteous—those who endure God's discipline and are instructed by divine **law**—are God's chosen heritage. When their enemies temporarily have the upper hand, God upholds them (verse 13). God will give them the **justice** for which they long.

94:16-23. The psalmist's experience gives substance to this confidence. Note the dramatic introduction by means of two questions. On **soul** see above on 6:1-3; 42:1-2*a*. On **land of silence** see above on 6:4-5; 88:10-12. When the psalmist was at the end of his resources, God's **steadfast** (saving) **love** sustained him. He was assured that in spite of appearances the just God does not take the side of the oppressor. He defends the righteous. The cruelty of **the wicked,** recoiling upon them, destroys them.

Psalm 95. Worship of the Creator-King

This psalm is an invitation to participate in the enthronement festival and the ritual of covenant renewal (see Introduction and on Psalm 47).

95:1-5. With song and a joyful cry the procession bearing the ark approaches the temple. They hail God, who rules the divine beings of the heavenly council (see above on 58:1-5; 82:1-5). God is the creator and owner of the universe who dwarfs the creation.

95:6-7*c*. These verses state the relationship to God on which **worship** is based. The congregation owes its existence to the creator God and must accept God's absolute authority. **As sheep** survive only because of the shepherd who finds pasturage for them, the congregation lives by God's continuous guidance.

95:7*d*-11. This passage is a direct speech of God mediated to the worshipers by a priest or prophet. It describes the sin which negates the relationship between God and people. This sin is an evil mixture of stubbornness (hardness of heart) and the attempt to coerce God into doing what the people wish (testing him). The incident **at Meribah** and **Massah** during the exodus period is the classic example of this rebellion (cf. Exodus 17:1-7; Numbers 20:1-3). There the people demanded water in the desert. They received the water but lost the greater blessing of entering Canaan (**my rest**). All died **in the wilderness** under God's wrath and loathing during the forty years of wandering.

Psalm 96. The Universal King

This psalm was composed for the enthronement festival (see Introduction and on Psalm 47). The leading themes of the festival are creation (verses 1-5) and judgment (verses 10-13). These come together in an invitation to all nations to join the sacred procession (verses 7-9).

96:1-9. The creator and judge of the earth requires the worship of all its inhabitants (verses 1, 7). On **new song** see above on 33:1-3. God's **name** is a divinely authoritative presence with the people (cf. I Kings 8:44). The worshipers are urged to see in this presence the source of all blessing (verse 2) and the authority to which they must submit (verses 7-8; cf. 29:1-2). *All* divine power is included within the might of the LORD. Therefore the **gods of the peoples**—that is, the gods of other nations—can have no reality beyond the images which represent them (verses 4-5). On **in holy array** see above on 29:1-2).

96:10-13. No distinction between nature and history is made here. The same decrees of God establish the ordered universe and judge the nations. The description of the LORD's coming in judgment (verses 11-12) draws on the pagan imagery of the annual resurrection of the fertility god. In Canaanite mythology when Baal escaped from the underworld, bringing the lifegiving rain, the gods in heaven rejoiced and the earth exulted in the rebirth of its powers. In this psalm God's stabilizing and order-producing justice causes the universal **joy.** Even the chaotic **sea** joins the rejoicing (see above on 74:12-14).

PSALM 97. KING ABOVE THE GODS

This is another hymn for the enthronement festival (see Introduction and on Psalm 47). It celebrates God's coming to the people as king.

97:1-5. The whole **earth** is summoned to rejoice in the LORD's universal kingship. **Many coastlands** refers to the remote islands and peninsulas of the Mediterranean. Using the standard imagery of the theophany, verses 2-5 describe God's coming to reign over his people (see above on 18:7-18). God's **justice** is the dais on which the heavenly **throne** stands (see above on 7:6-11).

97:6-9. The harmony of the heavenly bodies testifies to God's ordering justice. By observing them people of all races can see God's authority in action (verse 6; see above on 96:10-13). Pagan deities are mere **worthless idols** (cf. 96:4-5). The only divine beings other than the LORD are members of God's heavenly council, who are servants and **bow down before him** (see above on 58:1-5; 82:1-5). **Zion** (Jerusalem) and the **daughters** (smaller cities) **of Judah rejoice** when they hear God's world-ruling majesty declared in the temple.

97:10-12. God's moral government of the universe is filled with meaning for the covenant community. God **loves those who hate** what is opposed to the divine will. God protects the loyal adherents to the covenant faith against their enemies, filling their lives with **light** and **joy.** All their songs of thanksgiving are therefore responses to **his holy name**—God's majestic, awe-inspiring presence with them.

PSALM 98. THE WARRIOR-KING

This hymn for the enthronement festival emphasizes the coming of God as warrior-king (on these terms see Introduction).

98:1-3. In the holy war context (see above on 20:6-9) **steadfast** (saving) **love** and **faithfulness** refer to **victory** over God's and the people's enemies. The fame of these triumphs fills **the earth.** On **new song** see above on 33:1-3.

98:4-9. The worldwide rejoicing is symbolized by the **song** and instrumental music of the festal procession. Since the procession carries the ark, its rejoicing is **before the King** (see below on 99:1-5). **Trumpets** here are straight metal tubes blown by priests. The **horn** is the curved ram's-horn *shophar*, less accurately translated "trumpet" in 47:5; 81:3; 150:3 (see above on 81:1-5*b*). On the **lyre** see below on 150:1-2. Verses 7-9 closely parallel 96:11-13.

PSALM 99. THE HOLY KING

This is a hymn for the enthronement festival (see Introduction). The refrain (verses 3, 5, 9) emphasizes that the LORD's presence with the people in awe-inspiring majesty places a gulf between God and worshipers. This holiness gives a sacred distinctiveness to the **holy mountain** (the temple, verse 9), where it is revealed to all.

99:1-5. These verses celebrate God's worldwide dominion and the **justice** by which God establishes the universe and rules history (see above on 7:12-16; 68:5-6; 96:10-13). God's heavenly throne (see above on 7:6-11) has its earthly counterpart in the ark which the festal procession carried into the temple. The ark was a portable box, surmounted by two **cherubim**—winged figures with animal bodies and human heads. They formed the sides of a throne of which the outstretched wings were the seat (verse 1*b*). The golden lid of the box served as **footstool** for the invisible King.

99:6-9. God's justice is seen in the covenant with Israel. **Moses and Aaron** and **Samuel** were mediators of that covenant, interceding with God on behalf of the people and mediating God's revelation and law to them. Since the covenant involved both blessing and curse, God's action through mediators was sometimes forgiveness and sometimes punishment (verse 8). The **pillar of cloud** was a symbol of God's presence. It was associated with the tabernacle, the place of revelation in the time of Moses (cf. Exodus 33:9-10; 40:34). The tabernacle was transferred successively to Samuel's shrine at Shiloh and the Jerusalem temple, the heirs of the tabernacle as Israel's central shrine.

PSALM 100. REJOICING IN GOD

This is a hymn for the presentation of a thank offering (on this category see Introduction). It shows that at its best Old Testament thanksgiving arises, not from benefits received, but from the character of God.

100:1-2. The procession approaching the temple is reminded that worship is an occasion for **gladness.** The worshipers are called on to **know**—to experience for themselves—**that the LORD is their God.** The LORD is the final authority of their lives, their creator, and the one who shepherd-like provides for their needs (cf. 95:7). In verse 3*b* "and not we ourselves" is the reading of most Hebrew manuscripts (see the Revised Standard Version footnote). But **and we are his,** differing by one letter, seems the more likely original.

100:3-5. As the singing procession nears the temple **gates,** it is exhorted to **enter . . . with praise.** Their praises will acknowledge that God's presence (**his name**) is the source of their blessing. God's nature is to perform acts of **steadfast love,** and God's character remains consistent and reliable throughout all time. For the Hebrew time was neither an abstract concept nor the mere ticking of a clock. It was the flux and flow of human experience. Hence **for ever** equals **all generations.**

PSALM 101. A SEVENFOLD PLEDGE

This is a royal psalm (on this category and the title see Introduction). It is the king's response to prayers offered on his behalf at his coronation (cf. Psalm 72). The king's conduct was of vital concern to the nation. If he incurred divine wrath by failure to mediate the LORD's justice to the people, all would suffer. Hence, addressing himself to God, the king here proclaims before his people the principles of private life and public administration by which he will live.

101:1-3*b*. The king summarizes his guiding principles as **loyalty** (the word usually translated "steadfast love," "mercy," or "kindness") and **justice**. He promises to fix his mind on **blameless** conduct and unswerving trustworthiness. In verse 2*b* the more probable reading is "truth will abide with me." Even in the privacy of his palace his inner life will be upright and free of anything pertaining to evil (verses 2*c*-3*b*).

101:3*c*-8. The king will despise the deeds of those who violate the covenant and the distorted thinking which leads to rebellion (verses 3*c*-4). His justice will fall hard on slanderers and haughty oppressors (verse 5). He will form his government of loyal men devoted to **blameless** conduct (verse 6) and exclude crooks and liars from his court (verse 7). He will purge Judah and Jerusalem of all whose crimes show that they are guilty before God (**wicked**). His justice, like God's, will be exercised in the **morning** (cf. 59:16).

PSALM 102. EXILE AND ILLNESS

This is an individual lament (on this category and the title see Introduction). It includes two prophecies (verses 13-22, 28) each introduced by a hymn (verses 12, 25-27). Since the prophecies are concerned with the coming of God as king, the introductory hymns are similar to enthronement psalms (see above on Psalms 95–97). This is one of the penitential psalms (see above on Psalm 6).

102:1-11. The psalmist is stricken in the prime of life (verses 23-24) by a deadly disease. He is harassed by mocking **enemies** who use magic spells against him (verse 8). He describes his plight in the conventional language of the lament (see above on Psalm 22), but with vivid images—an inner life blighted like sun-withered **grass** (verse 4*a*), the loneliness of a bird in the desert (verse 6), the total abandonment of being tossed aside by God (verse 10).

102:12-28. In his mind his suffering and salvation are bound up with those of the nation. In a prophetic vision he announces that the time of deliverance has come (verse 13). The exiles, no longer rebellious, yearn for Jerusalem and mourn over its ruins (verse 14). On the heavenly throne God hears **the groans** of the exiles and will come to save them from national death (verses 19-20). The LORD will bring all **nations** under rule (verses 15, 22). This great salvation will be recorded as a witness to later generations. Like the events of the exodus, it will be recited in the worship of the temple (verses 18, 21; cf. Psalm 105; Isaiah 43:18-21).

PSALM 103. A FATHER'S COMPASSION

This hymn is for the presentation of a thank offering (on this category and the title see Introduction).

103:1-5. The psalmist summons his whole being to grateful acknowledgment of the saving presence of God (**his holy name**). This has touched his life in many ways—forgiveness, healing, rescue from death, and long life which has retained the vigor of a soaring eagle (cf. Isaiah 40:31). On **my soul** and **the Pit** (Sheol) see above on 6:1-3, 4-5.

103:6-18. He has received these benefits from God's **justice** toward the **oppressed**, which in the Old Testament is the same as saving love. This gracious God is described in Israel's ancient confession of faith (verse 8; cf. 86:15; Exodus 34:6). God delivered the people from Egypt and gave them the law through **Moses.** Though God may punish, **anger** is a transient quality of the divine nature. In contrast, God's **steadfast love** is immense, eternal, and unchanging (verses 9-11, 17-18). **He knows** our frail, death-dominated human existence (verses 14-16) and with a father's compassion **pities** those who are reverent. Because God understands the LORD forgives to the uttermost (verse 12).

103:19-22. The final call to praise embraces all that exists—the members of the heavenly council who hear the LORD's commands and do the LORD's work (verses 20-21; see above on 58:1-5), the creation over which God rules, and the psalmist's own joy-filled **soul**. On God's **throne in the heaven** see above on 7:6-11.

PSALM 104. THE WONDERS OF CREATION

This hymn praises the majesty of God the creator (on this category see Introduction; cf. 19:1-6). Older than Genesis 1, it demonstrates that concern with creation was not a late phenomenon in Israel but formed part of the cult traditions of Jerusalem from an early date. Th poet's natural science is that of Mesopotamia and Canaan. Verses 1-5 are based on the Mesopotamian picture of the universe and on the Canaanite conception of the weather god as the "rider of the clouds" (see above on 18:7-18; 65:9-13). Verses 10-24 also celebrate the LORD's power to give the rain.

Verses 20-30 closely resemble sections of the Egyptian Hymn to the Sun attributed to Pharoah Akh-en-Aton. However, many scholars believe that the Egyptian poem is itself based on Canaanite models. In Israel, as in the rest of the Near East, interest centered, not in the creation of matter out of nothing, but in the conferring of order upon chaos. The psalmist unfolds the ordering of the universe in seven stages.

104:1-4. ***The Organization of the Heavens.*** God "pitches" the sky **like a tent** and builds a palace on the unstable surface of the heavenly ocean (cf. Genesis 1:7). God creates **clouds** and **winds** and **fire and flame** (lightning). On the cloud **chariot** see above on 65:9-13.

104:5-9. ***Formation of the Earth.*** The earth is firmly anchored in the ocean. Originally the primeval sea covered the land. At the command of God's thunder-voice it retreated, revealing the **mountains** and **valleys** (see above on 74:12-14; cf. Genesis 1:9).

104:10-13. ***Provision of Water.*** The underground ocean surges up in the form of **springs,** and the heavenly ocean is released as rain.

104:14-18. ***Food for Humans and Beasts.*** God provides vegetation, both wild and cultivated. Even the **wild goats** and rock **badgers** of the **high mountains** find sustenance. Olive **oil** was used for cleansing the skin.

104:19-23. ***Organization of Time.*** In ancient Israel, where the lunar calendar was in use, the **moon** controlled the **seasons** and the **sun** controlled day and night. **Darkness** was a real thing, created by God.

104:24-26. ***The Sea.*** The most marvelous work of God's wisdom was the taming of the primeval ocean. Now it becomes a home for God's creatures and a highway for commerce. Grim old **Leviathan** (see above on 74:12-14), thoroughly domesticated, plays in the water.

104:27-30. ***Control of Life.*** When God withdraws the divine presence, the animals suffer. God takes away their life and by a creative **spirit** (literally "breath"; cf. Genesis 2:7; 6:17) forms their successors.

104:31-35. The hymnic conclusion prays that the rule of God, whose presence is accompanied by earthquake and volcano, will continue **for ever.** It expresses the psalmist's joy in contemplating the wonders of God's work. Those who rebel against one who creates such a perfect order have forfeited their right to live.

Psalm 105. God's Saving Deeds

This is a hymn for covenant renewal (on this category see Introduction). Verses 1-15 are quoted in I Chronicles 16:8-22.

105:1-6. The priests command the heirs **of Abraham** to pray for God's presence (verses 1*a*, 6). They are to be diligent in their attendance at the feast (verse 4), to listen to the story of Israel's beginnings on which their worship is centered and from which their theology has come (verses 2, 5). As told in the cult, "history" is the record of what God **has done.** Every episode is said to be God's deliberate act (verses 1*b*, 5). These acts are detailed throughout verses 9-44.

105:7-15. The priests' account of Israel's early history devotes more space than usual to the patriarchs (verses 7-22; cf. Deuteronomy 6:20-25; 26:5-11; Joshua 24:2-13). The **covenant . . . with Abraham** is an act of God's justice. It is not an agreement between two parties but a divine **promise** which was **sworn** to by God (verses 8-9). Since it depends solely on God's faithfulness to the oath, it endures **for ever.** Verse 14*b* refers to the protection of Sarah from abuse by foreign **kings** (Genesis 12:10-16). Verse 15 suggests that the **prophets** and **anointed** kings of Israel were present by anticipation in the patriarchs.

105:16-22. The patriarch **Joseph** is the model of Israelite wisdom. Because of his righteousness he passed the hard testing of God and became capable of teaching the rulers of Egypt, the traditional home of **wisdom.** The **staff of bread** is a small stake on which loaves were placed for transporting or for storage.

105:23-44. The account of the exodus includes the sojourn in Egypt (verses 23-25), the plagues (verses 26-36), the miracles in the wilderness (verses 37-42), and the entrance into Canaan (verses 43-44). However, the deliverance at the sea, the revelation at Sinai, and the rebellion in the wilderness are omitted. On **the land of Ham** (verse 23) see above on 78:9-55. In the description of the plagues the fifth and sixth—cattle disease and boils—are omitted. The order differs from that in Exodus 7:20–12:50.

105:45. The purpose of God's historic acts was to create a people obedient to the will. The congregation responds with one word, "Hallelujah"—**Praise the LORD!**

PSALM 106. A RECORD OF REBELLION

This psalm is a community lament for covenant renewal (see Introduction). In its present form it dates from after the

Babylonian exile (verses 27, 47). In describing the Essene covenant ceremony the Manual of Discipline found among the Dead Sea Scrolls says, "The priests shall recount God's saving deeds, and the Levites shall recount 'the sins of the Israelites.' " This double use of the exodus event probably reflects ancient practice. Psalm 105 was the part spoken by the priests, and Psalms 78 and 106 that of the Levites.

106:1-5. The psalm begins with acknowledgment of God's righteousness and mercy. Then follows a personal prayer for prosperity.

106:6-46. The lament is a confession of national sin which uses the exodus period to set up a contrast between the forgiving God (verse 45) and the rebellious people (verses 13, 21). As in Psalm 78, Israel's sin is testing God. If God does not fulfill demands promptly on order, Israel will turn to more amiable deities. The psalm is full of the idea of God's poetic justice (verses 15, 24-27, 34-36; see above on 7:12-16).

On **his name's sake, the land of Ham,** and **Moses** as intercessor see above on 23:1-4; 78:9-55; 99:6-9 respectively. On the identification of pagan gods with the demonic powers who rebelled against God in the heavenly council (verse 37) see above on 58:1-5. On the specific instances of Israel's rebellion cf. as follows:

(1) **the Red** (literally "Reed") **Sea** (verses 6-12)—Exodus 14:10-12;
(2) quails and manna (verses 13-15)—Numbers 11:4-33;
(3) **Dathan** and **Abiram** (verses 16-18)—Numbers 16:1-35;
(4) the golden **calf** (verses 19-23)—Exodus 32:1-14;
(5) the spies (verses 24-27)—Numbers 13:1–14:10;
(6) **the Baal of Peor** (verses 28-31)—Numbers 25:1-13;
(7) **Meribah** (verses 32-33)—Numbers 20:1-13;
(8) **the idols of Canaan** (verses 34-39)—Exodus 34:11-16; Leviticus 18:21;
(9) the pattern of rebellion, foreign invasion, repentance, and deliverance (verses 40-46)—Judges 3:7–16:31.

106:47-48. The lament ends with a prayer for the return of the dispersed Jews to their homeland. Verse 48 is the benediction and doxology closing Book IV of the Psalter (see Introduction). It is not a part of this psalm.

PSALM 107. SALVATION AND LORDSHIP

This psalm consists of a community thanksgiving (verses 1-32) and a hymn (verses 33-43; on these categories see Introduction). Some interpreters have argued for the unity of the psalm. But it seems more probable that the hymn and verse 3 are postexilic additions to an earlier poem. This is borne out by the strophic arrangements of the first part, with a double refrain in verse 6, 13, 19, 28 and 8, 15, 21, 31.

107:1-32. The community thanksgiving is a liturgical introduction to the presentation of individual thank offerings. The priests lead the congregation in calling on those who have experienced God's salvation to bring their offering and testify to God's saving **love** (verses 2, 22, 32). The summons to thanksgiving is addressed to wayfarers who have received divine guidance (verses 4-9), liberated **prisoners** (verses 10-16), the **sick** who have been **healed** (verses 17-22), and seafarers rescued from the **storm** (verses 23-32).

The sovereignty of God is emphasized throughout. Imprisonment and illness are the punishment of sin (verses 11, 17). God raises the storm which is eventually stilled (verses 25, 29; on the allusion here to God's victory over the primeval ocean see above on 74:12-14). In ancient thought the underworld was entered by seven **gates** (verse 18; see above on 6:4-5; 18:7-18).

107:33-43. Elaborating the emphasis on God's sovereignty, the hymn insists on God's lordship over the powers of fertility (verses 33-38) and the course of history (verses 39-43). This is an effective denial of the power of the pagan deities, to whom ancient mythology assigned precisely these functions. The wise person will **consider** how God's justice supports **the needy** and overthrows the powerful. In these actions God's **steadfast** (saving) **love** is revealed.

Psalm 108. Awake, Give Thanks

This psalm is a combination of 57:7-11 (verses 1-5) and 60:5-12 (verses 6-13). See comment on these psalms. On the title see Introduction.

Psalm 109. Cursed but Confident

This is an individual lament (on this category and the title see Introduction). Here a suppliant in the temple seeks vindication from the Lord (see above on Psalm 7).

109:1-5. The psalmist cries for help to the God whom he worships. He is **beset** by enemies who bring **lying** charges against him, although he has done them good and prayed for them when they were in trouble.

109:6-19. In the ancient Near East the curse was a potent means of attacking an enemy. The magical formula might be recited over a statue of the victim which incorporated cuttings of their hair or nails. The potent words made the curse become a reality. These verses are a series of such curses, but it is not clear against whom they are directed. Many have understood them as the psalmist's curses against his enemies, collectively designated by singular pronouns, or against a leader among them. But it is more likely that he is here repeating before God the terrible curses against himself by which his enemies have sought to destroy him. They wish that he be found **guilty** of a crime and executed, that his sons be robbed of their inheritance and die childless (verses 10-13), and that his very **name be blotted out** (verses 13, 15; see above on 83:1-8).

109:20-31. Basing his petition on the **steadfast** (saving) **love** of the Lord the psalmist prays that the curses of his enemies may recoil on their own heads. Their power has already reduced him to a pitiable condition of weakness, over which they gloat (verses 22-25). He pleads that God will cancel their curses with a blessing (verses 27-29). He vows that he will publicly proclaim God's goodness if his prayer is answered (verses 30-31; see above on 7:17). On **thy name's sake** (verse 21) see above on 23:1-4.

PSALM 110. THE PRIEST-KING

This royal psalm was probably used at the coronation ritual (on this category and the title see Introduction). It consists of two divine speeches (verses 1, 4), spoken by a priest or prophet, and the congregational response to each (verses 2-3, 5-7).

110:1-3. The LORD invites the king to **sit at my right hand**—probably at the right side of the ark. This position of honor indicates that the king is God's vicegerent, his earthly deputy. Mesopotamian art often depicts the king with his foot on the neck of a conquered enemy. The congregation prays that the king's power, symbolized by his **scepter,** will spread outward from Jerusalem and overthrow his enemies. The people will fight for him in the sacred battle array of the holy war (Revised Standard Version footnote; see above on 20:6-9). The king's vigor will be renewed as the dew refreshes the earth at dawn.

110:4-7. The second oracle (verse 4) refers to Genesis 14:17-24. There Abraham recognizes **Melchizedek,** king of Salem (Jerusalem), as both king and **priest** by offering him tribute and participating in a sacrifice conducted by him. The Davidic monarch is in the direct line of the kings of pre-Israelite Jerusalem. Like them he combines the offices of priest and sovereign. The Jerusalem cult stressed the justice of God (Melchizedek means "my king is righteousness"). The LORD has condemned **the nations**, and the LORD's priest-king will carry out the sentence (verses 5-6). During the ceremony the king replenishes his strength by drinking from a sacred spring—possibly Gihon (cf. I Kings 1:28-40)—a practice noted in the old Canaanite texts from Ugarit.

PSALM 111. THE BEGINNING OF WISDOM

This psalm is a hymn in the form of an alphabetic acrostic (on these terms see Introduction).

111:1-4. The opening "Hallelujah"—that is, **Praise the LORD** (cf. 112:1; 113:1)—sets the mood of the hymn. Here an individual offers public thanksgiving for **the works of the LORD.** In these acts are revealed the LORD's majestic power, perfect justice, grace, and mercy.

111:5-9. The psalmist concentrates on the exodus events which brought Israel into existence—the miracles of **food** in the wilderness, the conquest over the **nations** of Canaan, and the giving of eternally valid **precepts** (the law) which demand **faithfulness** and integrity. The whole complex of events is summarized as **redemption** and the establishment of the **covenant**, a binding agreement **commanded** by God and accepted by the people. Contemplating these wonders the psalmist cries out that God's **name** (presence) is unique and awe-inspiring.

111:10. This is the basic doctrine of Israel's wisdom teachers. In Old Testament thought **wisdom** is the ability to deal successfully with the tensions and problems of practical life. **Understanding** is the capacity to discern among conflicting possibilities what values and courses of action ought to be followed. The source of these qualities is not brain power but reverence for God, **the fear of the LORD.** The hymnic conclusion echoes the opening mood of **praise.**

PSALM 112. HE WILL NOT BE MOVED

This is an alphabetic acrostic, similar in form to Psalm 111. It is related in content to Psalm 1 and hence is to be classed as a wisdom psalm (on these terms see Introduction). It is a bold statement of the familiar Old Testament doctrine that righteousness is rewarded and wickedness punished in this life. The psalmist has no hope of personal immortality (see above on 6:4-5; 88:10-12). He looks for the continuation of his life in his family and the memory of his friends (verses 2, 6).

112:1-4. Whoever reverences God by joyfully keeping **his commandments** will have **wealth**. Their children will be honored and influential in the community. When trouble comes, the **light** of God's presence will shine into their **darkness.** God's saving power and justice are directed especially to the helpless and oppressed.

112:5-9. A similar **justice** characterizes all the social activity of one who reverences God. In particular it is expressed in the use of money. Firmly anchored in the reality of God's nature, such a person's inner life is stable and **righteousness** lasts, even when one is the victim of **evil tidings** (better "rumors") spread by his enemies. One's **adversaries** will go down, but one's **horn** (power) will increase. Even as he perishes, **the wicked man gnashes his teeth** in envy of the good person.

PSALM 113. KING ABOVE THE HEAVENS

This psalm is a congregational hymn (on this category see Introduction).

113:1-6. The priests call on the worshipers in the temple (**servants**) to **praise** God's saving presence with them. God is worthy to be praised continuously by all the inhabitants of the earth because the LORD is enthroned in **glory**—the LORD's authority over nature, humanity, and history. Psalm 7 speaks of God's throne in heaven. Here God towers over heaven itself with an authority which cannot be confined within the bounds of the universe.

113:7-9. God's throne is founded on justice (cf. 97:2). That justice is particularly concerned with the protection of the helpless and oppressed (see above on 68:5-6). When God's loyal worshipers (the **poor** and **needy**) are crushed and mourn in **dust** and ashes, God **raises** them to the highest places in the land. To have **children** was one of God's greatest blessings, since the only immortality for which the Hebrews could hope was the continuation of their name and memory in the family (see above on 6:4-5). A **barren woman** was in danger of being divorced and dismissed from her home. But God opens the womb of the childless and makes her a **joyous mother.**

PSALM 114. THE SEA FLED

This artistically constructed hymn was probably used in the covenant renewal ritual of the new year festival, when worship centered on the exodus event (on these terms see Introduction).

114:1-2. Strophe 1 emphasizes the unity of the people of God. Both the northern and southern divisions of the nation (**Israel** and **Judah**) were chosen by God and led out of **Egypt**—a land so foreign that its **language** was unintelligible. God made them the holy place of residence and kingdom.

114:3-4. Strophe 2 dwells on the miracles which accompanied the exodus—the crossings of the **sea** (Exodus 14:21-29) and the **Jordan** (Joshua 3:14-17) and the earthquake at Sinai (Exodus 19:18) when the mountains **skipped** like frolicsome **lambs.** The nature religion of Canaan depicted a vicious battle between Baal and Judge River (see above on 74:12-14). Here the sea flees at the mere approach of the LORD. The pagan myth has been historicized. The defeat of the sea has been equated with the deliverance of Israel.

114:5-6. The poet feels he has become a part of the events recreated in the worship of the temple. Therefore he asks the questions of strophe 3 in the present tense.

114:7-8. Strophe 4 reverts to the earthquake at Sinai. It adds the miracle of **water** from **the rock,** heightening the wonder by declaring that the rock itself became a **pool**.

PSALM 115. A LITURGY OF PRAISE

This is a hymn in liturgical form (on this category see Introduction). It was sung during a time of national distress.

115:1-8. The psalm begins with a congregational prayer. The people pray that God will help them, not to enhance their power, but to show the worldwide authority of God's **steadfast** (saving) **love** and consistent **faithfulness** (see below on Psalm 117). Even though **the nations** deny that the LORD can save Israel, the congregation boldly affirms the universal sovereignty of its God. The pagan deities are manmade **idols,** without life or power (cf. 96:4-5). Likewise the idolaters are impotent and futile.

115:9-15. Israel, the priesthood, and the non-Israelite worshipers of the LORD (those who **fear** him) are called on to commit themselves to God. Each group replies with a confession of faith in God's saving power (verses 9-11). The congregation affirms that the LORD has blessed and will bless again (verses 12-13). A priest pronounces a benediction on the congregation (verses 14-15).

115:16-18. The concluding strophe portrays the three-storied universe of ancient cosmology (see above on 18:7-18). In heaven God's rule is supreme, but God has given control of **the earth** to human beings. Because of human freedom, inequities and oppression exist. In the underworld the shades, sunk in forgetfulness, cannot **praise the LORD** (see above on 6:4-5; 88:10-12). In spite of the ambiguity of human existence and the long silence of death Israel will continuously praise its God.

PSALM 116. GRATITUDE FOR DELIVERANCE

This psalm is an individual thanksgiving (on this category see Introduction).

116:1-4. Unless it is interpreted in the light of verses 5-6 and 15, the opening cry of gratitude sounds grossly self-centered—love in return for services rendered. The psalmist was near death and the LORD **heard** his desperate cry. On **snares** and **Sheol** see above on 9:13-17 and 6:4-5 respectively.

116:5-11. The psalmist rejoices to think that his deliverance is evidence of the **gracious** nature of the LORD. God is the champion of the **simple**—those who lack the capacity to fend for themselves. God acts toward them with the justice which saves the oppressed and the mercy which understands their sorrow (cf. 103:13). The psalmist invites his **soul** (his vital powers; see above on 6:1-3) to **rest** after its turmoil. In his distress he lost neither his **faith** nor his life. But he has learned that trust in human power is deceitful and **a vain hope.**

116:12-19. These verses are spoken just before the presentation of the thank offering. The **cup of salvation** was probably held aloft before the altar and then poured out as libation (cf. Exodus 29:40). The worshiper pays his **vows** (see above on 7:17; 50:7-15) and offers the thank offering (Leviticus 7:12). Verse 15 means that the LORD is not indifferent to whether or not faithful servants are killed. On **son of thy handmaid** see above on 86:8-13.

PSALM 117. A CALL TO PRAISE

This psalm is a hymn for the begining of a temple service (on this category see Introduction). It calls on **all nations** to **praise the LORD**, whose creative power and control is world wide (see above on Psalm 97). It extols the LORD's **steadfast** (saving) **love** abundantly revealed to Israel (**us**) in the nation's history. As frequently in the Psalter, God's love is united to **faithfulness**—God's consistency. This quality guarantees that none of God's actions will be arbitrary or inconsistent with the divinely declared will.

PSALM 118. THANKSGIVING FOR VICTORY

This is a thanksgiving liturgy for the king's victorious return from battle (on this category see Introduction). The abrupt changes in thought result from changes in speaker and mood as the ceremony progresses.

118:1-4. The procession approaches the temple, and the priests call the congregation to general thanksgiving. Verse 1 is the same as 107:1. The groups mentioned in verses 2-4 correspond to those of 115:9-11 (see comment).

118:5-14. The king offers his personal thanksgiving. Hard pressed by numerous enemies he **called on the LORD** for aid (verse 5; cf. verses 10-12). He is confident that **with the LORD on my side** he has nothing to **fear** and that his trust is better than manpower or generalship. The LORD, who has always been his **strength** and the object of his praise, has given him victory. **In the name** (saving presence) **of the LORD** he has destroyed his enemies. This testimony comes from the tradition of the holy war (see Introduction and on 20:6-9).

118:15-18. The camp of the Israelites is resounding with **songs of victory,** praising the mighty (**right hand**) **of the LORD.** The king predicts a long reign in which he will tell of what God has done for him. His temporary setbacks and troubles were God's discipline.

118:19-25. Arrived at the temple gates the king requests admission (see above on Psalm 24). He calls the doors **gates of righteousness** because the temple is the place where God's justice is revealed. The priests remind him that only those whom God has declared innocent can enter (verse 20). He replies that his recent victory is sufficient evidence of God's favor (verse 21). The procession chants its praise of God's **marvelous** deed. God has made the **stone** which the nations despised the most important part of the building and has made possible this **day** of national rejoicing. The congregation prays for continued divine blessing.

118:26-29. The priests pronounce a benediction. Then they bid the procession with its garlands and palm **branches** to form a human chain of dancers up to the **altar.** The **horns** were projections at the corners of the altar which stood in the temple court (cf. I Kings 8:64). The king then concludes his thanksgiving within the temple (verse 28). The congregation answers with the words with which the ritual began.

PSALM 119. VENERATION OF THE LAW

This skillfully contrived poem expresses a deep piety centered in the **law** (see above on 19:7-14). It consists of twenty-two sections, one for each letter of the Hebrew alphabet. Each section contains eight lines, all beginning with the same letter.

The number of lines per section was perhaps suggested by the eight synonyms for law used in the poem. Four of these—**precepts, statutes, commandments, ordinances**—refer to separate legal units, commands and prohibitions in the strict sense. **Testimonies** is more general, signifying that the law is God's own witness to the divine will (cf. verse 72). The use of **word** shows that the psalmist regarded the law, not as an impersonal mass of legislation, but as the dynamic utterance of God. **Way** (literally "path") has the same connotation—guidance through the complex landscape of life. **Law** itself means basically "guidance" or "instruction."

The law, so conceived, is perfect (verse 96). It brings the promise of **salvation** (verse 41). Therefore it is the sure ground of **hope** (verse 49) and the source of **life** (verses 50, 93). Although it fills the worshiper with fear of God's terrible justice, it means **liberty** (verses 44-45), **peace**, and protection (verse 165). It is the same creative word by which the universe (verses 89-90) and the psalmist himself (verse 73) were made. It represents God's **name**—lifegiving presence (verse 55)—and **steadfast** (saving) **love** (verses 41, 64, 76).

People obey the law, not as a duty, but because it is true, and indeed is **truth** itself (verse 160). Such obedience cannot be mechanical. The servants of the LORD love the law (verses 48, 97, 113, 119, 131). It is their **delight** (verses 77, 103), and they value it above all treasure (verse 72).

But devotion does not insure obedience. The psalmist acknowledges that he wanders from the way, but his sin is never the result of willful rejection of the law (verse 176). Even in his erring the law is in the heart and at the center of his vital concern. Obedience produces wisdom (verses 32, 98, 100, 130). But obedience also *requires* wisdom (verses 32, 125), and the **understanding** necessary for obedience is the gift of God. The law can be obeyed only as God's presence enables the worshiper to hold fast to God's will.

This divine support is sorely needed. Many in the community

hold the law in contempt and hinder the servants of God in their obedience (verses 113, 115, 134). As the psalmist thinks of these enemies he passes into the style and mood of the lament (verses 25, 41-43, 53, 69-71, 78-80, 81-88; on this category see Introduction). The psalmist's obedience in spite of the difficulties which surround him becomes the basis of his cry for help (verses 143, 153-154).

This psalm has clear affinities with the thought of the wisdom teachers (see above on Psalm 1). This—plus the fact that the individual's, rather than the nation's relationship to the law is the main theme—indicates a date after the Babylonian exile. The "law" probably refers to the law of Israel as written in the Pentateuch, the first five books of the scriptures.

Psalm 120. Irreconcilable Foes

This is an individual lament (on this category and title see Introduction). A pilgrim, ascending toward the temple, prays for deliverance from the accusations of malicious enemies.

120:1-4. The psalmist's **distress** is caused by **lying lips**, and he wishes for these adversaries the fate which they have tried to bring on him. Verses 3-4 have the structure of a curse formula (see above on 109:6-19). The **arrows** shot by a professional soldier were war's deadliest weapon and the wood of **the broom tree** burned hottest and longest.

120:5-7. The psalmist's enemies are members of his own people. As citizens of the covenant community they should all live at **peace** with one another. Instead they behaved to him like rough mountaineers of **Meshech**, a region between the Black and Caspian seas, or wild tribesmen of **Kedar**, the Syrian desert. When he tries to be reconciled to them, they redouble their attacks.

Psalm 121. A Ritual of Dismissal

This is a liturgy (on this category and the title see Introduction). Some scholars consider it a pilgrim psalm sung on approaching Jerusalem. More probably, it was used for the dismissal of pilgrims leaving the temple on their homeward journey.

121:1-2. Looking to the east over the arid **hills** of the Judean wilderness, the pilgrim wonders what **help** he can rely on to complete the arduous journey. He affirms that the God who created the universe is able to sustain him on his way. These verses may, however, refer to the hills that surround Jerusalem. They would then state the confidence which fills the departing pilgrims as they contemplate the dwelling place of the mighty God (cf. 125:2).

121:3-8. The priests dismiss the wayfarer with a threefold benediction. Guarded by the ever-vigilant God he will suffer no disaster on the road. Sickness will not strike him, either from the heat of the **sun** or the baleful effects of the **moon,** which according to Mesopotamian thought could cause such diseases as leprosy and fever. The LORD will preserve his life and keep him from every peril from the time he leaves the temple until he enters his home and continuously thereafter. On **for evermore** see above on 22:25-26.

PSALM 122. MEMORIES OF JERUSALEM

This is a pilgrim psalm (on this category and the title see Introduction). Verse 5 seems to indicate that it dates from postexilic times.

122:1-2. A pilgrim taking leave of Jerusalem expresses the joy brought about by a visit to the city. He recalls his pleasure at being invited to join a group of travelers banded together for the dangerous journey (verse 1; cf. verse 8).

122:3-5. Three impressions of his visit are strongly with the pilgrim: the imposing structure of the **city** (cf. the **walls** strengthened by defense **towers,** verse 7), the procession of pilgrims from all the **tribes** of **Israel,** and the site where in former times the **thrones** of the Davidic kings stood. The law required that every male Israelite present himself at the sanctuary three times a year. Since the main function of the Davidic king was to mediate the justice of God to the nation God's throne was primarily one of **judgment.**

122:6-9. The psalmist concludes with a moving prayer for the spiritual and material well-being of the city and of those **who love** it. His motive is not patriotism but religious faith. He values the city, not because it is the nations's capital, but because it is the place where God's temple, the divine earthly **house,** is established.

PSALM 123. GORGED WITH CONTEMPT

This is a community lament (on this category and the title see Introduction). A pilgrim is suffering from the mockery and insult heaped on his nation by foreign oppressors. He pours out his complaint on the threshold of the temple. The most probable historical setting is the postexilic period, when Israel was under the direct rule of foreign powers.

123:1-2. The psalmist raises his **eyes** to God's heavenly throne, founded on righteousness (97:2), from which God administers justice (see above on 7:6-11). Speaking for faithful Israel the psalmist describes the nation's eager longing for God's delivering justice. As slaves, knowing that their life depends on their master's good will, watch the master's **hand** for some sign of favor, so Israel waits expectantly for God's response to its prayers.

123:3-4. The psalmist prays that God will quickly respond to the nation's petitions. The oppressors have lorded it over them so long that they are "fed up" with **contempt.**

PSALM 124. A VICTORY SONG

This community thanksgiving for victory contains strong overtones of the holy war ideology (see Introduction and on 20:6-9).

124:1-5. If the LORD were not **on our side,** the attack of a foreign enemy **would have swallowed us up alive.** The attacking army resembled the primeval ocean raging to engulf the ordered universe in chaos (see above on 74:12-14). Verses 4-5 are a striking example of motifs from Near Eastern mythology applied to Israel's history (see above on 114:3-4).

124:6-8. Israel was already between the **teeth** of the monster and enmeshed in the net of the **fowlers.** With immense relief and gratitude the congregation exclaims, **The snare is broken, and we have escaped!** Verse 8 ascribes the victory to the **name**—that is, saving presence—of the creator of the universe, who is also Lord of history.

PSALM 125. THE TRUE ISRAEL

This is a community song of confidence (on this category and the title see Introduction). It was composed in a time of foreign domination, probably after the Babylonian exile. Pagan control of the nation put a premium on cooperation with the conquerors. Jews had to summon all their powers to hold fast to the traditional faith against the pressure of conformists within and foreigners in positions of authority.

125:1-3. The opening verses are an assurance that **those who trust** the LORD have a stability of life which no power can move. They have the permanent protection of God's saving presence. The burning question was, "What will happen to the Holy Land? Will pagans and traitors continue to rule it?" The psalmist answers that those who remain true to the covenant faith (**the righteous**) are the true Israel. **The land** belongs to them. The **scepter** (domination) of the foreigner will not long continue.

125:4-5. The concluding prayer asks that God restore the land (**do good**) to those who adhere to the straight way of God's will. It asks that the oppressors (**evildoers**) and those who follow **their crooked ways** perish together. Then Israel will know **peace**—that is, complete well-being (see above on 28:3-5).

Psalm 126. A Harvest of Joy

This community lament probably dates from the difficult times after the return from the Babylonian exile about 538 B.C. (on this category and the title see Introduction). Many commentators, however, render verses 1-3 in the present or future tense. Thus they read the psalm as a prediction of restoration (verses 1-3) followed by a prayer for its fulfillment (verses 4-6). In this case it could have been composed during any time of difficulty in Israel's history. On **restored the fortunes** see above on 85:1-3.

126:1-3. Assuming the early postexilic date, these verses recall the joy with which the exiles greeted the decree of Cyrus of Persia permitting them to return to Palestine. In that act even the foreign **nations** recognized the power of the LORD. But drought, locusts, and bad harvests have reduced the returned community to poverty (cf. Isaiah 59:9-11; Haggai 1:9-11).

126:4-6. The people pray for a new manifestation of God's restoring power—one which will bring renewed life to the nation like the winter rains filling the dry **watercourses in the Negeb,** the semidesert in southern Palestine. Then the sower, who went out with a bag of seed and sorrow in the heart, will return with **shouts of joy** from the bountiful harvest.

Psalm 127. Wisdom Fragments

This is a wisdom psalm (on this category and the title see Introduction). Two independent proverb-like sayings are brought together, probably for use at the birth of a son.

127:1-2. No product of purely human effort can survive, neither one's family (**house**) nor the **city** in which it lives. Labor from dawn to dusk brings no lasting result. The LORD can give more good gifts to those the LORD loves during a night's **sleep** than they could accumulate in a life **of anxious toil.**

127:3-5. Nothing is really done unless the LORD does it. Like all else good in life **sons** are God's gift. They are an **inheritance** and also, in accordance with a basic doctrine of the wisdom teachers, a **reward** (literally "wage") for righteousness. Through them the house which God has built is continued, and the name and memory of the father are kept alive (see above on 113:7-9). Moreover, sons born in the vigor of **youth** protect their father **like arrows** of a professional soldier. It is well to come into battle with a **quiver full.** The law courts at which the elders presided in the open space at the city **gate** were often corrupt. But enemies would not dare to rig a case against one who came backed by stalwart sons.

PSALM 128. A PRIESTLY BLESSING

This wisdom psalm was probably used as a priestly blessing on pilgrims arriving at the temple (on this category and the title see Introduction). Its theological basis is the Old Testament doctrine that righteousness brings material reward—a doctrine favored by the wisdom teachers (see above on Psalm 1).

128:1-4. Verse 1 states that the blessing is given to those who reverence God and live in obedience to the divine revealed will. Verses 2-4 specify the nature of the blessing, apparently for a group of small farmers. They will not be robbed of the **fruit** of their **labor** by crop failure or the tax collector. Their wives will receive the gift of many **children,** who will stand **around your table** like young **shoots** at the base of an **olive** tree (see above on 127:3-5).

128:5-6. These verses indicate that the **prosperity** of the individual depends on the welfare of the community and on the God who resides in **Zion.** A prosperous Jerusalem is a center radiating well-being to the whole land. May the pilgrim live to be a grandfather and see Israel enjoying **peace** all his life (cf. 125:5*c*; see above on 28:3-5).

PSALM 129. NOT WORTH HARVESTING

This is a community song of confidence (on this category and the title see Introduction). It was composed in a time of foreign domination (see above on Psalm 125).

129:1-4. Israel's enemies have often overrun the Holy Land, scarring the covenant people as a plow scars a field. But the God of justice remained true to the covenant. God **cut the cords** (harness) so that the plowmen could work no more.

129:5-8. The congregation prays that those who now oppress the people of God may be dealt with like the enemies of the past. The flat roofs of Palestinian houses were made of mud plastered on reeds. A little **grass** could grow there, but the first hot wind of summer killed it so that it was not worth harvesting. Verse 7 reflects ancient harvesting techniques. **The reaper** grasped a handful of grain and cut it with a sickle. Then, holding it against the chest, it was tied into a sheaf. It was customary to greet reapers with a **blessing** (cf. Ruth 2:4). But those **who hate Zion**—foreign oppressors and native traitors—are outside the sphere of the LORD's blessing and stand under the LORD's curse (verse 8).

PSALM 130. OUT OF THE DEPTHS

This individual lament is one of the seven penitential psalms (see Introduction and above on Psalm 6).

130:1-4. The watery deep is a common Old Testament synonym for death or deep distress (cf. 42:7; see above on 6:4-5; 18:7-18). Almost submerged, the psalmist calls on God for aid. Verses 3-4 reveal the ground of his hope. He knows himself to be a sinner. He realizes that if God were to keep a record of deviations from the divine will, all would **stand** guilty. But the LORD is no bookkeeper of offenses. It is the LORD's nature to forgive. Because of God's forgiving love, even more than God's power, the LORD is to be **feared**—that is, worshiped with reverence.

130:5-8. Verses 5-6 state the attitude of true repentance. With the tense, strained expectancy of **watchmen** on the wall of a besieged city, the psalmist **waits** for the assurance of forgiveness. **The morning** was the traditional time when God revealed salvation (cf. 59:16). Like the young Isaiah the psalmist recognizes the universality of sin and his own oneness with a sinful people (Isaiah 6:5). He therefore calls on the nation of **Israel** to join him in penitence and in confident **hope** in the LORD's **steadfast** (saving) **love** and power.

PSALM 131. REPOSE OF SOUL

This is an individual song of confidence (on this category and the title see Introduction). The psalmist asserts that he does not indulge in claims to greatness. He is not proud of himself, nor does he pretend to understand the mysteries of the universe. Nevertheless his life was deeply troubled until he brought his turbulent **soul** (see above on 6:1-3) to quietness and repose. This was not an exercise in self-mastery. He stilled his disturbed spirit by holding fast to the LORD, as a **child** quiets its fears by clinging to its mother. He invites all **Israel** to share his unquestioning confidence in the God of the covenant.

PSALM 132. THE UNITY OF TEMPLE AND COURT

This royal psalm is written in dramatic liturgical form. It was probably sung during the annual ritual of the enthronement of the LORD when the ark was carried in procession into the temple (on these terms and the title see Introduction). It provides theological and historical justification for the close relationship between the Jerusalem temple and the Davidic monarchy. **David,** the first king of united Israel and the conqueror of Jerusalem, also planned the temple, though he did not build it. This psalm consists of two parts, verses 1-10 and 11-18, which were probably once independent poems. They may have been combined because both relate to the narrative in II Samuel 7.

132:1-5. A solo voice calls on the Lord to remember the difficulties David surmounted in finding a site for the temple and to give him credit. David's oath (verses 3-5) does not occur elsewhere in the Old Testament (cf. I Kings 8:17). However, it graphically illustrates the story in II Samuel 7 of the king's desire to provide a temple for the LORD. The use of the ancient name **Mighty One of Jacob** (cf. Genesis 49:24) emphasizes that under David all the descendants of Jacob lived in a political unity.

132:6-7. A choir takes the part of David and his followers. The ark has been captured by the Philistines (cf. I Samuel 4:10-11). In David's home town, Bethlehem **Ephrathah** (cf. Micah 5:2), they learn that it is at **Jaar** (Kiriath-jearim, also called Baale-judah, I Samuel 7:1-2; II Samuel 6:2). They decide to go there and **worship** at the **footstool** of God's throne, the golden lid of the ark. For a description of the ark see above on 99:1-5).

132:8-10. The congregation prays that the LORD will enter the sacred place with the throne. Here the tradition of David's bringing the ark to Jerusalem (II Samuel 6) blends with the cultic procession now carrying **the ark** into the temple. Since the ark was a portable shrine which traveled with Israel during the time of Moses, the permanent structure of the temple provides the LORD with a **resting place** (cf. verse 14). Since it was carried into battle with the armies of Israel (I Samuel 4:1-9) it is the throne of God's military **might.**

The procession bearing the ark consists of the king, the **priests**, and the people. In verses 9-10 a solo voice offers a threefold prayer:

(1) that the priests' robes of office be the **righteousness** and salvation of God, which they mediate to the people;

(2) that the loyal members of the covenant community (**saints**) be filled with **joy**;

(3) that the king enjoy God's favor, not only for his own sake, but because of the devotion of his ancestor David (cf. verses 1-5).

132:11-12. The second poem deals with two decisive and closely related choices of the God of Israel. God chose David as king and pledges **a sure oath** that his descendants would occupy the **throne . . . for ever.** The condition that the kings obey the law (**keep my covenant**) does not appear in the narrative of II Samuel 7:10-17. It may have been written into the tradition after a succession of bad rulers had shown the weakness of an unconditional promise.

132:13-18. The LORD's second choice was to establish Jerusalem as the divine dwelling place. Because of the LORD's presence the land is blessed with abundant food, its **poor** are cared for, its **priests** bring the **salvation** of God to the nation, and its people rejoice. God will make the successor of David, the **anointed** one, a **horn,** symbol of strength, and a **lamp,** symbol of illumination and life, for God's people. God will crush the king's **enemies.** The king's authority will gleam like his golden **crown.**

PSALM 133. BROTHERS TOGETHER

This is a wisdom psalm (on this category and the title see Introduction). It was intended to combat a practice which threatened to destroy the traditional structure of Israelite society. If brothers continued to live together after the death of their father, the estate remained undivided and the family's inheritance in the Holy Land was kept intact (the literal meaning of **dwell in unity** is "dwell together"). The development of commerce and the urbanization of society induced many young men to sell their share of the inheritance and go off on their own. The psalmist urges that the old custom is **good and pleasant.** It was decreed by the LORD, who blesses it with the continued **life** and vigor of society (not personal immortality, verse 3*d*; see above on 22:25-26).

Two metaphors illustrate the beauty of the ancient way. The first is the holy **oil** of anointing **running down** the hair and **beard** of the high priest, the successor of Aaron. The second is the **dew** gathering on the slopes of Mt. **Zion.** Mt. Hermon, in the far north, was a region of heavy dew, and the expression **dew of Hermon** had become proverbial. Some commentators believe verse 2*bc* to be an interpolation not fitting the poetic meter. Thus they make the metaphor merely a reminder of the beneficial effect of olive oil on the hair. Some also, regarding the flow of dew from Hermon to Zion as a geographical impossibility, emend verse 3*b* to read "which flows down on the arid highlands."

PSALM 134. EVENING WORSHIP

This hymn is a call to worship for the evening service of the temple (on this category and title see Introduction). The priests summon the people to praise and pronounce a blessing on the congregation. To **bless the LORD** is to acknowledge that all good is the gift of the LORD's might and grace. To be blessed by the LORD is to receive the gifts from that power which created the universe.

The temple is the center of the sphere of blessing. The worshipers are called **servants**—a term applied throughout the Near East to slaves, subjects of a king, or worshipers of a god. They stand in the temple courtyard with their **hands** held up toward the inner court containing the shrine, the dwelling of the LORD.

PSALM 135. LORD OF NATURE AND HISTORY

This hymn begins and ends with "Hallelujah" (**Praise the LORD**; on this category see Introduction).

135:1-4. On the opening call to praise see above on Psalm 134. Because **he is gracious**—that is, the LORD's kingly quality of hearing and acting on the petitions of subjects—the LORD's **name** is a saving presence. The most conspicuous example of grace is the election of **Israel** in the deliverance of the nation from Egypt.

135:5-7. The hymn proper begins with a solo voice praising the power of God in nature. God rules supreme over the members of the heavenly council (see above on 58:1-5; 82:1-5). God's authority over creation from the highest **heaven** to the lowest **deeps** of the ocean is unlimited. The LORD, not the pagan weather gods, gives the **rain** on which the fertility of Palestine depends. The LORD gathers the **clouds** from afar, fashions **lightnings** to accompany the storm, and unleashes the **wind** from the heavenly **storehouses.**

135:8-14. The Lord of nature is also Lord of history. Verses

8-12 are a condensation of 136:10-22 (see comment). They describe how God brought Israel out of **Egypt** and gave **Canaan . . . as a heritage.** Since God's power is independent of time, God will likewise deliver **his people** from their present troubles.

135:15-21. Contemplation of the LORD's greatness leads the psalmist to pour scorn on the pagan deities (see above on 115:1-8). The closing call to praise resembles 115:9-11 (see comment). The Levites (**house of Levi**) were the temple singers and servants.

PSALM 136. GOD'S SAVING LOVE

This is a hymn in praise of God's **steadfast love** (on this category see Introduction). This love is manifested in God's control over nature (verses 4-9) and rule in human affairs, typified by the deliverance from Egypt and the giving of the Holy Land (verses 10-22). The antiphonal response which follows each line was a regular part of the temple liturgy.

Israelite theology and worship arose from the same source. The nation was the creation of the LORD. It was brought into being by a series of mighty acts which both defined and illustrated the LORD's *hesed*—a Hebrew word which can be only partially translated by "steadfast love." It meant the LORD's consuming concern for a worthless slave people that led to their rescue. It meant the LORD's unshakable loyalty to the relationship to the people which the LORD's saving act had created.

136:1-3. Verse 1 is the call to thanksgiving commonly used in the temple worship (cf. verse 1 of Psalms 106; 107; and 118). Verses 2-3 are an expansion of this.

136:4-9. The pre-Israelite Jerusalem cult focused on the Most High God, whose power was revealed in the creation and control of the universe. When the temple was established in Jerusalem, Israel adopted this feature of worship. It was seen as a preliminary statement of Israel's traditional historic faith and another manifestation of the LORD's steadfast love. On the concepts of creation in this section, which closely parallels Genesis 1:1-19, see above on Psalm 104.

136:10-22. The recital of the LORD's mighty acts in the nation's founding includes traditional events. The LORD broke the power of Pharaoh **with a strong hand and an outstretched arm.** The LORD saved the people at the **Red** (literally "Reed") **Sea** and preserved them in **the wilderness.** The LORD destroyed the **kings** of the eastern Jordan region who opposed their march, and the LORD gave them a **heritage** in the Holy Land. This account omits the revelation at Sinai and the people's rebellion in the wilderness (see above on Psalms 105 and 106).

136:23-26. The worshipers have heard these deeds of the LORD dramatically recited at the covenant renewal festival (see Introduction). The acts are felt to be, not traditions from the remote past, but events taking place in the living present. They involve every true Israelite for all time. **He remembered,** not "our forefathers," but **us.** The concluding verse continues the opening call to thanksgiving.

PSALM 137. NO SONG OF ZION

This is a community lament (on this category see Introduction).

137:1-4. The exiles in **Babylon** gather on the banks of the irrigation canals which bring the **waters** of the Euphrates to the fields of the city. They come together for a ceremony of mourning over the destruction of Jerusalem and prayer for its restoration. There is no music. The **lyres** (see below on 150:3) hang silent on the poplar trees (Revised Standard Version footnote). The **songs of Zion** (cf. Psalms 95–99), with their emphasis on the might and majesty of the LORD, would only arouse the contempt and amusement of the conquerors. **The LORD's song** belongs to the ritual of a temple that is no more.

137:5-6. An individual testifies that, though he cannot sing the sacred songs, he will never **forget** the place of their origin. He will regard the opportunity to return as life's **highest joy.**

137:7-9. The psalm ends with two curses. **The Edomites,** who lived south and east of the Dead Sea, joined the Babylonian armies in the sack of **Jerusalem.** This was an especially heinous offense since, as descendants of Jacob's brother Esau, they were the nation most closely related to Israel. Verses 8-9 wish for blessing on the world power which shall destroy Babylon as it destroyed Jerusalem. The gruesome practice of verse 9 was a common feature of ancient warfare (cf. II Kings 8:12; Hosea 10:14).

Psalm 138. The Divine Presence

This is an individual thanksgiving (on this category and the title see Introduction).

138:1-3. The psalmist is standing in the forecourt of the **temple.** He prostrates himself toward the sanctuary in the inner court (verse 2) and gives thanks to God with his **whole heart** (inner being). **Before the gods** may mean either that he praises the Lord's infinite superiority over the pagan deities or that he calls the heavenly council to witness his act of devotion (see above on 58:1-5; 82:1-5).

He gives thanks to the **name** of God, his mysterious presence in the temple. He is thankful for God's **steadfast** (saving) **love** and **faithfulness** and for the supremacy of the Lord's creative and judging **word.** He has been through severe trouble, but the Lord has restored strength to his life (on **soul** see above on 6:1-3).

138:4-6. These reflections lead the psalmist into a hymn to the greatness of the Lord. Israel's testimony to its God has been heard by the nations. Their **kings** will eventually worship the Lord, who rejects the **haughty** and exalts the **lowly** (see above on 112:1-4).

138:7-8. The psalm closes with an expression of confidence that the Lord will deliver the psalmist from his **enemies** and a prayer that God will **not forsake** the one who owes life itself to God's work.

PSALM 139. THE EVER-PRESENT GOD

This psalm expresses the abstract concepts of the omniscience (verses 1-6), omnipresence (verses 7-12), and creative power (verses 13-18) of God. The language is remarkably personal and concrete. The psalm defies classification, but verses 19-24 suggest that it may have been used by a suppliant seeking God's vindication and help (see above on Psalms 4 and 7). On the title see Introduction.

139:1-6. God knows the psalmist's every movement, reads his **thoughts** before he thinks them, and understands the full meaning of each **word** he utters. Like a city wall God surrounds, and the LORD's protecting **hand** is always near. **Such** perfect **knowledge** is quite beyond the psalmist's comprehension.

139:7-12. Even if he would, the poet could not escape God's mighty presence. The meaning of **wings of the morning** is not clear, but it may refer to an ancient personification of the dawn as a winged creature. Since the **sea** lies to the west of Palestine, verses 8-9 mean that the universe from top to bottom and from side to side is filled with the presence of God and is under God's control. On the cosmology of these verses see above on 18:7-18. **Even the darkness** has no reality for the God whose presence is **light.**

139:13-15. The psalmist's thoughts on creation center, not in the formation of the universe, but in the making of his own person and personality. His being holds no mystery for the God who formed his **inward parts** (literally "kidneys," which in Old Testament psychology are organs of thought) and **knit** his frame together with bone and sinew. The ancient world believed that children were formed in the **earth** before they entered the womb. Egyptian art shows the potter-god fashioning a child of clay on a wheel.

139:16-18. Verse 16 develops the theme of the "book of the living" (see above on 69:19-29). Before the psalmist was born, the LORD recorded the number of days given him. This is a poetic statement of the comprehensive knowledge of God—incomprehensible, but **precious,** to the psalmist. Verse 18 is obscure (cf. the Revised Standard Version footnote). It appears to mean, "If I were to count God's thoughts till my strength failed, the task would remain unfinished."

139:19-24. That people should defy such a God and hold the LORD in contempt fills the psalmist with passionate hatred and loathing. He realizes that some **wicked way** may lurk unrecognized and undetected in himself. He prays that God will expose him with divine wisdom, eradicate the evil, and lead him in the **way** of permanent peace (see above on Psalm 1).

PSALM 140. PLOTS OF VIOLENT MEN

This is an individual lament (on this category, the title, and **selah** see Introduction). It closely resembles Psalms 59 and 64 (see comments).

140:1-8. Three prayers describe the psalmist's predicament and seek divine aid (verses 1-3, 4-5, 6-8). He is beset by enemies, **evil men** bent on violence, godless and proud (verses 1, 4-5). In a **plot** to bring him to ruin (verses 2, 8) they have brought lying charges against him. He compares their malicious **lips** to those of a serpent which has **poison** under its **tongue.** Their violence is like that of a hostile army (verse 2), and their cunning is that of a hunter laying snares (verse 5; see above on 9:13-17). Verse 7 recalls former occasions when God protected the psalmist from hostile men.

140:9-11. This cry for vengeance is reminiscent of ancient Near Eastern curse formulas (see above on 17:13-14; 109:6-19). The **burning coals** suggest the fate of Sodom (Genesis 19:24). The other curses have the character of poetic justice, especially the personification of **evil** as a hunter stalking the hunters (see above on 7:12-16).

140:12-13. The closing expression of confidence states the psalmist's certainty of the **justice** of God which supports the helpless against the oppressor (see above on 68:5-6; 112:1-4). Because this is God's nature, the faithful in Israel will remain forever in God's saving **presence.** They will have continuous cause for thanksgiving.

PSALM 141. TEMPTATIONS

This is an individual lament (on this category and the title see Introduction).

141:1-2. The psalmist offers his prayer at the time of the **evening sacrifice** of grain and frankincense (cf. Leviticus 2:1). Holding his **hands** out palms upward—the ancient gesture of supplication—he asks that his **prayer** itself be considered a sacrifice. In this request we can see the beginning of the spiritualization of the sacrificial system.

141:3-7. Written in the form of a prayer, these verses tell the reasons for the psalmist's cry for help. Many Israelites have renounced their allegiance to the LORD and have prospered (see above on Psalms 73 and 125). They are friendly with the psalmist, inviting him to their feasts (verse 4) and offering to anoint him with **oil** like an honored guest (verse 5). He fears that this association will lead him to some corrupt word (verse 3), thought, or deed (verse 4). He prays for divine protection from all temptations, declaring that he would rather take harsh discipline from **a good man** than lavish hospitality from **the wicked.**

Verses 5-7 are obscure. Apparently they contain a **prayer** that those who spurn the covenant law will be condemned in God's heavenly council (verse 6; see above on 7:6-11), broken as a field stone shatters under a farmer's hammer, and given over to the dark power of the underworld (see above on 6:4-5; 88:10-12).

141:8-10. The concluding verses renew the apeal for help. On **the snares of evildoers** see above on 9:13-17.

PSALM 142. NO HUMAN HELPER

This is an individual lament (on this category and the title see Introduction).

142:1-3*b*. A note of confidence breaks through the call for help. The God of perfect knowledge (cf. 139:1-6) already knows that the psalmist's **spirit** (vital power; see above on 31:1-8) is at a low ebb.

142:3*c*-6*b*. The cause of the psalmist's distress is the plots of his enemies against him. On the trap set by the enemy see above on 9:13-17. A helper traditionally appeared on the **right** side (cf. 110:5; 121:5). But though the psalmist looks anxiously, no human defender comes (cf. 60:11). Therefore he renews his appeal for aid to the LORD, the only **portion** (possession) he has.

142:6*c*-7. The psalmist acknowledges his helplessness before his enemies. The **prison,** like the underworld, is a common symbol for distress. Both are narrow and confining, and the root meaning of "salvation" is "to make wide" (see above on 18:19). The psalmist pledges the vow of a thank offering if his prayer is answered (see above on 50:7-15). He imagines the scene as he presents the offering. The worshiping community will crowd around him, sharing his joy in God's goodness.

PSALM 143. JUSTICE FOR A SINNER

This is an individual lament (on this category, the title, and **selah** see Introduction). It is the last of the penitential psalms (see above on Psalm 6).

143:1-6. Persecuted by vicious enemies the psalmist seeks vindication and vengeance from the LORD. He cannot base his appeal on his innocence (contrast Psalm 17) since any human being brought to trial before God would be found guilty. He therefore appeals because of his need (verses 3-4). His foes have reduced his **life** and his **spirit** (vital powers; see above on 31:1-8) to the vanishing point. He is already as if in the realm of death (see above on 6:4-5). God's justice is known to act most vigorously in just such a case, as the wonderful deliverance of Israel from Egypt testifies (verses 5-6; see above on Psalm 136).

143:7-10. The renewed cry for help expresses the psalmist's alienation from God, which is almost as complete as that of the shades in **the Pit** (the underworld; see above on 88:10-12). He prays for instruction and for the guidance of God's mighty but beneficent presence (**good spirit**). On **soul** see above on 6:1-3.

143:11-12. His closing prayer appeals to God's justice and **steadfast love** (see above on Psalm 136). He asks that the LORD **preserve** his **life** and **destroy** his **enemies.** On **thy name's sake** and **servant** see above on 23:1-4; 27:7-14 respectively.

PSALM 144. BEFORE BATTLE

This royal psalm was spoken by the king on the eve of battle (cf. Psalm 20; on the category and title see Introduction).

144:1-4. In a series of military metaphors the king acknowledges that the LORD is the source of his power in war (verses 1-2). The theological basis is the ancient holy war concept, "The LORD is a soldier" (cf. Exodus 15:3; II Samuel 22:35). The holy war requires absolute trust in the LORD and none in the troops or their officers (see Introduction and on 20:6-9). Hence the meditation on the frailty of human nature (verses 3-4; cf. 39:4-6; 90:4-6).

144:5-11. The king then calls on God to **come down** and rescue him from enemies whose **right hand** (power) is founded on treachery (verses 5-8, 11). On the accompaniments of the theophany see above on 11:4-7*a*; 18:7-18. If the victory is granted, the king promises a thanksgiving service. He will himself lead the singing of a psalm of the type of Psalm 124, accompanying himself on the **ten-stringed harp** (see below on 150:3). On **new song** see above on 33:1-3.

144:12-15. Looking beyond the victory the king prays for the general welfare of his nation in its population, crops, and cattle. He confidently expects that the covenant **people** of the LORD, who is ruler of nature and history, will enjoy these **blessings.**

PSALM 145. THE NAME OF THE LORD

This hymn for a solo voice is in acrostic form (on these terms and the title see Introduction). The verse beginning with "n" is missing in the Hebrew. It is supplied in the Revised Standard Version from the Greek Septuagint as verse 13*cd*.

145:1-7. The singer praises the various qualities which unite in the **name** of God—that is, God's saving presence with the people (verses 1-2; cf. verse 21). The unlimited power of God's kingly majesty (verses 1, 3) is revealed in God's wonderful **works** (verses 4-7)—an expression usually used of the exodus event (see above on Psalm 136). The LORD's deeds also make plain **goodness** and **righteousness,**—that is, God's faithfulness to the covenant with Israel.

145:8-13*b*. The merciful character of the covenant God is reinforced by the quotation of an ancient covenant formula (verse 8; cf. 103:8; Exodus 34:6). **His compassion** is described as wide as the created world (verse 9). **Kingdom** in verses 11-13*b* is not a geographical or political unity but God's kingly authority which rules all time and space (see above on 100:3-5).

145:13*c*-21. Verses 13*c*-20 describe God's consistency to the **words** and **deeds** of salvation and judgment. God upholds the weak, feeds human and beast, protects those who sincerely call on the LORD, preserving **all who love him,** and destroys enemies against divine authority. These deeds are manifestations of justice (verse 17; see above on 68:5-6; 112:1-4). Such a God is worthy to be praised by everything made—especially by the members of the covenant community (**saints**), by the singer himself, and by every human being (**all flesh**).

PSALM 146. THE JUSTICE OF GOD

This is a hymn for a solo voice (on this cateory see Introduction). Psalms 146–50 are called "Hallelujah Psalms" because they begin and end with this one-word call to praise (**Praise the LORD**).

146:1-4. The psalmist summons his **soul** (vital powers; see above on 6:1-3; 42:1-2*a*) to the praise of the LORD. He declares that **no help** can be expected from any human being (**son of**

man). All humans are subject to death, and their **plans** are as fragile and fleeting as their bodies (see above on 6:4-5; 88:10-12).

146:5-10. The theme of this hymn is the **justice** of God which reaches out to deliver the helpless and to destroy **the wicked** (see above on 68:5-6). Only in this justice can human hope and happiness be grounded. It is the operation of that kingly power which created the universe and rules it eternally (verses 6, 10; see above on 96:10-13). Verses 7-9 show God's justice in action on behalf of easily exploited or defenseless members of society: **the hungry, . . . prisoners** (see above on 79:11-13), **. . . the blind, . . . sojourners** (resident aliens), **the widow and the fatherless.**

Psalm 147. The Paradox of God's Deeds

This hymn is one of the "Hallelujah Psalms" (see above on Psalm 146; on this category see Introduction). It consists of three brief poems (verses 1-6, 7-11, 12-20) expressing the paradoxical nature of God's dealing with the world.

147:1-6. The God who gathers the **outcasts** (exiles) **of Israel,** tenderly caring for the sorrowful and weak, counts the countless **stars** and calls them by **their names.** Infinite in wisdom toward the universe, God is infinite in compassion toward its weakest inhabitants.

147:7-11. The Lord's unlimited power summons the **rain** to bring fertility to the soil and **food** to the animals. But the Lord does not respect power in **man** or beast. The Lord delights in the reverent devotion of those who anchor their lives on the divine **steadfast love.** On **lyre** see below on 150:3.

147:12-20. The God who rules the universe has taken up residence in **Zion** and made it a center of blessing and strength. God's **word** is all-powerful. When the Lord speaks the **snow,** the **hoarfrost,** and biting **cold** grip the land. This is rare enough in Palestine to be regarded as a natural wonder. At the Lord's command the warm **wind** releases the imprisoned **waters.** This world-controlling **word** was given to Israel in the covenant. The command that sends forth the snow has been enshrined in **his statutes and ordinances**—that is, the law.

Psalm 148. Praise in Heaven and Earth

This hymn is one of the "Hallelujah Psalms" (see above on Psalm 146; on this category see Introduction). It calls for **praise** to the LORD **from the heavens** and **from the earth.**

148:1-6. The psalmist summons the members of the heavenly council (see above on 58:1-5; 82:1-5), and the heavenly bodies, and the heavenly ocean. He will form a great choir for the praise of the God who created them by the divine **word**, gave them permanence, and established the limits of their movements and powers.

148:7-13. This heavenly choir should have an equally inclusive couterpart on earth. It would include such marvelous creations of God as **fire** (lightning), **snow,** the **stormy wind,** and the deep sea with its mysterious creatures (see above on 104:5-9, 24-26). The more mundane landscape and creatures of the earth and its human inhabitants of all ranks and ages should join to praise the LORD, whose **name** (saving presence) **is exalted** in power and whose **glory** (authority) rules the universe.

148:14. Israel has special reason to praise the LORD. The LORD has exalted it by drawing it **near to him** and binding it in the covenant. The LORD has taken up residence in Jerusalem (see above on 68:15-16; 87:1-3). On **horn** and **saints** see above on 75:1-5 and 16:3-4 respectively.

Psalm 149. A Hymn of Victory

This hymn is one of the "Hallelujah Psalms" (see above on Psalm 146; on this category see Introduction).

149:1-3. The call to praise summons the **faithful** members of the covenant community—**the sons of Zion**—to song and sacred dance in praise of Israel's **Maker.** Their God has created Israel by the deliverance from Egypt and the covenant at Sinai. On **new song** see above on 33:1-3. On the musical instruments see below on 150:3, 4.

149:4-9. The worshipers are celebrating a **victory** and appear in the temple with **swords in their hands.** As part of the ritual they recline on **couches,** possibly for a sacred meal (verse 5). The titles **humble** and **faithful** are appropriate to soldiers in the holy war, where trust in the LORD was more important than military skill (see Introduction and on 20:6-9). The victorious warriors rejoice in the acclaim of their fellows (verses 4*b*-5*a*). In the flush of victory they dream of a greater triumph to come. The LORD's **judgment** on the pagan nations has been **written** (determined), and Israel will be the LORD's instrument for the execution of the sentence (verses 7-9). The treatment of the foreign rulers here is less harsh than that sometimes visited on defeated princes (cf. Numbers 31:8-12; Joshua 10:24-27). This psalm could belong to any period of Israel's history. The kind of thought it contains gave birth to the idea of the final battle at the end of the age.

Psalm 150. The Last Hallelujah

This hymn is one of the "Hallelujah Psalms" (see above on Psalm 146; on this category see Introduction). Possibly it was used as an introduction to the covenant renewal ritual (see Introduction) when the mighty acts of God in delivering the nation from Egyptian bondage were recited.

150:1-2. The praise in the **sanctuary** is echoed by the heavenly choir above the **firmament,** the blue dome of the sky (see above on 148:1-6).

150:3. The raucous blast of the ram's-horn **trumpet** (the *shophar*; see above on 81:1-5*b*) opened and closed the worship. There is less certainty about the other instruments of the impressive temple orchestra. The word here translated **lute** is elsewhere in the Revised Standard Version rendered "harp." If it was like the harps found in Egyptian tombs, it consisted of strings stretched from a long soundbox to an arm curving from one end of the box. Josephus, Jewish historian of the first century A.D., describes it as having twelve strings, but in earlier times it may have had only ten (see above on 92:1-4).

On the other hand **harp** here represents the word usually translated "lyre" in the Revised Standard Version. From representations in Mesopotamian reliefs the Semitic lyre seems to have been quadrilateral in shape, with strings stretched over a bridge on a soundbox to a crosspiece at the other end. Josephus says it had ten strings and was played with a pick. However, the reliefs show fewer strings, and David played the lyre "with his hand" (I Samuel 16:23). Both harp and lyre were made of wood (I Kings 10:12).

150:4. The **timbrel** was a small hand drum to accompany the **dance** (cf. 149:3). **Strings** are mentioned also in 45:8 (and perhaps 33:3; see comment), but the instruments so designated are not known. The **pipe** was probably a sort of flute—a tube of cane or metal with finger holes, sounded by blowing across the end, or perhaps transversely across a hole.

150:5. Two kinds of **cymbals** are mentioned. The difference between them is uncertain. It has been suggested that those of one type were flat and struck horizontally. The other type was cone-shaped and struck vertically. Probably both kinds were of bronze.

150:6. The psalm and the Psalter end with a "Hallelujah"—a call to every living thing to **praise the LORD.**

THE PROVERBS

Robert C. Dentan

Introduction

Name and Character

The proverbs in the book of Proverbs were not written in the style of folk sayings. The Hebrew word translated "proverb" can indeed mean a folk saying, but it is also used for a variety of other, more artificial literary forms. It can mean a parable or allegory (Ezekiel 17:2), a taunt song (Isaiah 14:4), or a prophetic oracle (Numbers 23:7). It can also mean a polished literary maxim or a more lengthy moral essay. It is in the last two senses that the word is chiefly used in Proverbs, especially in chapters 1–29. In chapters 30–31 the term covers such diverse forms as a meditation, a private revelation (30:2-4), a prayer (30:7-9), numerical lists of interesting things (30:11-31), and a descriptive poem (31:10-31).

All the material in Proverbs 1–29 is educational in character. It was composed with conscious literary art for the instruction of the young. The larger part is in the form of terse maxims running to no more than a verse or two. A smaller part is in the form of short essays covering as much as a whole chapter. Its educational purpose explains in large part why the book was written in poetic form. Poetry, with its regular rhythmic patterns, unusual turns of phrase, and striking images, is more easily memorized than prose. The schoolroom setting is also the chief clue to the interpretation of the book and should be continually kept in mind.

Authorship

The book is traditionally ascribed to Solomon, but this is a mere convention. It was in Solomon's court that ancient oriental "wisdom" was first introduced to Israel. It later became customary to attribute all wisdom books to him. The actual authors of Proverbs were the successive generations of wisdom teachers—or "wise men"—who had charge of the moral and practical training of young men of the court and upper classes who were being prepared for positions of responsibility in society, business, politics, and diplomacy. The best description we have of such a wisdom teacher is that found in Ecclesiasticus 51:13-30. There both the teacher's early training and the subsequent practice of his profession are described.

From the time of Solomon on, these wisdom teachers played an important role in Israel. They were recognized, along with the prophets and priests, as spiritual leaders to whom the people might look for religious instruction and moral insight. The wise men operated largely within the traditional framework of society and based their teaching chiefly on rational and experiential premises. Thus there was frequently tension between them and the prophets, who were often social radicals claiming immediate divine inspiration. Nevertheless on many points the teaching of the wise men and the prophets is strikingly similar (cf. 11:1; 15:8; 17:5, 15; 21:3, 30, 31).

The wise men were the intellectuals of the ancient world. Like all intellectuals they sometimes strayed into dangerous, certainly unorthodox, realms of speculation. Ecclesiastes and Job are products of this kind of private, unconventional intellectual activity. However, Proverbs—with the possible exception of chapters 30–31—is a collection of maxims and essays composed by wisdom teachers of unimpeachable orthodoxy. Its units were designed for practical use in instruction. Each was presumably intended to be memorized by the pupil and further expounded orally by the teacher.

Date of Composition

The book in its present form cannot be older than the time of King Hezekiah (late eighth century B.C.), who is mentioned in 25:1. In actual fact it is probably much younger than that. Individual "proverbs" may, of course, be as old as Solomon—or even older. But it is generally agreed that the book as we have it comes from the time following the Babylonian exile, perhaps as late as the fourth century B.C. The developed style of chapters 1–9, as well as the social and intellectual setting they suggest, strongly point to this period. The dating of the other, smaller collections of which the book is composed is a further problem.

Contents

The book falls into certain natural divisions, which are for the most part marked off by separate subtitles. The nucleus consists of the two collections designated as "The Proverbs of Solomon" (10:1 and 25:1; the similar phrase in 1:1 is intended to cover the whole book). The first of these, 10:1–22:16, can be further subdivided on the basis of form and subject matter into two collections—chapters 10–15 and 16:1–22:16. The second collection, chapters 25–29, is entitled "Proverbs of Solomon which the men of Hezekiah king of Judah copied." It is likewise to be divided into two collections, chapters 25–27 and 28–29.

The most exhaustive study yet made of the content, literary form, and cultural background of these four collections led its author to the conclusion that chapters 10–15 are the oldest, chapters 28–29 the next oldest, with 16:1–22:16 and chapters 25–27 coming somewhat later. All of them are preexilic. Interesting and important as these conclusions are, however, they offer only a reasonable working hypothesis and cannot be taken as definitive.

Between the two "Solomon" collections an editor has inserted two smaller sections, each entitled "The words of the wise" (22:17; 24:23). The first of these (22:17–24:22) is of special interest. It was apparently written in deliberate imitation of an Egyptian work, The Instruction of Amen-em-Opet, even to the extent of its division into "thirty sayings" (22:20). In 22:17–23:11 nearly all the material has direct parallels in Amen-em-Opet's book, which probably dates from the end of the second millenium B.C. The second collection of "words of the wise" (24:23-34) is apparently just an appendix to the first. It is too brief to provide any clue as to date.

Chapters 1–9 is largely a collection of extended essays. In all probability this material dates from the post-exilic period. It was prefixed to chapters 10–29 as a general introduction. The last two chapters (30–31) are a miscellaneous appendix, containing material of entirely different character from the rest of the book. Each chapter has at its head the name of an otherwise unknown foreign wise man (Agur and Lemuel). In the Septuagint some of this material is placed in the middle of the book rather than at the end (see below on 30:1–31:31).

Wisdom

Proverbs belongs to the general class of wisdom literature. This means, from one point of view, that it was produced by a group of teachers collectively called the wise men. It also means that the theme of the book is something called "wisdom." This concept is important not only for understanding Proverbs and the history of the wise men in Old Testament times but also for the development of New Testament Christology. In I Corinthians 1:24 Christ is called "the wisdom of God," and in Colossians 2:3, he is said to contain "all the treasures of wisdom." In John 1:1-14; Colossians 1:15-18; and Hebrews 1:2-3 the underlying idea is likewise clearly dependent on the concept of "wisdom," though the word "wisdom" does not actually appear.

The wisdom literature, taken as a whole, is the philosophical literature of the Hebrews. It is concerned with the proper governance of life through an understanding of ultimate goals and general principles. It is distinguished from the philosophical literature of the Greeks by its predominant concern for practical activity rather than metaphysical speculation. The word "wisdom" in its basic, non-philosophical use outside the wisdom literature means merely skill—for example, in dress-making (Exodus 28:3), the art of government (Genesis 41:39-40), or even wickedness (II Samuel 13:3). Even in its highest philosophical development the Hebrew word never quite lost its connection with this basic sense of practical skill.

In the wisdom literature proper, "wisdom" means primarily skill in the management of one's life, a knowledge of the true ends of human existence, the general rules which enable one to attain them, and the ability to put those rules into practice. These are goals and rules which can be learned and taught. Therefore it also becomes possible to designate as "wisdom" the totality of such knowledge conceived as a body of learning that has been handed down from ancient days and can be transmitted to posterity.

From this point on it is not difficult to see how the concept developed into an almost metaphysical idea—the Hebrew thinkers' closest approach to Greek philosophy. Wisdom came to be thought of as a constituent part of the universe and, indeed, of God. This is the stage represented by 8:22-31. There is further development in a genuinely metaphysical direction in the Wisdom of Solomon, and in the writings of the first century Jewish philosopher Philo. It was from the use of it by these later writers that the term became available to the early Christian church as it searched for a suitable vocabulary in which to express its judgment as to the meaning of Christ's character and work.

This theologically and cosmically significant "wisdom" appears only in the latest parts of Proverbs, notably in chapters 8–9. But the whole book takes on added meaning when it is seen that this was the direction in which the wisdom movement had been tending from the first.

The Influence of Foreign Wisdom

The wisdom movement did not originate in Israel. It was introduced from abroad and never entirely lost the marks of its foreign derivation. In Egypt and Mesopotamia, where civilized societies had long been highly organized, there had grown up a class of skilled officials—educated men who had mastered the art of government as well as the complex and mysterious arts of reading and writing. They had long been engaged in developing a philosophy of how people should live and work in society. It was not until the time of Solomon that Israel first aspired to be a civilized people among the other great nations of the world. From these earlier nations it had to borrow the techniques, and almost certainly the personnel, for establishing the elaborate governmental organization which was necessary. Along with the methods of organization of foreign courts came the educational procedures and the moral philosophy which animated them.

The most striking example of foreign influence in Proverbs is that already mentioned in 22:17–23:11, in which every proverb but one can be paralleled in The Instruction of Amen-em-Opet. In addition the book as a whole shows many affinities with other well-known Egyptian wisdom books and with various Mesopotamian wisdom texts. Recent studies have also disclosed a large Phoenician influence on the book. Two sections of Proverbs are explicitly attributed to otherwise unknown foreign wise men: "Agur son of Jakeh of Massa" (30:1) and "Lemuel, king of Massa" (31:1).

The foreign origin of wisdom explains the absence in Proverbs (as well as in Job and Ecclesiastes) of any reference to the distinctive ideas or institutions of Israel or the facts of its history. The wisdom literature of the Apocrypha (Tobit, The Wisdom of Solomon, Ecclesiasticus, and Baruch) represent a later stage of the movement. Here the situation is altogether different. These books present wisdom as an integral part of traditional Hebrew religion. But the Old Testament wisdom literature shows no conscious effort in this direction. It makes no attempt to harmonize the universal truths taught by the wise men of the ancient orient with the particular revelation given by God to Israel.

However, this foreign thought necessarily underwent an unconscious transformation as it passed through the filter of the

Hebrew mind. Careful study of ancient Hebrew wisdom shows that even the early parts of Proverbs have subtle differences of emphasis from their foreign prototypes (for example, see below on 1:1-6; 21:1-3). But the general reader is likely—at least on first approach—to find the similarities more striking than the differences.

The Philosophy and Theology of Proverbs

The character of wisdom thinking was largely determined by its foreign origin. It is this that gives it, first of all, the stamp of *universalism.* It is concerned with humanity as such and the general principles that govern life everywhere. It does not deal specifically with the Israelite and the divinely revealed laws to which Israel was subject under a special covenant with God.

Another characteristic, partly to be explained by the practical, educational function of the wise men, is their apparent *utilitarianism.* Wisdom teaching, with a few notable exceptions (for example, 15:16, 17; 23:4-5; and 28:6), is concerned with pragmatic success in ordinary life. It does not deal with response to supernatural challenges or the search for transcendent goals. It aims to produce good citizens rather than saints or spiritual heroes.

The need to have clear-cut rules for conduct, easy to use in classroom instruction, leads the wise men to present on the whole *a mechanical view of retribution.* They are inclined to speak of immediate success as the reward of the good life and immediate disaster as the punishment for wickedness. Both reward and punishment are the result of an impersonal law inherent in the sequence of human events, although certainly subject to God's overruling sovereignty.

For pedagogical reasons, wisdom philosophy also tends toward *oversimplification of human character.* All people are divided roughly into three sharply defined classes:

(1) the "wise" or "righteous," who know and do what is right and are successful;

(2) the "simple," who are capable of becoming wise although they are not yet;

(3) the "fools," who are utterly corrupt, incapable of moral growth, and doomed to destruction.

Finally, because of their upper-class mentality and their concern for the stability of human institutions, the wise men incline—in contrast to the prophets—toward *conservativism* in their political and social views.

The wise men of Proverbs—unlike those responsible for Job, Ecclesiastes, or the wisdom literature of the Aprocrypha—show little specific concern for theological matters. This is not to say that they were indifferent to theology. But their immediate task did not seem to involve theological principles to any great extent. That they considered themselves thoroughly orthodox is shown by the fact that they normally refer to God by the distinctive Israelite name Yahweh ("the LORD"). This is their one direct point of contact with official Hebrew religion, but it is certainly a significant one.

Since the purpose of the wise men is practical, the only attributes of God they mention are those connected with creation and the moral government of the universe:

God's omniscience (15:3, 11; 20:12; 24:12),
power (16:1, 3, 4, 7, 9, 33; 18:10; 21:1, 30, 31; 22:2),
justice (11:1; 12:22; 14:31; 15:8; 16:11; 17:2, 5, 15; 19:17; 21:3; 28:5).

While the law of retribution functions impersonally, on the whole Yahweh is presumably its author. Certainly Yahweh is its guarantor, and on occasion is represented as setting it in operation.

Because of its pedagogical concern with God as guardian of the moral order Proverbs has little to say of God's love and mercy (only in 28:13 and perhaps 3:12). But it would be an error to suppose the wise men were unconscious of these aspects of the divine nature or indifferent to them. God's merciful overruling of human plans in order to deliver even the wicked is the major theme in the Joseph story, which is a typical product of the older wisdom school (Genesis 50:20; cf. Proverbs 16:9). The thought of God's compassion is a recurrent one in the wisdom literature of the Apocrypha. In Proverbs a direct concern with theological speculation for its own sake is found only in the poem on cosmological wisdom in 8:22-31 and in the enigmatic words of Agur (30:1-4).

It is clear that the wise men became increasingly concerned with religion and theological matters as the movement developed. This is shown by the fact that the latest part of Proverbs (chapters 1–9) is much more explicitly religious than the earlier. The latest editor, furthermore, was so profoundly religious that he placed the whole book under the motto "The fear of the LORD [Israel's religion] is the beginning of knowledge" (1:7). This tendency would lead ultimately to the complete identification of universal wisdom with national Hebrew religion. Later wisdom and the law are equated in Ecclesiasticus (19:20; 24:23; cf. Baruch 4:1).

The Poetry of Proverbs

The entire book is written in the common patterns of Hebrew poetry. Each verse therefore normally falls into two parts, the second of which "rhymes" in thought with the first. This is achieved either by repetition ("synonymous parallelism," see 27:2) or by stating the converse ("antithetic parallelism," see 15:1) or by simply completing the sentence ("synthetic parallelism," see 22:6). The antithetic type overwhelmingly predominates in chapters 10–15; 28–29 and seems to mark these collections as the oldest. In the later collections (including 16:1–22:16; 25–27) there is greater variety, and the antithetic type is in the minority.

The acrostic—a type of poem in which each line begins with a successive letter of the Hebrew alphabet—is found in Proverbs only in the "praise of the good wife" (31:10-31). A distinctive wisdom type of poetry is the numerical proverb, which calls attention to a certain number of similar objects or phenomena—for example, 6:16-19; 30:11-31. It is thought that this type may have originated in the telling of riddles. There are many examples of it in the Ras Shamra texts, clay tablets excavated at the ancient Canaanite city of Ugarit in Syria.

Each proverb, whether long or short, is designed to give

aesthetic pleasure as well as moral instruction. Each is polished like a jewel. The most careful attention is paid to alliteration, assonance, puns, and other subtleties of sound and association—few of which, unhappily, can even be suggested in translation. The individual proverbs are meant to be read, not in rapid succession, but leisurely, separately, with a careful savoring of all the nuances of each. The wise man's aesthetic delight in his art is shown by the remark of one of them that

> A word fitly spoken
> is like apples of gold in a setting
> of silver (25:11; cf. 15:23).

The wise men believed that truth should be adorned with beauty.

I. Commendation of Wisdom (1:1–9:18)

In these chapters teaching takes the form of developed essays rather than brief maxims. It is generally agreed that they contain the latest material in the book and were assembled in order to provide an introduction to the other collections. They consist in large part of the praise of wisdom. The climax, in chapters 8–9, is the eloquent and universal appeal spoken by wisdom herself, personified as a woman. The extended warnings against the "loose [or "strange"] woman" which are also so characteristic of these chapters (2:16-19; 5:1-23; 6:20-35; 7:1-27) are meant quite literally to put young men on their guard against sexual immorality. But they also serve to furnish the scene with a counterpart figure who acts as a dramatic foil to personified wisdom. The background is obviously that of a developed, sophisticated society.

A. Introduction (1:1-7)

1:1. ***Title.*** The name of **Solomon** is an indication of the kind of book rather than of authorship (see Introduction).

1:2-6. ***Preface.*** The Instruction of King Amen-em-Opet (see Introduction) begins with a preface very similar in character. However, the Egyptian book was intended only for court officials. Proverbs obviously has a more democratic outlook and offers wisdom to all who are capable of receiving it.

1:7. ***Motto.*** This was placed by the latest editor over the whole book. **The fear of the LORD** means simply "religion"—or more specifically "Israel's religion." Hebrew had no special word for this concept (see below on 29:25). The word translated **beginning** can also mean "best part."

B. THE DANGER OF BAD COMPANIONS (1:8-19)

1:8-9. ***Parental Instruction.*** Training by parents is the basis for later happiness. Fathers and mothers are the first and most important teachers (cf. 4:3-4; 31:1-9; Deuteronomy 6:7).

1:10-19. ***A Warning Against Criminals.*** The wisdom teacher, who is responsible for the later education of youth, takes the role of father and addresses his pupil as **my son.** In the ancient world, as today, the promise of quick wealth had great appeal for many young people. Organized robber bands existed to exploit their impatience. The pledge of brotherhood and equal shares in verse 14 was no doubt as hollow then as it is now. Verse 17 seems to say that even a **bird** will avoid a trap set for it, yet foolish people rush into an evil life however obvious the consequences. The prominence given to the warning seems to indicate that robbery was a particular problem at the time when the final editing of the book took place.

C. WISDOM'S PUBLIC CALL TO REPENTANCE (1:20-33)

For dramatic appeal **wisdom** is personified as a prophetess, the word "wisdom" being feminine in Hebrew. Like the older prophets she is represented as appearing in the principal place of public gathering, around **the city gates.** She threatens those who will not listen to her message and, incidentally, promises security to those who accept her (verse 33). In verse 22 **simple ones** are callow youths who are capable of learning. **Scoffers** are skeptics who reject the principle of retribution. **Fools** are the incorrigibly wicked in morals as well as mind (cf. Matthew 5:22).

D. The Blessings of Wisdom (2:1–3:35)

2:1-22. ***The Benefits of Pursuing Wisdom.*** In Hebrew chapter 2 is one long, loosely constructed sentence. In it the wisdom teacher describes to his pupil the advantages that will come from the diligent pursuit and apprehension of wisdom. The pupil must listen to the teacher and exercise intelligence (**heart**) to grasp the meaning of words (verse 2). But he must also **seek** for wisdom passionately on his own initiative (verses 3-4). If he does this, he will come to a genuine personal **knowledge of God** (verses 5-8). He will acquire an understanding of what is good and right (verses 9-11) and be delivered from the influence of criminals (verses 12-15; cf. 1:10-19) and immoral women (verses 16-19). Finally, in a positive sense, he will be set firmly on the right way and given the companionship of those **good men** who will ultimately possess **the land** of Israel (verses 20-22).

2:16-19. These verses introduce the reader to the **loose woman,** who is so prominent in this part of Proverbs. Like the criminals of chapter 1, the adulterous wife seems to have been a special problem when these chapters were written. More will be said of her in connection with chapters 5 and 7. Verse 17 is particularly remarkable for the high view of marriage that it implies. The wife is not the property of her husband but stands to him in a relation of companionship. Marriage is not a legal-economic contract but a **covenant** solemnly witnessed before God, requiring lifelong loyalty.

3:1-12. ***Wisdom the True Religion.*** The older Hebrew wisdom—partly because of its foreign origin (see Introduction)—had little to say about specifically religious attitudes and obligations. But there was obviously an increasing tendency toward connecting traditional wisdom teaching with Israel's faith. This poem is the most religious section in the book. Every one of its six two-verse strophes except the first, which is merely introductory, contains the name of God.

In verse 1 **teaching** represents the word more commonly, but less accurately, translated elsewhere in the Old Testament as "law." The qualities particularly praised in this section are **loyalty** (the word usually translated "steadfast love" or "kindness") and **faithfulness**—qualities which are also attributed to God. Humility is commended in verses 5-8. The fulfillment of cultic obligations is commended in Proverbs only in verses 9-10. The offering of **first fruits** to the deity was not unique to Israel.

3:13-26. ***The Value of Wisdom.*** The opening clause—**Happy** (or "Blessed") **is the man**—is typical of the wisdom teachers. The transcendent value of wisdom is shown by the fact that it is useful not only to humans (verses 13-18) but even to God (verses 19-20). Here one can see the first steps toward the idea of cosmic wisdom, which will be developed at such length in 8:22-31. Belief in God as creator was fundamental in the faith of the wise men (see Introduction). The rewards of wisdom are **long life**, prosperity and happiness (verses 16-17), and protection from various forms of disaster (verses 23-26; cf. Psalm 91:3-13).

3:27-30. ***Love for Neighbors.*** For all their utilitarianism the wise men insist on the obligation of unselfish generosity toward others, especially the poor and helpless.

3:31-35. ***The Justice of God.*** With the growth of reflective thought in Israel came a theological problem—how to reconcile the apparent success of the wicked and the suffering of the innocent with the wise men's teaching of inevitable retribution. This became acute in Job and Ecclesiastes, but from verse 31 it is evident that many had long been troubled about it. This wise man, like his colleague in Psalm 37 and the "friends" of Job, answers doubts by simply reaffirming the fact of God's justice.

E. In Praise of Wisdom (4:1-27)

This chapter contains three lectures, or essays, in general praise of wisdom. While their thought is similar, there are slight differences of emphasis. Each one begins with a renewed address to the **sons** or **son** (verses 1, 10, 20).

4:1-9. ***The Best Possession.*** The traditional character of wisdom is made clear in the opening verses. It is not something which each one must dig out for oneself but is passed on as a tradition from generation to generation (verses 3-4). This poem assumes that a young man entering on an independent career will be interested in building up his estate and acquiring valuable possessions. The point the teacher wishes to impress is that wisdom is the most valuable possession of all (verses 5, 7). It has been suggested that verses 6-9 view wisdom as a bride and her acquisition as a wedding ceremony.

4:10-19. ***The Way of Wisdom.*** The idea of **the righteous** as those who belong to the **light** while **the wicked** belong to **darkness** is familiar from the New Testament (cf. John 3:19-21; I John 2:10-11; Ephesians 5:8-14). It is also known from the Dead Sea Scrolls. We find the same contrast here in ancient Hebrew wisdom (verses 18-19). The righteous one lives life in a **dawn** which is becoming continually brighter, while the wicked stumble around through the night in impenetrable darkness.

4:20-27. ***The Sure Path.*** The comparison of life to a journey is a commonplace of ethical teaching. In rabbinical literature the rules of conduct are called Halakah ("a way of walking"). Jesus spoke of the need of choosing the right road (Matthew 7:13-14). The wise man here makes use of the same imagery (verses 25-27).

F. Warnings Against Immoral Women (5:1–7:27)

5:1-23. ***The Loose Woman.*** This part of the book is particularly concerned with the problem of sexual immorality. This concern is undoubtedly an indication of the later date of the collection. It comes from a time when the strict moral standards of ancient Hebrew society were being threatened by contact with new influences from abroad. It is striking that the word translated **loose** is literally "strange," meaning at least that the woman's moral standards seemed foreign to the people of Israel (see below on 7:1-27). Verses 9-10 imply—and 6:26-35; 7:19-20 make clear—that the problem is not prostitution but adultery. Chapter 5 falls into three parts.

5:1-6. These verses are introductory. After the usual general exhortation the specific problem is set forth and the woman described. Her charm is acknowledged, but the student is warned that the charm conceals a deadly poison. **Sheol** is the dark underworld to which all the dead must go.

5:7-14. The exhortation becomes more explicit. In ancient Hebrew society the punishment for adultery was death (Deuteronomy 22:22). This law was evidently no longer carried out. Here the danger is only that the adulterous young man may lose his property to the injured husband and fall into the hands of moneylenders in order to pay the damages imposed (verses 9-10; cf. 6:33).

5:15-20. These verses speak positively of the need to confine sexual attention strictly to one's own wife. The language is picturesque—at one point reminiscent of the Song of Solomon (cf. verse 19 with Song of Solomon 4:5 and 7:3). The emphasis on the sexual side of marriage is due to the context, not to a purely physical conception of the marriage relationship (cf. 2:17).

5:21-23. This section concludes with an appeal to the authority of God and the validity of an unchangeable, universally valid moral law.

6:1-19. ***Digression: Various Moral Precepts.*** These verses are more closely related to later collections than to chapters 1–9. They are probably an intrusion in this section, since 6:20–7:27 continues the theme of chapter 5.

6:1-5. ***Against Suretyship.*** The wise men were emphatic in proclaiming the obligation of charity. They were equally emphatic in declaring that young men must curb their generous, but rash, impulses to guarantee debts for friends (cf. 11:15; 22:26-27). From a commonsense point of view, this could lead only to disaster.

6:6-11. ***Laziness.*** Observation of nature was one of the interests of the wise men (I Kings 4:33). This was sometimes for its own sake (see 30:18-19, 24-31) and sometimes, as here, in order to draw moral lessons. Laziness was a particularly obnoxious vice, since it is obviously so natural to the young and so objectionable to employers (10:26). It can lead only to failure and poverty.

6:12-15. ***Crookedness.*** The wise men believed in straightforward speech and honest behavior. They warn against the person who says one thing with the lips but through sly signals indicates something quite different.

6:16-19. ***Seven Things God Hates.*** The numerical proverb is a favorite device in wisdom poetry (see Introduction; cf. 30:15-31). This one begins with a list of five organs of the body sometimes used in detestable ways: **eyes . . . tongue . . . hands . . . heart** (the mind) . . . **feet.** The last two items are the **false witness** and the **man who sows discord,** who deliberately creates trouble among those who would otherwise be at peace.

6:20-35. ***Another Warning Against Adultery.*** The exhortation begins, as usual, in general terms. **The evil woman** of verse 24 is identified as an **adulteress** in verses 26 and 29. Verses 27 and 28 resemble folk proverbs. Both are commonsense warnings that one cannot play with fire without getting **burned.** The proper translation of verse 30 is not quite certain. But a comparison of verses 30-31 and 32-35 suggests that adultery is far more dangerous from a prudential point of view than stealing. The thief may lose no more than his property. The adulterer, confronted by an enraged husband, may be beaten, lose his position in the community, and even lose his life. No bribe can save him (verse 35).

7:1-27. ***The Wiles of the Adulteress.*** This is the most elaborate of the four warnings against adulterous women found in chapters 1–9. In a vivid and extended narrative the wise man pictures the wiles she uses to lead impressionable youth astray. Certain details in this chapter have led one scholar to suppose that the

loose (literally "strange") **woman** of these passages is a non-Israelite, perhaps the wife of a foreign merchant living in Israel. Her debased fertility-cult religion required her to have intercourse with a stranger. While the argument has considerable merit, it seems on the whole more natural to understand her as a wealthy Hebrew woman of the late postexilic period whose morals have been corrupted through contact with the pagan world.

7:1-5. Anticipating the introduction of the **loose woman,** the wise man advises his pupil to make wisdom his female companion (verse 4).

7:6-23. These verses describe a typical seduction scene. The woman, in the absence of her **husband**, goes out into the city street at the time of the evening promenade to find herself a lover. Acting like an ordinary prostitute she makes shameless advances to an inexperienced **young man.** She tells him there is a banquet waiting to be consumed at her home, for she has just been offering a sacrifice in the temple and the accompanying meal is not yet eaten (verse 14; in the so-called peace offering only a small part of the animal was sacrificed, the rest being eaten by the worshipers, Leviticus 3:3-4). She is able to offer luxuries such as only great wealth can provide. Since her husband, evidently a successful merchant, is away on a long business trip, there will be no danger. Finding the lure irresistible, the foolish youth goes to his doom. The result of such folly, described in matter-of-fact terms in 6:33-35, is here portrayed only in metaphorical language (verses 22-23).

7:24-27. The conclusion states the familiar idea that the pursuit of loose women is **the way** that leads **to Sheol** (see above on 5:1-6).

G. The Contrast Between Wisdom and Folly (8:1–9:18)

8:1-36. ***Wisdom Speaks.*** As in 1:20-33, wisdom herself, rather than the wise man, is represented as speaking. Standing at the city gate, where the streets come together, she declares her worth and offers her blessings. No doubt this is the way prophets and other religious teachers of ancient Israel often presented their message. Wisdom characteristically directs her appeal to all **the sons of men,** not just to the people of Israel.

8:4-21. Particularly notable in wisdom's speech is her emphasis on straightforwardness as opposed to crookedness (verses 8-9) and humility as opposed to **arrogance** (verse 13). Her high dignity is shown by the fact that **kings** rule by wisdom (verses 15-16; cf. Isaiah 11:2).

8:22-31. Wisdom was present with God at the creation of the world (cf. 3:19). As indicated in the Introduction, this passage is of primary importance for the development of a doctrine of cosmic wisdom, and for the later doctrine of the Logos (Word), so basic to an understanding of New Testament Christology. Here, however, the conception seems to be merely poetic, not philosophical. The dignity of wisdom as the most important of possessions is enhanced by representing her as the first of God's creations. Poetically she is pictured as standing by God's side when the rest of the world was made (cf. John 1:1).

The meaning of the word translated **master workman** in verse 30 is uncertain (cf. the Revised Standard Version footnote). Nothing else in the passage suggests that wisdom played an active role in creation—although she undoubtedly does so in the later development of the doctrine. There are an unusual number of Canaanite-Phoenician expressions in this remarkable passage. It therefore seems probable that the conception derives ultimately from Canaanite sources and that "wisdom" was originally a pagan goddess of wisdom.

8:32-36. The note of direct appeal returns at the end of the poem. The **life** promised in verse 35 is not everlasting life but a rich and full life in one's present existence.

9:1-6. *The Invitation of Wisdom.* This section of Proverbs closes appropriately with a challenge to choose between the two ways open to humans: the way of wisdom and the way of folly. Wisdom, again personified, is represented as inviting guests to a rich banquet she has prepared. Since only the most luxurious houses have pillars, her seven-pillared house is evidence of the wealth at her command. **Seven** is possibly derived from some originally cosmological or mythological conceptions, for this passage, like 8:22-31, shows traces of Canaanite influence. If the picture is that of a house, rather than a temple, the **pillars** are to be understood as ranged around an interior courtyard. Wisdom's final invitation forms the ultimate pattern for the similar appeals in Ecclesiasticus 24:19; 51:23-26 and Matthew 11:28-30.

9:7-12. *Digression: Incorrigibility of the Scoffer.* This passage is plainly a later addition. It obscures the intended parallelism of verses 1-6 and 13-18. The tone is pessimistic. While the appeal in verses 1-6 is addressed to the **simple**—the young and inexperienced—this paragraph is chiefly concerned with the **scoffer**—that is, the skeptic and hardened evildoer, for whom wisdom's appeal always falls on deaf ears.

9:13-18. *The Invitation of Folly.* Like wisdom, folly is personified. Her portrait is evidently modeled on that of the "loose woman" who has been so prominent in the preceding chapters. In contrast to wisdom, who sends out her messengers to summon guests to a magnificent feast, she **sits** lazily **at the door**. Like a common prostitute, she loudly invites passers-by to a meal that consists only of **bread** and **water.** She suggests—perhaps quoting a proverb—that her food is more delightful because forbidden. There is nothing to warn the unwary youth that her house is only the entrance chamber of **Sheol** (see above on 5:1-6).

II. The First Solomonic Collection (10:1–22:16)

Chapters 1–9 are to a large extent general and introductory. The main part of Proverbs (chapters 10-29) consists of several collections of brief moral maxims, most of them consisting of a single verse. Occasionally, as in chapter 24, they consist of two verses, and only rarely of longer units. In a few instances an attempt has been made to arrange the proverbs according to subject matter (for example, 10:18-21; 11:24-26; 26:1-12, 20-28). But on the whole their arrangement within the collections is unsystematic. The commentary deals only with verses of particular interest or presenting some particular problem. The first Solomonic collection is marked by the title **The proverbs of Solomon**, which applies to all of the material through 22:16 (on "Solomon" see Introduction). The style and content of the proverbs show, however, that this collection is made up of two smaller collections which were originally independent—chapters 10-15 and 16:1–22:16.

A. Part I of the First Solomonic Collection (10:1–15:33)

This collection consists overwhelmingly of proverbs composed in antithetical parallelism (see Introduction). It may well be the oldest collection in the book. The predominant theme of the proverbs is the contrast between the wise person and the fool, the righteous and the wicked. They are concerned more with general attitudes than with specific acts.

10:1*b*-2. *The Wise One and the Fool.* These verses introduce the two pairs of contrasted terms which provide the theme of the whole collection—wisdom versus folly and righteousness versus wickedness. Wisdom and folly are intellectual and moral terms. They imply the ability or inability to apprehend the principles by which life should be lived and to order one's life accordingly. **Righteousness** and **wickedness,** on the other hand, are in Hebrew essentially legal terms. The righteous is the one who is "innocent" of any violation of the law, while the wicked is "guilty." In the practice of the wise men the two pairs of terms are really equivalent and are generally used interchangeably. In verse 1 no distinction is intended between **father** and **mother**. The variation is merely for the sake of parallelism.

10:3. *Retribution.* The retribution doctrine is plainly stated and its operation put under the control of God (cf. verses 27-32).

10:4-5. *Sloth.* Laziness is one of the vices most frequently condemned by the wise men (cf. verse 26; see above on 6:6-11). Verse 5 illustrates the fact that the background of this collection—so far as it can be determined—is that of an agricultural society (cf. 12:10, 11; 13:23; 14:4).

10:7. A *Lasting Name.* For the pious Hebrew the only possible immortality was that of **memory,** kept alive by one's children. This will be achieved only by the wise and righteous.

10:12. *Love Above Hatred.* The wise men of Israel, like those of Egypt, regarded the calm, cool, unargumentative life as the best. Better than **hatred,** which **stirs up strife** on every side (cf. 6:19), is **love.** Love "is not irritable or resentful" (I Corinthians 13:5), seeks to promote harmony, and finds excuses for the misdeeds of others (cf. 17:9). This verse is quoted in James 5:20 and probably alluded to in I Corinthians 13:4-7 and I Peter 4:8.

10:15. *The Advantages of Wealth.* A number of proverbs in this book appear to be merely cynical when taken out of context—for example, 13:7, 8; 14:20; 18:11; 19:4, 6, 7; and 22:7). But their purpose is pedagogical: to make the young man realize how important it is to preserve his patrimony and not allow it to be dissipated by sloth and luxurious living (but cf. 11:28).

10:18-21. *Controlling the Tongue.* The wise men were characteristically concerned with the importance of keeping one's speech (**tongue . . . lips**) under proper control. The New Testament wisdom book shows the same concern (James 3:1-12). Simply talking too much was regarded as evil (verse 19).

11:1. *Honesty.* Like the prophets and the lawgivers of ancient Israel the wise men were concerned with promoting honest practice in business. Significantly, they are not content merely to say it "is the best policy." They also place it under divine sanctions (cf. 20:10, 23).

11:2. *Pride.* The willingness to learn is an essential quality of the seeker after wisdom. Thus it is evident that pride—the confidence that one already has the required knowledge—is a prime deterrent in the quest. Humility is a basic virtue.

11:8. *Dramatic Retribution.* The thought of a reversal in the fortunes of the good person and the sinner is a common feature of teaching literature.

11:9-14. ***Wisdom's Social Value.*** Wise people are a source of advantage not only to themselves but also to the society of which they are a part. These verses are good evidence that in spite of their individualistic emphasis the wisdom teachers had by no means forgotten that all people live in society and are responsible for it. Verses 12 and 13 show that the emphasis on silence is not merely self-regarding (cf. 10:18). It is against malicious gossip because of the injury it causes to others.

11:15. See above on 6:1-5.

11:16, 22. ***The Need for Good Sense in Women.*** Though most proverbs are concerned with men, a few deal with qualities desirable in women. This was probably an effort to provide the young man with guidance in his search for a wife (cf. 12:4). The meaning of verse 16 is not entirely clear, but verse 22 is a good example of how humor can be used to teach a lesson. Here it is that intelligence is a far more important quality in a wife than beauty.

11:24-26. ***Generosity.*** Everyone who is generous with their goods will receive generously in return (cf. 21:26; 22:9; Matthew 5:7; 7:2). Verse 26 refers to the practice of hoarding **grain** in time of famine.

11:28. ***Life's Ultimate Aim.*** Despite their generally utilitarian point of view the wise men were quite aware that the achievement of wealth and security is not the ultimate aim of life (cf. 15:16, 17; 23:4, 5; 28:6, 11). To be **righteous**—that is, the right kind of person—is far more important. On the image of the **green leaf,** a favorite one in a dry country, cf. Psalm 1:3 and Jeremiah 17:8.

12:1. ***Discipline.*** The word translated "discipline" means both "chastisement" and "education"—an indication that the wise men believed that severity was part of the educational process (cf. 13:24). The intelligent pupil will understand why the teacher is strict and will submit gladly (cf. 13:18; 15:32; 29:1).

12:4. ***Value of a Good Wife.*** A young man's success in life will be greatly abetted by the wise choice of a wife (cf. 11:16, 22; 21:9, 19). The most elaborate treatment of this theme is in 31:10-31.

12:9. *Comfort Above Ostentation.* The common sense of the wise men shows itself in their advice that one should not dissipate one's resources in trying to keep up with neighbors. Comfort and basic necessities are more important (cf. 13:7).

12:10. *Kindness to Animals.* Kind treatment of animals is obviously good business, since it means taking care of one's own property (cf. 14:4). However, the maxim is not prudential but a natural expression of the kindly and generous ethical philosophy of the wise men.

12:11. *Industry.* Hard work is the price of success (cf. verses 24, 27). Verses 10 and 11 both show the interest in agriculture that is characteristic of this section.

12:16-23. *Reticence, Truth, and Kindliness.* Many verses in this chapter exhibit the wise men's concern with self-control in speaking (cf. 10:18-21). Verse 16 recommends reticence in showing bad temper. Verse 23 advises against garrulity in any situation. Verses 17, 19, and 22 all assert that one's word must be absolutely dependable (cf. 13:5); God requires it. Verse 18 says the **words** of the wise are always kindly.

12:25. *The Effect of a Good Word.* As in verse 18 the emphasis is a positive one. Kind words create health and joy.

13:2-3. *Words Have Power.* Verses 2*a* and 3*a* assert that the proper use of speech brings great benefits (cf. 12:25). Verse 3*b* (and perhaps verses 2*b*) says that its improper use brings one to **violence** and **ruin.**

13:7-8. *The Value of Money.* Verse 7 is intended to teach the same moral as 12:9: better to be **rich** and act **poor** than to be foolishly ostentatious and have nothing. The meaning of verse 8*b* is uncertain, but the Revised Standard Version makes a good guess. As in 10:15 the purpose is to commend habits of thrift to young men inclined to dissipation. It is not to represent the attainment of wealth as the chief purpose of life (cf. 11:28; see below on 14:20-21, 31).

13:11. *Easy Come, Easy Go.* As in modern society there was always a tendency for young men to prefer get-rich-quick schemes to laborious toil (cf. 1:10-19). This proverb represents one aspect of the wise men's attempt to inculcate habits of industry, which are more conventionally advocated in verse 4. The translation in the Revised Standard Version is based on the Greek Septuagint rather than the Hebrew. But it does give the probable meaning: what comes too easily is likely to vanish just as easily (cf. 19:2; 20:21; 28:20, 22).

13:12. ***Longing and Fulfillment.*** This is a good example of the wise men's capacity for psychological observation. Though they were primarily teachers of the good **life** they were also interested in studying the world and human behavior as objects of interest in their own right. Just as 30:18-19, 24-31 illustrate their interest in the world of nature, this verse shows their interest in the operations of human nature. Anxiety and unfulfilled longing result in psychological depression and even physical illness. A desire suddenly satisfied often seems to release new psychic and physical energies (cf. 15:13). The idea of verse 12*b* is repeated in verse 19*a*. But verse 19*b* has no obvious connection and is perhaps misplaced.

13:17. ***Dependability.*** The pupils of the wise men were being prepared for positions of trust in society. They would frequently be employed as messengers for others, and in later life might be trusted with important missions of state. No quality was more important than absolute fidelity to their employers and to the commissions given them (cf. 25:13; 26:6).

13:19. See above on verse 12.

13:20. ***Good Companions.*** Character is deeply affected by those with whom one habitually associates, hence the great importance of choosing them carefully (cf. 14:7; 22:24-25; 24:1).

13:23. ***Misfortunes of the Poor.*** The meaning is uncertain. It may be that, although God has provided adequately for the poor, human **injustice** often deprives them of their due. Possibly the moral is the same as in 10:15.

13:24. ***Strictness with Children.*** This verse is a classic statement of the wise men's theory of pedagogy. The insistence that strict **discipline** is an expression of love is specially noteworthy (cf. 3:12).

14:6. ***The Scoffer.*** Education implies both capacity and receptivity. The scoffer has neither and is wasting time (cf. 9:7-12).

14:10, 13. ***Human Solitude and Sadness.*** These are two further examples of the wise men's keenness of observation (see above on 13:12). Every **heart** has depths that are inaccessible to others (verse 10). Though the wise men were, on the whole, cheerful and optimistic (see below on verse 30), they were by no means unaware that even the greatest joys of life are tinged with sadness (verse 13).

14:15. ***Credulity.*** While one should be open to truth and willing to learn, only the fool **believes everything** that is heard.

14:20, 21. ***Concern for the Poor.*** Verse 20 is a purely prudential proverb, similar to 11:15 and 13:8, 23. But verse 21 shows how unfair it would be to draw the conclusion that the wise men were mere materialists, interested only in success and unconcerned for the poor (cf. 15:27; 21:26; 22:9; see below on verse 31).

14:26, 27. ***True Religion Means Life.*** On **the fear of the LORD** see above on 1:7 (cf. verse 2). **Life** means a full life in the present world. **Death** means premature death that comes before life has been fully lived. On the **confidence** which comes from righteousness cf. 28:1.

14:28. ***The King.*** This verse and verse 35 contain the only references to the king in the older collection of chapters 10–15, and these are merely incidental. Contrast the frequent references to the king and court life in 16:1–22:16. Verse 28 says that the fortunes of the king are involved in those of his **people.** Verse 35 says that he prefers courtiers who have acquired wisdom.

14:30. ***Health Through Calmness.*** This verse may constitute a first essay in psychosomatic medicine (see above on verses 10, 13, and 13:12). The wise men were aware that there is close interrelationship between the states of the spirit and of the body. Tranquility and cheerfulness incline toward health. **Passions** such as anger and fear produce sickness (cf. 15:13, 15, 30; 17:22; 18:14).

14:31. ***More on the Poor.*** This verse is particularly significant.

It makes the care of the poor a religious duty, based on God's special care for them (see above on verses 20, 21; cf. 15:25; 17:5; 19:17; 22:22-23). To abuse God's creatures is an affront to their **Maker.**

14:34. See above on 11:9-14.

14:35. See above on verse 28.

15:1. ***Anger.*** Calmness and self-control are among the principal virtues admired by the wise men (cf. verses 4, 18; 12:16; 14:17, 30; 16:32; 19:11; 25:15). In the famous formula of Exodus 34:6 God is said to be **slow to anger** (verse 18). In Egypt also the ideal was that of the quiet, imperturbable person.

15:3. ***God's Omniscience.*** This chapter has far more to say about God than those preceding it in this collection (chapters 10–15). One dare not disobey the moral law, since God, who presides over it, knows all that happens. God is aware of what goes on **in every** earthly **place**, in **Sheol** (verse 11*a*; **Abaddon,** like Sheol, is a name for the underworld where all the dead go), and in **the hearts of men** (verse 11*b*).

15:4. See above on verse 1.

15:8, 9. ***God's Justice.*** Ritualistic religion, practiced without regard for ethical principles, is obnoxious to God. But God gladly hears the prayers of the honest (cf. verse 29; 21:3, 27; 28:9). One might suppose the wise man was here simply echoing one of the prophets. But such sentiments are also found in foreign wisdom literature—for example, the Egyptian: "More acceptable is the character of one upright of heart than the ox of the evildoer."

15:11. See above on verse 3.

15:13, 15. ***More Psychosomatic Proverbs.*** Cheerfulness produces health (see above on 14:30). The mood of these proverbs is much more characteristic than that of 14:13.

15:16, 17. ***Poverty Sometimes Above Wealth.*** Poverty with the assurance of God's presence and favor is better than riches. A vegetable dinner where there is **love** and harmony is better than a sirloin steak with quarrelsome people (cf. 16:8, 19; 17:1; 19:1).

15:18. See above on verse 1.

15:23. *The Pleasure of Speaking Well.* The wise men delighted in the well-chosen word, the well-shaped and graceful speech (cf. 25:11).

15:25. See above on 14:31.

15:26. See above on verses 8, 9.

15:28. *The Thoughtful Answer.* The good person does not speak before thinking; the bad has instant answers to every question (cf. 29:20).

15:29. See above on verses 8, 9.

15:30. *Another Psychosomatic Proverb.* See above on 14:30. **The light of the eyes** means the cheerful expression of one who brings **good news.**

B. Part II of the First Solomonic Collection (16:1–22:16)

The second of the two collections included under the title "The proverbs of Solomon" (10:1*a*) contains a nearly equal mixture of synonymous, antithetic, and synthetic proverbs (see Introduction). They are more concerned with specific acts rather than general attitudes. They show more concern for city and court life, and were perhaps assembled explicitly for the training of court officials.

16:1-9. *Man Proposes but God Disposes.* Most of these proverbs have to do with God's all-powerful guidance of human affairs (cf. 20:24; 21:1, 30, 31; 29:26). Ultimate decisions are not in human hands but in God's (verses 1, 3, 7, 9; cf. verse 33). Although self-justification is natural, only God is ultimately in a position to pass judgment (verse 2; cf. 21:2). The **arrogant** person is headed to disaster (verse 5; cf. verse 18). God permits **the wicked** to flourish only to illustrate how wickedness is punished in the long run (verse 4). One lives harmoniously and well by learning to submit to God's **ways** (verses 6, 7); to lead the right kind of life (in submission to God) is better than wealth (verse 8; cf. verse 19; 15:16). In verse 6 it is interesting to note how a technical cultic term ("to make atonement for," Leviticus

1:4) is given a purely inward and ethical interpretation. Verse 9 is strikingly illustrated by the Joseph story (Genesis 45:5-8; 50:20).

16:10-15. ***The King.*** Cf. 14:28, 35; 25:2-7. Such proverbs are good evidence that this part of the book is to be dated before the fall of the monarchy in 586 B.C. As is to be expected in a book greatly concerned with training for court life, the monarchy is idealized and regarded as the instrument for God's rule on earth (verse 10). Such views were common in the ancient Near East. Verse 11 probably intends to say that part of the king's task is to enforce God's demands for honesty and justice (cf. verse 13).

16:18-19. ***Humility.*** Cf. 11:2; 22:4. Like 15:16, verse 19 declares there are **better** things than wealth—in this case the humbling of one's **spirit** (cf. Matthew 5:3, 5).

16:25. See above on verses 1-9.

16:26. ***Hunger as an Incentive.*** This verse is a general observation without any obvious moral content (see above on 13:12).

16:27-30. ***Four Kinds of Evil Men.*** Special emphasis is laid on the misuse of speech through unkind gossip (verse 28), enticement to evil ways (verse 29), and hypocrisy (verse 30).

16:31. ***The Blessing of Old Age.*** Since a long life was one of the chief rewards promised by the wise men, gray hair was in itself a sign of wisdom. It was therefore a badge of pride (cf. 20:29).

16:32. ***Calmness of Spirit.*** This verse is a classic expression of the wise men's ideal of the quietness and self-control of the righteous (cf. 15:1, 4, 18; 25:28; 29:11, 22; see above on 10:12).

16:33. See above on verses 1-9.

17:1. See above on 15:16, 17.

17:3. ***God's Judgment of Men.*** Refiners separated precious metals from lead, iron, and other impurities by melting them in the **crucible** of a **furnace.** The purity of a sample could be tested by attempting further refinement of it. In view of the general outlook of the wise men, as well as the use of the same metaphor regarding reputation in 27:21, this proverb evidently refers simply to God's knowledge of character. It does not seem to involve the prophetic idea of purification of the individual or the nation through suffering found in Isaiah 1:25-26; Zechariah 13:9 and Malachi 3:3.

17:5. *Care of the Poor.* See above on 14:20, 21, 31. The second line adds a warning against rejoicing at the misfortunes of others (cf. 24:17).

17:6. *Grandchildren a Blessing.* Another reward promised those who sought wisdom (see above on 16:31) was children and grandchildren. Thus a man may legitimately take pride in them. They in turn should be proud of him.

17:8. *Taking Bribes.* Like verse 7, which warns nobles to behave nobly, this verse is addressed to officials (cf. verses 15, 23, 26; 18:5, 16-18; 28:16, 21). Those charged with the administration of **justice** have an obligation to be just. A **bribe** seems to have almost **magic** powers, but it is abhorrent to God (verse 15). The judge's aim must be simply to condemn the guilty and acquit the innocent. He should be entirely fair. He should not be swayed by the wealth and social standing of the guilty or by the insignificance of the innocent. That the corruption of justice was a perennial problem in ancient Israel is shown by the fact that the prophets were also deeply concerned with it.

17:9. See above on 10:12.

17:10. *The Teachable and the Unteachable.* An intelligent person learns sufficiently from verbal **rebuke.** The **fool** fails to learn even from **blows** (cf. verse 16; 26:11; 27:22).

17:15. See above on verse 8.

17:16. *Tuition for Wisdom.* It is evident from this verse that the wise men normally received fees for their instruction.

17:17. *Friendship.* The wise men accounted friendship one of life's highest values (cf. 18:24; 27:10).

17:18. See above on 6:1-5.

17:22. See above on 14:30.

17:23. See above on verse 8.

17:24. *Concentrating on the Present Task.* The **fool** is always dreaming of things far away and of possibilities yet to be realized. The wise person knows that **wisdom** is to be found and practiced in the present situation.

17:26. See above on verse 8.

17:27–18:8. ***Control and Economy of Speech.*** The first of these proverbs advises one to speak calmly. The second advises speaking rarely, adding—somewhat cynically, it might seem—that this is a good way to acquire a reputation for wisdom (see above on 10:18-21).

But the **fool** has no desire to be educated (18:2). His **opinion** is already formed, and he wishes only to express it (cf. 18:13; 29:9). His words cause trouble for himself and others (18:6, 7). The words of some are like sugar-coated poison, contaminating the springs of individual and social life (verse 8). Wise speech is like a deep, refreshing stream in an arid land (18:4). On 18:5 see above on 17:8.

18:11. See above on 10:15.

18:13. See above on 17:27–18:8.

18:14. See above on 13:12; 14:30.

18:16-18. ***The Wise Administration of Justice.*** It is unfortunately true that a bribe has great power and often gains one entrance where the pure merits of his case would not bring him (verse 16; see above on 17:8). The wise men apparently thought a mere description of this possibility should be sufficient warning to an honest official. A conscientious judge will not pass judgment until he has heard both sides of the question (verse 17). Under Hebrew law it was permissible to make certain difficult decisions by the casting of **lots** (cf. Joshua 7:16-18; I Samuel 14:40-42; Acts 1:26). Verse 18 suggests that sometimes this is the safest and fairest thing to do.

18:20-21. See above on 10:18-21 and 17:27—18:8.

18:22. ***Marriage a Divine Blessing.*** Marriage is the proper state for a young man to aim at, although the choice of the right **wife** presents many problems (cf. 11:22; 12:4; 19:14; 21:9; 31:10-31).

18:23. See above on 10:15.

18:24. ***Friendship.*** One close friend is better than a multitude of casual and uncertain acquaintances (cf. 17:17).

19:1. See above on 15:16, 17. The sense of this verse is better given in 28:6.

19:3. ***Accepting Responsibility for Failure.*** One should not blame God for disasters brought about by one's own **folly.**

19:4. ***The Advantages of Wealth.*** This and verses 6, 7 are more proverbs intended to encourage the young man to acquire thrifty habits and preserve his inheritance (see above on 10:15). Verse 1 shows clearly, however, that the wise men did not intend to represent wealth as life's greatest good (see above on 15:16, 17). Verse 6 shows how wealth can be used to gain influence. Generosity is a favorite virtue of the wise men, although here it has a practical rather than a philanthropic motive (cf. 11:24-26; 21:26; 22:9).

19:5. ***False Witnesses.*** Here is another aspect of integrity in the law courts (cf. verse 28; see above on 17:8; 18:16-18). This proverb is almost identical to verse 9—illustrating the fact that the individual proverbs had a long history as independent units and as parts of other collections before being assembled in their present form.

19:10. See above on 16:10-15.

19:11. See above on 15:1.

19:12. See above on 16:10-15.

19:13, 14. ***Family Relations.*** A man's life can be made miserable by a bad son (cf. verse 26; presumably he has not been properly educated; cf. verse 18; 13:24; 23:13-14). He can also suffer from an unsuitable wife (cf. 21:9; 27:15-16). But a good wife is a gift **from the LORD** (see above on 18:22). Verse 14*a* is an example of the emphasis throughout the book on keeping an **inherited** fortune rather than acquiring a new one (see above on 10:15).

19:15. See above on 6:6-11.

19:17. See above on 14:31.

19:21. See above on 16:1-9.

19:22. See above on 15:16, 17.

19:24. This is almost a doublet of 26:15; see below on 26:13-16.

19:28. See above on verse 5.

20:1. ***Danger in Wine.*** Young men needed then, as today, to be warned against the dangers of over-indulgence in wine as well as against the temptations of immoral women. The longest passage on this subject is 23:29-35, where it is combined with the warning against women (23:27-28; cf. also 31:3-7). The wise man's disapproval of strong drink was not moral but prudential. Wine used in excess is likely to lead to carousing and brawling, which can prevent a successful career.

20:2. See above on 16:10-15.

20:5, 6. ***Understanding Others.*** Although people's deepest thoughts are concealed from their fellows, a patient, intelligent person will be able to discover them. One must be cautious in trusting others, however. Their professions of trustworthiness rarely match their real character.

20:8. See above on 16:10-15.

20:9, 10. ***The Ways of God.*** An unusually large group of proverbs deals with profound theological-moral issues. Verse 9 is unique in Proverbs in expressing the thought of universal human sinfulness. Verse 10 speaks of God's concern for justice and common honesty (cf. verse 23; see above on 11:1).

Verse 12 implies that God, who made the **ear** and **eye,** is certainly able to hear and see (see above on 15:3). Verse 22 enjoins the pupil of the wise men not to practice revenge; God can be trusted to punish **evil** (cf. 24:29; 25:21-22).

Verse 24 asserts God's ultimate sovereignty over the created order and the will of men (cf. 16:1-9, 33). Verse 25 warns against the dangerous and superstitious habit of making **vows** without due consideration—and then being sorry afterward. Verse 27 seems to identify **the spirit of man** as a divine element that makes it possible for him to understand and judge himself. If this is the correct interpretation, it comes very close to the idea of conscience.

20:11. ***A Child's Behavior.*** The wise men recognized that "the child is father to the man"—that his **acts** give indication of what his adult character will be like. This proverb has obvious implications for child training (cf. 22:6).

20:12. See above on verses 9, 10.

20:13. See above on 6:6-11; 19:24.

20:14. ***Business Ethics.*** This proverb pictures the almost universal hypocrisy in the commercial enterprise. The **buyer,** when bargaining, pretends to be dissatisfied with the thing he is bidding for. His later **boasts** show what he really was thinking.

20:16. ***Against Suretyship.*** Cf. 27:13, which is almost a doublet. See above on 6:1-5. The words are supposedly addressed to the creditor. "If a man has been foolish enough to guarantee another's debt, exact everything you're entitled to!" Deuteronomy 24:10-13 authorizes the taking of a **garment . . . in pledge**—though under strict limitations.

20:18. ***The Need for Deliberation.*** Important enterprises can be carried out successfully only by consultation and careful planning.

20:22-25. See above on verses 9, 10.

20:26. ***Advice to the King.*** In contrast to many warnings to the would-be courtier to show proper respect for the throne (see above on 16:10-15) this proverb and verse 28 are for the guidance of the king himself. On **loyalty and faithfulness** see above on 3:1-12.

20:27. See above on verses 9, 10.

20:28. See above on verse 26.

20:29. See above on 16:31.

20:30. See above on 13:24.

21:1-3. ***God's Omnipotence and Justice.*** Like numerous other proverbs in this collection, verses 1, 30, and 31 express God's absolute sovereignty over creation (cf. 16:1-9, 33; 20:24). While the idea of God's mysterious guidance of the course of events is common to much oriental wisdom literature, the Hebrew wise men's conception of God's absolute independence of—and control over—the created order is quite without parallel. Verse 1 says that God controls the decisions of kings as easily as a farmer directs the **water** in an irrigation ditch.

Verses 30 and 31 sound like the prophetic literature in declaring that **victory** is from God alone (cf. Isaiah 8:9-10; 31:1-3). Verse 2 denies that anyone is really capable of judging their own conduct; ultimately this is in God's hands (cf. 16:2). Verse 3 agrees with the prophets in teaching that God prefers ethical conduct to mere ritual exercises (cf. 15:8, 9; Hosea 6:6;

Amos 5:21-24). The same thought is expressed in verse 27, without explicit mention of God.

21:5. See above on 6:6-11; 13:11.

21:9. This is repeated in 25:24 (cf. 27:15-16). See above on 11:16, 22; 19:13.

21:13. *Care of the Poor.* See above on 14:20, 21, 31; cf. 17:5; 22:9, 16. Those who fail in charity toward the poor will be treated the same way.

21:14. *Gifts to Pacify.* It is well for a young man to know that a judiciously chosen gift, offered at the right moment, can often avert even justified anger. Only a thin line, of course, separates this kind of gift from an outright **bribe** (see above on 17:8; 18:16-18).

21:19. Cf. verse 9. See above on 11:16, 22; 19:13.

21:22. Cf. 24:5.

21:23. See above on 10:18-21; 17:27–18:8.

21:25. See above on 6:6-11.

21:26. Cf. 11:24-26; 22:9.

22:1. *The Value of Reputation.* A man with a reputation for wise and honest dealing will often be able to accomplish more than a rich man. Therefore one should cultivate the good opinion of others.

22:2. *Rich and Poor.* In the view of the wise men God has created social distinctions, but the poor must be helped. This proverb well illustrates their conservative political philosophy (cf. 29:13). The conclusion intended to be drawn is that God cares for **rich and . . . poor** alike and that each has responsibilities toward the other. Verse 7 says it is a simple fact that the rich have certain advantages over the poor (see above on 10:15). In verse 9 generosity toward the poor is declared to be a source of blessing (see above on 14:31; 17:5; cf. 21:26).

22:6. *Training Children.* Education produces character, according to this oft-quoted proverb (see above on 20:11). To be effective the **discipline** must be severe (verse 15; see above on 13:24; cf. 23:13-14).

22:7, 9. See above on verse 2.

22:13. See below on 26:13-16.

22:14. See above on chapters 5; 7.
22:15. See above on verse 6.
22:16. See above on verse 2.

III. The "Thirty Sayings" (22:17–24:22)

This collection is in some way directly dependent on the Egyptian Instruction of Amen-em-Opet. The translation of an obscure Hebrew phrase as **thirty sayings** in 22:20 (King James Version: "excellent things") is based on the fact that Amen-em-Opet's book contains thirty chapters. In 22:17–23:11 most of the proverbs consist of two verses each. Every proverb but one (22:26-27) has a more or less close parallel in the Egyptian book, though the order is different. The quotations below from this work are from the translation by J. A. Wilson in *Ancient Near Eastern Texts*, edited by J. B. Pritchard, pp. 421-25.

22:17-21. *Tithe and Preface.* Cf. 1:1-6.

22:22-23. *Care of the Poor.* See above on 14:31; cf. Amen-em-Opet chapter 2: "Guard thyself against robbing the oppressed and against overbearing the disabled." The Hebrew proverb adds the theological motive.

22:24-25. *Avoid Irascible Companions.* See above on 13:20; cf. Amen-em-Opet chapter 9: "Do not associate to thyself the heated man, nor visit him for conversation."

22:26-27. *Against Suretyship.* See above on 6:1-5; 20:16. As noted above, this proverb alone in 22:17–23:11 has no parallel in the Egyptian book.

22:28. See below on 23:10.

22:29. *The Result of Good Training.* Cf. Amen-em-Opet chapter 30: "As for the scribe who is experienced in his office, he will find himself worthy (to be) a courtier." The rare Hebrew word translated **skillful** is also used of scribes in Psalm 45:1 (Revised Standard Version "ready") and Ezra 7:6. The Egyptian parallel makes clear the precise sense of the proverb.

23:1-3. *Greed at the King's Table.* Cf. 25:6-7; Amen-em-Opet chapter 23: "Do not eat bread before a noble, nor lay on thy mouth at first. . . . Look at the cup which is before thee, and let it serve thy needs." Here the parallel is not as close as in some other instances. But both documents are concerned with discouraging greedy and disgusting habits at table.

23:4-5. *The Deceitfulness of Riches.* Cf. Amen-em-Opet chapter 7: "Cast not thy heart in pursuit of riches. . . . If riches are brought to thee by robbery, they will not spend the night with thee; at daybreak . . . they have made themselves wings like geese and are flown away to the heavens." The substitution of the Palestinian **eagle** for the Egyptian "goose" is characteristic of the freedom with which the original was used.

23:9. *Talking with Fools.* Cf. 20:19; Amen-em-Opet chapter 21: "Spread not thy words to the common people, nor associate to thyself one (too) outgoing of heart."

23:10-11. *Respect for Boundary Markers.* Cf. 22:28; Deuteronomy 19:14. There was always a temptation for the powerful and unscrupulous to move boundary markers to their own advantage. Cf. Amen-em-Opet chapter 6. "Do not carry off the landmark at the boundaries of the arable land, . . . nor encroach upon the boundaries of a widow, . . . lest a terror carry thee off." The Hebrew text introduces the characteristic Old Testament conception of God as the **Redeemer** (literally "legally appointed vindicator"); (cf. Job 19:25; Psalm 103:4; Isaiah 44:6).

23:12. *Introduction and Subtitle.* This verse introduces the collection 23:12–24:22, which completes the "words of the wise" (22:17). This section contains no parallels to Amen-em-Opet (see above on 22:17–24:22).

23:13-14. *The Education of Children.* See above on 13:24; cf. 20:30; 22:6, 15. See also the maxim from the Mesopotamian book of Ahikar: "Withhold not thy son from the rod, else thou wilt not be able to save [him from *wickedness*]. If I smite thee, my son, thou wilt not die, but if I leave thee to thine own heart [thou wilt not live]" Translation by H. L. Ginsberg, *Ancient Near Eastern Texts*, edited by J. B. Pritchard; p. 428.

23:17-18. *Envy of the Wicked.* The success of **sinners** was a growing problem with the wise. As in 3:31-35; 24:19-20; and

Psalm 37 the answer given here is overly simple: "Wait long enough and you will see the law of retribution working out!"

23:19-21. ***Avoiding Wine and Gluttony.*** See above on 20:1. Here the young man is warned against carousing, since it can lead only to poverty.

23:26-28. See above on chapters 5 and 7.

23:29-35. ***The Folly of Drunkenness.*** See above on verses 19-21 and 20:1. This is a good example of the wise men's use of vivid description, mixed with humor to convey their lessons (cf. chapter 7; 11:22; 26:13-15). Verse 35 pictures both the deadening effects of alcohol and the incorrigibility of the confirmed **drunkard.**

24:1-2. See above on 23:17-18.

24:3-7. ***The Praise of Wisdom.*** Wisdom has the advantage over **strength** (cf. 21:22). The **fool** is incapable of getting it (verse 7; cf. 17:16; 26:7; 27:22). Wisdom is sweeter than **honey** (verses 13-14; cf. Psalm 19:10).

24:10-12. ***Rescue of the Innocent.*** The text of verse 10 appears to be corrupt. The purpose of verses 11-12 is to encourage an active concern for the rights of the oppressed. To plead ignorance of the facts is no excuse. God the All-knowing will hold one strictly to account both for one's sins and for one's failure to respond to human need (cf. Luke 10:25-37; James 4:17).

24:13-14. See above on verses 3-7.

24:17-18. ***How to Treat Enemies.*** The fine sentiment of verse 17 is somewhat spoiled by verse 18 (but cf. Romans 12:19). The utilitarian motive is introduced for teaching reasons. Verses 28-29, which offer a similar injunction as an absolute ethical principle, are more congenial to modern and Christian taste. Cf. 25:21-22.

24:19-20. See above on 23:17-18.

24:21-22. See above on 16:1-9, 10-15; cf. I Peter 2:17.

24:23-34. ***Appendix to the "Thirty Sayings."*** This brief section is apparently an appendix to 22:17–24:22, as indicated by the title (verse 23*a;* cf. 22:17*a*). In the Septuagint 30:1-14 appears between verses 22 and 23.

24:23*b*-26. See above on 17:8; 18:16-18.
24:28-29. See above on verses 17-18.
24:30-34. See on 6:6-11; 26:13-16.

IV. The Second Solomonic, or "Hezekiah," Collection (25:1–29:27)

A new title (25:1) separates chapters 25–29 from the rest of the book. But, as in the case of the first "Solomon" collection (10:1–22:16), internal evidence shows that these chapters consist of two smaller collections—chapters 25–27 and 28–29. In the Septuagint 30:15–31:9 is inserted between chapters 24 and 25.

A. Part I of the Second Solomonic Collection (25:1–27:27)

More than half the proverbs in chapters 25–27 show no real parallelism in construction. They have a greater concern with the life of simple people, especially peasants, than with that of the court. A theological motivation appears only in 25:21-22. The secular character of this collection has led most commentators to consider it probably the oldest in the book. In contrast, however, a recent study presents evidence for viewing it as the latest of the four "Solomonic" collections. The greater length of many of the sections appears to show a more developed literary style. The interest in common life is seen as pointing to a broadening of intellectual horizons.

25:1. ***Title.*** There is no reason to doubt that the reign of **Hezekiah** (II Kings 18–20) was marked by a surge of literary and cultural activity.

25:2-7*b*. ***Preface.*** Though the major interest of this collection is with common life, this preface shows that it originated at court. Verses 6-7*b*, which advise the courtier to be modest, are echoed in Luke 14:7-11.

25:7*c*-10. *Lawsuits.* One should avoid going to court if possible and settle disputes privately (cf. Matthew 5:25).

25:11, 12. *The Well-chosen Word.* Cf. 15:23. The proverb of comparison (**is like**) is especially characteristic of this section.

25:13. Cf. 13:17.

25:16, 17. *Moderation.* Just as too much sweet is sickening, so is too effusive a friendship. Cf. verse 27; 30:7-9.

25:20. *Suitability to the Occasion.* Even **songs** are sometimes out of place. The text of the verse is corrupt, but the translation probably comes close to the thought.

25:21-22. *Feed Your Enemy.* The motive, though utilitarian, is higher than in 24:18: "you will make him ashamed of himself." This proverb is quoted verbatim in Romans 12:20. In the Old Testament the great example of the forgiving spirit is Joseph (Genesis 50:15-21). He represents the spirit of ancient Hebrew wisdom at its best. It is noteworthy that the motive for Joseph's attitude is said to be a purely theological one (Genesis 50:20).

25:28. Cf. 16:32.

26:1-12. *The Fool.* These proverbs describe what a fool is like and how the fool is to be treated. Verses 4 and 5, which appear contradictory, are probably to be interpreted as complementary. Verse 4 means "Don't act the way fools act!" Verse 5 advises to "treat a fool as he deserves!" On verse 12 cf. 11:2.

26:13-16. *The Lazy Person.* Verses 13-15 show the ability of the wise men to use humor for pedagogical purposes (cf. 11:22; 23:29-35). Any excuse is sufficient to keep lazy people at home and away from work (verse 13; cf. 22:13, where the form is more complete). He turns **on his bed** like a creaky gate. Some seem too indolent even to feed their own faces (verse 15; cf. 19:24).

26:17. *Mind Your Own Business.* An Akkadian proverb says: "When you see a quarrel, go away without noticing it."

26:18-19. *The Practical Joker* is headed for serious trouble.

27:1. *Don't Count on Tomorrow.* Chapter 18 of Amen-em-Opet (see above on 22:17–24:22) says in a similar vein, "Do not spend the night fearful of the morrow. At daybreak what is the morrow like? Man knows not what the morrow is like."

27:2. Cf. 25:6-7*b*.

27:4. This proverb may be concerned with the same situation as 6:34-35.

27:5-6. ***Frankness in True Love.*** Love ought to be expressed, not hidden, even if it takes the form of rebuke. Only hypocrisy is always smooth and effusive (verse 6; cf. verses 14; 29:5).

27:7-9. ***Observations on Life.*** See above on 13:12. Verse 8 speaks of the pathos of the homeless man. If the Revised Standard Version is right in substituting the reading of the Septuagint for the Hebrew of verse 9*b*, this proverb simply means that external **trouble** is as disquieting to the inner life as luxurious unguents are soothing.

27:10. ***Friendship.*** Cf. 17:17. It is better to make friends among neighbors, who are close at hand, than depend on relatives who are **far away.** Line *b* is meaningless in the context and probably out of place.

27:13. This is a doublet of 20:16. See above on 6:1-5.

27:14. See above on verses 5, 6.

27:15-16. This is perhaps an expansion of 19:13*b* (see comment).

27:17-20. ***More Observations on Life.*** Verse 17 says that social life, not solitude, brings out one's true humanity. Verse 19 probably means that one learns to understand oneself through watching others. Verse 20 testifies that one's reach is always greater than one's grasp. On **Sheol and Abaddon** see above on 15:3.

27:21. ***People Judged by Their Reputations.*** Just as refiners separate precious from base metals (see above on 17:3) so most people will be judged in the long run by the opinions of those with whom they associate. The point is probably the same as in 22:1 (see comment).

27:22. See above on 17:10.

27:23-27. ***The Value of Country Life.*** These verses may reflect a pessimistic view of the increasingly luxurious and sophisticated life of the city. Wealth, in the form of gold or silver, whether inherited or earned in trade, quickly vanishes. But a good herd of animals will provide dependable **food** and **clothing.**

B. Part II of the Second Solomonic Collection (28:1–29:27)

Chapters 25–29 are closer, at least in form, to chapters 10–15 than to other parts of the book. The great majority of the proverbs are antithetical (see Introduction). There is similar concern with the general contrast between the wise and the foolish. A number of proverbs are directly concerned with the office of the king, the administration of justice, and the condition of the poor. The collection may therefore have been assembled as a "Mirror for Princes"—instructions for those destined to rule or hold official positions in the state (cf. 31:1-9). Probably this collection should be dated soon after chapters 10–15.

28:1. *Righteousness as a Source of Security.* One who is wise and does what is right has nothing to fear. This verse vividly contrasts the apprehensiveness of evil people, who stand in constant fear of well-deserved retribution, with the confidence of **righteous** people, sure of their own integrity. Other proverbs in this chapter express in more conventional ways the thought that religion (verse 14), straightforwardness (verse 18), and a wise humility (verse 26) are the best resources for confident living. See above on 14:26, 27; cf. 29:25; Psalm 91.

28:2. *The Importance of Wise Government.* Verses 2, 15, and 16 contain three different Hebrew words for **ruler.** All are general terms used of various kinds of officials, including kings. Verse 2 refers to constant changes in government such as occurred in the northern kingdom at certain periods. Verse 5 associates the sound administration of justice with sincere religion. Verse 15 pictures the unhappy fate of a badly governed people. Verse 16 promises long life to incorruptible officials. Verse 21 satirizes the dishonesty of some whose favorable judgment can be won by the smallest of bribes (just **a piece of bread**).

28:3. *Care of the Poor.* The opening phrase of this proverb should probably be corrected to read "A man of position." Cf. verses 8 and 27, which promise prosperity to those who are concerned for **the poor.**

28:4. ***The Law.*** This does not refer to civil law or the "law of Moses" but to the "instruction" or "teaching" given by wise men, prophets, and priests. Cf. verses 7, 9.

28:5. See above on verse 2.

28:6. ***Poverty Sometimes Above Wealth.*** This is almost identical with 19:1. It is further evidence that the wise men's teaching was not merely utilitarian. Cf. verse 11. See above on 11:28; 15:16, 17.

28:7. See above on verse 4.

28:8. ***Usury.*** This echoes the law which forbids the taking of **interest** on loans (Exodus 22:25; Leviticus 25:36). In a simple society loans were acts of charity; to take interest was to capitalize on another's misfortune.

28:9. See above on verse 4.

28:11. See above on verse 6.

28:13. ***Confession Obtains Mercy.*** This proverb is doubly unique. It is the only one which advises confession (publicly?) and the only one which speaks of God's mercy. Cf. Psalm 32:1-5; I John 1:9.

28:14. See above on verse 1.

28:15, 16. See above on verse 2.

28:17. ***Don't Help a Murderer.*** The sense of this is not entirely clear—nor is the reason for its inclusion in the book.

28:18. See above on verse 1.

28:19-25. ***Avarice.*** Verse 19*a* commends farming as an honest way to achieve security. Verses 19*b*, 20, 22, and 25 condemn all schemes to get rich quickly. They probably represent a reaction against the rise of a mercantile society. See above on 27:23-27; also 13:11. On verse 21 see above on verse 2. The situation envisaged in verse 24 may be that of a son who claims that what belongs to the family belongs to him. Therefore it is not robbery to take it.

28:26. See above on verse 1.

28:27. See above on verses 3; 14:20.

29:2, 4. ***The Importance of Wise Government.*** Verse 2 speaks of the happiness of a people whose officials are upright. Verse 4 advises against heavy burdens on the nation (cf. I Kings 12:4,

9-11). Verse 12 suggests that the head of state, by his example, sets the moral tone of his whole administration. Verse 16 adds that the doom of a wicked administration is sure. Though the power of a king is evident to everyone, verse 26 declares the final decision is really in the hand of God (cf. 16:1-9).

29:7. ***Care of the Poor.*** Genuine concern for the needs of the poor is a sign of wisdom. The absence of it is equally a sign of folly. These words are probably directed to officials, as verses 13 and 14 certainly are. Frequently in the course of a lawsuit rich and poor will appear together before the same judge. He must remember that both are God's creatures and that God is concerned for them both (verse 13). An administration in which the poor are treated fairly is in a sound condition and will endure (verse 14).

29:8, 9. ***Scoffers and Fools.*** The **scoffers** are the intellectually perverse who deny that the law of retribution exists (cf. 14:6; Psalm 10:4, 11). The **fool** is more interested in loudly expressing an opinion than in learning (see above on 17:27–18:8). Unlike the wise man fools cannot control their passions (verse 11; cf. verse 22; see above on 10:12; 15:1; 16:32). One who speaks before there is time to think is even worse than a fool (verse 20; cf. 15:28).

29:10. ***The Wicked Hate the Righteous.*** If the translation of the Revised Standard Version is correct—as it probably is—both lines of this verse declare that the life of the righteous is imperiled by the wicked. The thought is unique in Proverbs, which tends to picture only the blessings of the righteous. It is perhaps intended as a word of caution to officials who are determined to perform their duties without fear or favor. Cf. verses 25, 27.

29:11. See above on verses 8, 9.

29:12. See above on verses 2, 4.

29:13, 14. See above on verse 7.

29:15. See above on 13:24.

29:16. See above on verses 2, 4.

29:17. Cf. verse 15; see above on 13:24.

29:18. ***Importance of Religious Teaching.*** A nation needs rulers who are not only wise but also willing to listen to prophets and wise men. On **the law** see above on 28:4.

29:19. ***Discipline of Servants.*** Even more than children (cf. verses 15, 17) slaves require stern correction. Scolding is not enough. Beating is needed (cf. Exodus 21:20-21).

29:20. See above on verses 8, 9.

29:21. See above on verse 19.

29:23. See above on 11:2.

29:24. ***Partners in Crime.*** Anyone who accepts stolen property is putting their own life in danger (cf. 1:10-19). A **curse** spoken against the **thief** will destroy the **partner** also—even though the partner is only a passive accomplice.

29:25. ***Don't Fear Other People.*** Security comes from putting one's trust in God (see above on 28:1; cf. Psalm 56:11). The Hebrew word used here for **fear** means literally "trembling, animal terror." It is something quite different from the "fear of the LORD"—a different word with the connotation of awe and reverence. Fear of the LORD includes trusting God.

29:26. See above on verses 2, 4.

29:27. See above on verse 10.

V. MISCELLANEOUS APPENDIX (30:1–31:31)

The material in these last two chapters is quite different from that in the rest of the book. It is miscellaneous in character. In the Septuagint only 31:10-31 is found here. 30:1-14 follows 24:22, and 30:15–31:9 follows 24:34.

A. THE WORDS OF AGUR (30:1-9)

We cannot be sure just how far **The words of Agur** are supposed to extend. They may include verses 1-9 or possibly verses 1-4. On the basis of the division in the Septuagint (where, however, the proper name does not occur) many assume the title covers verses 1-14. The most extensive modern study of this material takes the whole chapter to be the intended unit.

30:1. ***Title and Beginning.*** Only the phrase **The words of Agur son of Jakeh** is clear. The Hebrew word *massa* here and in 31:1 might be a common noun meaning "oracles" or "prophecy" (King James Version) or a place name, **of Massa.** The latter is more likely. Such a name—referring either to a tribe or a place—is mentioned among "the descendants of Ishmael" (Genesis 25:14). Nothing further is known of Agur, Jakeh, or Lemuel (31:1). They were probably wise men of the non-Israelite "people of the east" who were already famous in Solomon's day (I Kings 4:30) and who are mentioned in Job (1:3).

30:1*b*. The words following the title certainly do not include the proper names **Ithiel** and **Ucal,** as in most English versions. They are a corruption of some such sentence as "The inspired utterance of the man who struggled with God, struggled with God, and prevailed." The precise translation is uncertain. But the sentence apparently describes some visionary experience which led to the revelation that follows in verses 2-4.

30:2-4. ***The Mystery of the Divine Nature.*** As in Ecclesiastes and Job—but not the rest of Proverbs—God is represented here as inaccessible to human wisdom. God can be known only as God chooses to be revealed (cf. Job 28:20-27; Ecclesiastes 9:1).

30:5-6. ***The Value of Revelation.*** These lines were probably added by an orthodox Hebrew wise man who wished to correct what seemed to him the foreign, skeptical tone of verses 1-4. Verse 5 is apparently borrowed from Psalms 12:6 and 18:30.

30:7-9. ***Two Petitions.*** Like much of the rest of the chapter this is a numerical proverb (see Introduction). It is in the form of a prayer asking for **two** favors—a trustful spirit and a happy mean between being either excessivly poor or disgustingly rich. The similarity between verse 8*c* and Matthew 6:11 is striking.

B. Various Proverbs: Numerical and Otherwise (30:10-33)

This section consists mostly of numerical proverbs (see Introduction). There are several proverbs of simpler form, none of which has any clear relation to its context. Verse 10 warns about the effectiveness of curses (cf. 29:24). Verse 17 threatens those who fail to honor their parents. Verse 20 presents a fascinating vignette of a shameless woman. Verses 32-33 warn that it is better to be quiet than arrogant. Angry and arrogant speech will lead to trouble.

30:11-14. ***Four Objectionable Persons.*** This may originally have been a more explicit numerical proverb, listing four types hateful to God—the unfilial, the self-righteous, the proud, and the greedy.

30:15-31. ***Nature and Human Nature.*** None of these five numerical proverbs has any moral or theological content. They represent another activity of the wise men—careful, systematic observation of the world (see above on 13:12). Thus they illustrate the beginnings of the scientific spirit. Verses 21-23 picture **four** situations in which people become intolerable. The others consist of observations of animals and natural objects and show a rudimentary interest in classification. Similar lists were produced by Egyptian wise men. Verses 15-16 speak of **four** objects which cannot be **satisfied.** Verses 24-28 describe **four** little things which nevertheless arouse wonder because of their cleverness. Verses 29-31 picture **four** things which have stately movement. What the author intended by the last two is uncertain (cf. the Revised Standard Version footnote). Verses 18-19 humorously compare aspects of nature with the mystery of human courtship.

C. The Words of Lemuel (31:1-9)

31:1. ***Title.*** See above on 30:1. The verse illustrates the role that parents played in the early education of youth (cf. 1:8-9).

31:2-9. ***The Duties of Kings.*** Kings must avoid the corruptions of luxury. Sexual indulgence saps their vitality (verse 3). Alcohol makes them indifferent to responsibilities (verses 4-5)—drink being useful only to the miserable (verses 6-7). A king's primary duty is to those who cannot take care of themselves (verses 8-9; see above on 29:7).

D. THE GOOD WIFE (31:10-31)

In Hebrew this poem is an alphabetical acrostic; that is, each line begins with a successive letter of the alphabet. The Hebrew wife here appears as the responsible head of the household (cf. 11:16, 22; 12:4; 18:22; 21:9, 19). She provides for food and clothing, purchases property, engages in trade, and exercises charity. Physical beauty is a matter of indifference. What is important is intelligence, kindness, industry, and above all a religious spirit.

THE BOOK OF ECCLESIASTES

Harvey H. Guthrie, Jr.

INTRODUCTION

Name and Place in the Bible

The Hebrew title of the book is "Koheleth," meaning "Preacher" (see below on 1:1). Ecclesiastes is the Septuagint translation of this word. After a good deal of controversy, Ecclesiastes was included in the Writings, the final section of the Hebrew Bible. It is read in the synagogue on the third day of the feast of booths.

Date and Authorship

The book is attributed to Solomon (see below on 1:1). However, the language and style indicate a third century B.C. origin, which would be hundreds of years after Solomon. In spite of some opinion to the contrary, it is probably basically the work of one author. His disciples were responsible for certain additions, including the two epilogues (12:9-11 and 12-14).

Relation to Wisdom Literature

The background of Ecclesiastes is the wisdom of the ancient Near East (see Introductions to Job and Proverbs). Wisdom was cultivated by both the average person and the professional wise man of the royal courts. It sought to express in terse, polished sayings or parables the nature and meaning of life's realities. Its aim was wise conduct based on accurate observation and mature reflection. It rested on the conviction that a basic order underlay life.

Wisdom did not become theologically important in Israel until the Babylonian exile. Then, the fall of the nation, in 586 B.C., shut off the continuing national history in which God was revealed. Theological interest then moved more toward nature and individual morality, and wisdom became increasingly important. The doctrine of reward and punishment for individual action arose. The wise behavior cultivated by the wise men was expressed in more specifically Israelite terms. Wisdom came to be thought of as a personified agent of God (cf. Proverbs 8–9). The scriptural law and prophets came to be seen more as the revelation of wisdom than as a record of God's historical activity. All this led to a rather rigid orthodoxy, characterized by extreme confidence in its own understanding of life and the purposes of God and by a rather narrow, prudential moralism. Job and Ecclesiastes are, in different ways, protests against the imposition of such doctrine on the reality of existence.

Its Message

Ecclesiastes states the central idea in ancient wisdom—an acknowledgment of the limits of human understanding. "The fear of the Lord is the beginning of wisdom" is an often repeated motto. The author never denies the sovereignty of God. What he does deny is the ability of a finite human to grasp the meaning of life. He asserts that the human perspective is too limited to permit any pronouncement on the meaning of things (see below on 1:3-11). It is too partial to formulate any theory about the individual occurrences of life. His counsel, therefore, is that the ambiguity of life is to be accepted for what it is—not evaded by pompous orthodoxy (cf. 5:18-20; 7:15-22; 8:1-9).

Ecclesiastes thus represents, in terms of a specific time and culture, a double protest. Faith is always tempted to shore up its own uncertainty with dogmatism. Human understanding has a constant tendency to overrate its potentiality. Ecclesiastes speaks out against both these failings. The inclusion of Ecclesiastes in a canon that also contains writings against which it protests is a witness to the Bible's location of divine revelation in finite human history.

I. The Heading of the Book (1:1-2)

1:1. ***The Superscription.*** Solomon is identified as the author of the book in the phrase **the son of David, king in Jerusalem.** Proverbs and Wisdom of Solomon also claim him as the author of wisdom writings. This tradition arose because it was in Solomon's court that wise men became official participants in Israel's life. Thus Solomon was considered the originator of the literature that came from the wise men—just as Moses was considered originator of all the law and David of the psalms (on Solomon's wisdom cf. I Kings 3:16-28; 10). But Ecclesiastes must come from a later time than Solomon's (see Introduction).

The Preacher is the English translation of the Greek "Ecclesiastes." The Hebrew word is *koheleth,* whose root has to do with gathering an assembly or performing some function in it. Whether it is a proper name or the designation of an office—and whether the writer uses it of himself or for some other reason—are questions on which there is no agreed answer.

1:2. ***The Theme of the Book.*** The word translated **vanity** denotes a breath—exhaled air that disappears. Over half its occurrences are in Ecclesiastes. It is the equivalent of the name of the first man in the Bible to die, Abel. This may be no accident. The author restates his theme in 12:8. It is that, so far as we humans can observe, all that makes up life soon vanishes and loses significance.

II. The Vanity of Life (1:3–6:12)

1:3-11. ***A Poem: Nature's Cycle is Pointless.*** The major subdivisions of the book seem to begin with poetic, or semipoetic, passages (cf. 3:1-8; 7:1-14; 9:17–11:8). This poem turns quickly from human **toil** (the word connotes suffering, trouble, strained labor) and the succession of generations (verses 3-4) to the earth which is their setting. The earth too is characterized by monotonous movement to which nothing a person can say can give significance. (A possible translation of verse 8*a* is **all** "words" **are full of weariness.**) This implies a criticism of the efforts of the wise men to frame sayings catching the meaning of life.

1:9. The phrase **under the sun** occurs throughout the book. It sets limits around the author's claim to truth (cf. verse 13). He does not attempt to overthrow the wisdom tradition. He stands in that tradition in his claim merely to observe accurately what life offers. He does not seek to go beyond the outer limits of human wisdom. On that basis he implies that orthodox wisdom has imposed a false order on life. But his own position is no absolute denial of life's significance. **Under the sun,** or **under heaven** (verse 13), strictly limits the area of which he speaks. The repetition of the phrase is a clue to its significance for the author, whose skepticism is not final.

1:12–2:26. *Reflections on Pointlessness.* The author proceeds to state how all that even a Solomon had been and possessed could lead only to the conclusion reached in the preceding poem. Neither faithful following of the methods of the wise men (1:13-18), nor sheer physical pleasure, nor the things money can buy can make life anything more than vanity (2:1-11). All human **business** is pointless—at least so far as can be observed under the sun.

2:18-26 is devoted to human toil (see above on 1:3). Everything gained by toil is left behind at death. The only reward for gain is the exhaustion it produces (vss. 18-23). Yet some enjoyment is to be found in devoting attention and energy to what each moment brings. That enjoyment **is from the hand of God**. God has given the toil, and has given us the ability to see the meaninglessness of it. The wonder of this uncomforting mystery must be recognized. It can impart a thrill to life (2:24-26).

3:1-8. *A Poem on "Times."* Again, a poem begins a major section (see above on 1:3). The author here turns to the times marking life's movement. Two words in verse 1 are central to the poem. **Season** has connotations of "being determined," "fixed," "appointed." **Time** basically means "occurrence." It refers to the given moments of existence. The use of **season** at the beginning implies that, for the author, the moments of life enumerated in the poem with concise beauty are fixed in an unchangeable way. Verses 9-15 imply that God is responsible for this.

3:9-15. *The Author's Basic Conclusion.* The answer to the question of verse 9 is central to the author's philosophy. The stuff of life described in the poem—human **business** (verse 10)—is not something about which the author is utterly skeptical. He asserts that **everything** is **beautiful in its** own **time,** and that God has made it so. The word "beautiful" denotes fittingness of arrangement.

3:11*b* is the most controversial sentence in the book. The crucial word is **eternity.** Some have tried to defend the King James translation "world." Others have suggested various emendations—for example, "toil," "mystery," "forgetfulness." But it is best to take the text as it stands. God has put eternity, an intimation of the wholeness of which the recurrent times are parts, into the human mind. Yet it is only intimation. We are unable to corroborate it on the basis of honest observation of the succession of times we know here under the sun. Thus the author is not absolutely skeptical. He has faith in the meaning of the totality of things under God. But he is rigorously skeptical of any human claim to state that meaning. Human wisdom can neither add nor subtract anything from the totality of what God has ordained (verse 14).

3:15*b* is difficult to translate. It reads literally "God searches out what is pursued." In the light of what has gone before, the two halves of the verse may summarize the two sides of the author's thought. From the human vantage point **that which is, already has been** and **that which is to be, already has been.** Human wisdom can discern no order or pattern. But **God seeks**

what has been driven away. That is, in the totality of the eternity of which we have only an intimation, what seems recurrently pointless is pursued, brought back, and given meaning. It is God's unfathomable eternity that both gives life its meaning and, to our limited view, makes life tragic.

Thus in verse 12 the counsel to enjoy each time is not entirely hedonistic. Though we may not see it, there is significance in what we occupy ourselves with (verse 13). Meaningless as the verdict of human wisdom on things has to be, the ultimate issues are in God's hand (verses 14-15).

3:16–5:9. ***Miscellaneous Thoughts on Life's Content.*** The author has stated his central thesis. Now come various loosely organized observations on how life bears out what has been said.

3:16–4:3 insists that observation of life reveals no moral order. The author can find no time of righteousness among those times of which life is made up (3:16-17). Human life is no different from that of the beasts in its meaningless movement toward death (3:18-21). Further, what takes place in it makes death desirable (4:1-3). These observations are contrary both to the earlier Israelite conviction that history consists of moments which reveal the righteousness of God and to the later emphasis on individual rewards and punishments.

4:4-12 is basically variations on the theme of the meaninglessness of toil, which has already been stated. Verses 9-12 reveal the author's honesty of observation in their insistence that companionship lightens the oppressive human load.

4:13-16 stands a quoted or invented proverb on its head. The final sentences say that what is extolled at the opening passes away like everything else. Terse and allusive language makes this section difficult to translate, but the point is clear.

5:1-7 indicates that the author takes the Israelite worshiping community for granted. However, he holds that what religion provides deserves no more enthusiasm or confidence than anything else under the sun. Religion is the means by which human beings acknowledge the reality of the God of eternity. But its word here under the sun is not more final than the word describing the vanity of life.

Four pieces of advice are given:

(1) Because God is so far above the human sphere, religion should not be attended by the busy activity that takes it too seriously (verse 1).

(2) Because there is no possibility of direct correspondence between our words and the reality of God, not too many words should be uttered in prayer (verses 2-3).

(3) Because of the realism the author always values, one must not be rash in making sacred vows (verses 4-5).

(4) In no event should one put oneself in the position of having to make excuses before God's representative (verses 6-7). **Messenger** probably refers to a priest.

5:8-9 counsels the reader not to be surprised at political oppression. The final part of verse 8 probably means that each official has to oppress those beneath him in order to satisfy the demands of his superior. The difficult verse 9 probably means that the profit of the land is taken over by the officials mentioned and that no cultivated field is exempt from royal taxes (cf. the Revised Standard Version footnote).

5:10–6:12. ***Maxims on the Possibility of Enjoying Life.*** The first half of the book ends with a series of proverbs on paths to enjoyment. Some are brief, some more extended. The first four of these (5:10, 11, 12, 13-17) have to do with wealth and goods. They are negative.

5:18-20 is positive. The author insists that the only enjoyment there is must be found in taking life honestly as it comes—not asking for more and not investing a given time with more significance than it has. The ability to do this is the **gift of God** (verse 19). Again, the author does not advocate a sheer hedonism. The point is that enjoyment of life comes, not by what one can attain, but by a power over which one has no control.

6:1-9 develops the above from the negative side. This leads to the sixth proverb in the series in verse 9. The author meditates on the mystery of why some people do not have the gift spoken of in 5:18-20. He comes to the conclusion that those who do not have it, though they have **no burial** (never die), would have done better to have been born dead. The concluding proverb holds that satisfaction is better than perpetual longing.

6:10-12 concludes by repeating the themes of 1:3-11 and 3:1-8. Life is endless repetition (verse 10). No word uttered, even by the wise, can give it meaning (verse 11). The meaning of the totality of life is beyond the ken of human beings, who die so soon (verse 12).

III. Advice Based on Reality (7:1–9:16)

The book is loosely organized, and the outline used here is arbitrary. However, chapter 7 does seem to mark a turn from the author's presentation of his philosophy to more practical advice on the basis of that philosophy. Again a major subdivision begins with poetry.

7:1-14. *Six Poetic Pieces of Advice.* The author may very well here be employing proverbs from wisdom circles, not his own compositions. His opening chapters, however, put them in a new framework. They make it clear that the good to which traditional wisdom directs people is really only relative good. Thus the author is rooted in his background, but is critical of it.

7:1*a* praises the value of a good reputation. There is a play on the Hebrew words for **name** (*shem*) and **ointment** (*shemen*). Verse 7*b* fits with what the author has said in chapters 1–6.

7:2-4 holds that wisdom lies in acting in accord with the tragic nature of life as outlined in chapters 1–6 (see above on 3:9-15).

7:5-7 speaks for wisdom instead of foolish pleasure. Foolish laughter is likened to the **crackling of** a fire of **thorns** that generates no heat. But, characteristic of the author's realism, the conclusion is that even wisdom can be bought. **Oppression** in verse 7 probably denotes ill-gotten gain.

7:8-10 is based on 1:3-11 and 3:1-8. The point is that each event should be accepted for what it is. Heated comparison with previous events is foolish.

7:11-12 acknowledges the practical, proximate value of both wisdom and wealth as defenses against life's difficulty and perplexity.

7:13-14 concludes this series on the note so often struck by the author: No one can change what God has ordained. Take the good for what it is when it comes. When evil comes, accept the fact that our limited perspective does not permit us to see how it fits into the totality of things (cf. 3:9-15).

7:15-22. ***Be Satisfied with Relative Good.*** Outside its context, this would be the crassest kind of cynically prudential advice. But it must be read in the light of the author's philosophy. The heart of the section is the poetic proverb of verse 19. The wisdom the author praises there has been defined in chapters 1–6 as recognition of the limited nature of the human perspective. In the light of this, one should not impute unqualified righteousness to any one act or position. Furthermore, action should be taken in this light without regard to what others may think (verses 21-22).

7:23-29. ***The Limitations of Wisdom.*** In spite of his reservations, the author never denies the value of wisdom. Here he tells of his personal knowledge of one theme stressed by the wise men—the dangers of the wicked woman (cf. Proverbs 2:16-19; 5; 6:20–7:27). But wisdom is able only to deal with the individual times, not eternity (cf. 3:9-15). It can deal with the parts but not **the sum of things** (verses 25, 27-28*a*).

8:1-9. ***Wisdom Recognizes the Necessity of Compromise.*** Some details of translation and interpretation in this section are debated. But its point is clear: compromise is the characteristic of wise conduct. As an example the author pictures a wise man in the service of an arbitrary king. He holds that the wise man is absolved from responsibility for actions of which he himself might not approve. His wisdom makes him master of the situation, for he recognizes reality for what it is.

8:10-15. ***Seek Enjoyment in the Midst of Aimless Order.*** The text of verse 10 is difficult and the subject of debate. Verses 11-13 are probably an addition by some later, more orthodox annotator. The main thrust of the section is in line with what precedes it: wisdom cannot discern any absolute moral order in the way things work out. Thus the wise thing is to enjoy what there is to enjoy. The end of verse 15 again makes clear that the author is no absolute nihilist.

8:16–9:12. ***God's Ways Are Inscrutable.*** The main point of the book, already stated in 3:9-15, is repeated in 8:16-17. Human study of **the work of God** cannot lead to a knowledge of the purpose of life. Honest observation shows that fortune does not necessarily come to the good (9:1-6). Life's prizes are not necessarily gained by ability (9:11-12). Death's overtaking of all is the only sure thing (9:3-6, 10*b*), and wisdom dictates making the best of things (9:7-8). Again the author does not categorically deny meaning (verse 7*b*). But he does demand honesty on the basis of observation.

9:13-16. ***Wisdom Is Nevertheless Worth It.*** A realistic parable in verses 13-15 is followed by a saying on the value of wisdom. The point here, as elsewhere, is that the wisdom which honestly discerns the aimlessness of life is more to be desired for the freedom it brings than is the power in which one may delude oneself.

IV. Concluding Proverbs (9:17–12:8)

Again a subdivision is marked by poetry.

9:17–10:20. ***A Series of Poetic Proverbs.*** This section consists of a collection of maxims, very much like those found in Proverbs. The author may not have created them all himself, and some may have been added as the book brought others to the minds of copyists. In the context of the whole book, what is said reflects the philosophy of the writer. Life is aimless (10:5-7). Though wisdom's value may not be apparent, **foolishness** is plainly worthless (10:1-3, 12-15). Prudence characterizes the wise person's behavior (10:4, 20). And there is conviction about the value of **wisdom** (9:17-18).

11:1-8. ***Life Must Be Lived.*** Like the one following it (11:9–12:7), this section has the flavor of the author's own advice. Though interpreters have debated the meaning of some of its figures—for example, in verse 1—the meaning of this striking poem is clear. Our limited view here under the sun, our inability to see enough to find meaning in the totality of life, must not paralyze us. We cannot control the forces by which life is shaped. Therefore let us act, and enjoy things as they come.

11:9–12:7. ***Enjoy Youth While You Have It.*** This passage is a pathetically beautiful description of old age and the inexorable approach of death (12:2-7). The point of it all is advice to enjoy the vitality and optimism of youth while it is possible (11:9–12:2). This is all the counsel with which the author can honestly leave his readers. Many interpreters have found 12:1*a* hard to reconcile with the author's viewpoint. Some have tried to emend **Creator**—for example, to "wife" or "grave." Others have taken the clause to be a pious interpolation. But such theories are unnecessary. In the light of the author's philosophy, 12:1 is the most pathetic statement in this section. It is saying, "Affirm meaning in life while you can, before age and experience, if you are honest, lead you to my position" (again cf. 3:9-15).

12:8. ***The Theme of the Book Repeated.*** See above on 1:2.

V. Postscripts on the Author and His Teaching (12:9-14)

12:9-11 is praise of the author by a disciple probably responsible for the "publication" of the book. He has forgotten the ascription to Solomon in 1:1. Verse 10 indicates that the disciple truly appreciated the master. **Uprightly** is the central word. It recalls that the author never compromised the truth as he saw it in order to say what was pleasing.

12:12-14 seems to be a second epilogue by a more pious person. Possibly this was the editor responsible for softening the sharp words of the writer at some points in the book.

THE SONG OF SOLOMON

Robert C. Dentan

INTRODUCTION

Author and Date

The title of this book in Hebrew is "The Song of Songs [that is, "the most beautiful song"] which is Solomon's." The beauty of the song is undeniable. It is filled with rapturous expressions of basic and tender human emotion and of delight in the loveliness of nature. But its attribution to Solomon is no longer taken seriously. Apart from the title verse—which is certainly much later than the book itself—the claim that Solomon wrote it is based on the fact that his name occurs in certain passages (1:5; 3:7-11; 8:11-12). There is also an ancient tradition that makes him the author of many songs (I Kings 4:32), some of which presumably might be of this character. The way Solomon's name occurs in the text of the song, however, in no way supports the contention that he wrote it. On the contrary it would more naturally be interpreted to imply that he did not. The almost universal consensus of modern scholars, therefore, is that the book is anonymous.

The song exhibits a variety of forms and lacks any progress of thought or clear plan of composition. This makes it likely that different parts come from different hands. When compared with the rest of the Old Testament the book has a certain unity, seen particularly in the use of uncommon words and rare grammatical forms. These, however, may be best explained as deriving from a common geographical background and the use of a particular Hebrew dialect. The Hebrew is probably that of northern Israel, though as we have it now the book obviously comes from the vicinity of Jerusalem (cf. 2:7 and 3:5).

The date of the book is almost as uncertain as its authorship. Clues seem to point in different directions. Since it contains a Persian word ("orchard," 4:13) and one possibly Greek ("palanquin," 3:9), it is impossible to date the text in its present form earlier than the late Persian or Greek periods. On the other hand, the use of Tirzah in parallelism with Jerusalem, apparently as a capital city, suggests the early period of the divided monarchy (see below on 6:4-10). Such apparently contradictory data lead many scholars to believe that the book contains material from various periods of Israel's life. They hold that its text has undergone considerable transformation in the course of its history.

Place in the Bible

Because the book does not mention God or contain any religious or ethical ideas, its position in the Jewish canon of scripture was long a precarious one. According to a famous passage in the Mishnah, a second century collection of Jewish interpretations of the Old Testament, its canonicity was one of the points disputed between the rabbinical schools of Shammai and Hillel near the beginning of the Christian era. But Rabbi Akiba in the second century A.D. could declare that "all the ages are not worth the day on which the Song of Songs was given to Israel." Between the two dates the question of canonicity had been settled, probably on the basis of its alleged Solomonic origin. This was done by a rabbinical council at Jamnia around A.D. 90, when Judaism was being consolidated and reorganized after the fall of Jerusalem.

Apparently a secular interpretation of the song was common up until the date of its final acceptance into the biblical canon. Portions of it were frequently sung at wedding feasts. After it was formally and generally recognized as scripture, however, a religious interpretation prevailed. The contents of the book were allegorized. It was understood to be an account of the relation between God, the husband and lover of Israel, and God's people, who were the bride. It came to be associated liturgically with the Passover, perhaps because of its obvious connection with spring (2:11-13; 6:11; 7:12). At one time it was read during the public services of the festival.

The allegorical interpretation was accepted by Christians, but the figures of Christ and the church were substituted for God and Israel (cf. the chapter headings in the King James Version). Sometimes the book was interpreted as a dialogue between Christ and the soul. Theodore of Mopsuestia (fifth century A.D.) revived the view that the poem was purely secular. He considered it a long song written by Solomon for Pharaoh's daughter. His opinion was later considered heretical. In modern times the allegorical interpretation has largely fallen into disfavor. It is usually assumed that the subject of the song is sexual, not spiritual, love.

Original Character

Four views of the original form and purpose of the song are still current:

(1) It was written as *a drama*, with either two characters or three.
(2) It was *a collection of wedding songs*, intended to be used at various stages in a marriage ceremony.
(3) It was *a fertility-cult liturgy*.
(4) It was assembled as *an anthology of separate love songs* without inner coherence or external organization.

On quick reading the drama theory is appealing, since the poem has a certain dramatic atmosphere. It is made up of speeches delivered by various characters, including at least a maiden (1:5-6), a lover (1:9-11), and a chorus (5:9; 6:1). Some think there are two lovers, a king (1:12), and a shepherd (2:16). The chief argument against the dramatic interpretation is the impossibility of getting any agreement on what story it is supposed to tell. There are as many plots as interpreters. Further, there is no external indication of the speakers and no dialogue in the strict sense, since each speech is an independent unit. A final argument is that the ancient Hebrews were unfamiliar with the drama as a literary form.

During the latter part of the nineteenth century, the view that the book was originally a collection of wedding songs gained great popularity. It was observed that Syrian wedding festivities, lasting for over a week, were marked by dances and songs, by saluting the bridegroom and his bride as king and queen, and by elaborate descriptions of their physical beauty. Unfortunately, however, it is not clear that nineteenth century Syrian ceremonies have any bearing on the wedding rites of ancient Hebrews. This interpretation of the song is therefore less widely accepted than it used to be.

An interpretation that has gained increasing popularity in recent years sees in the song the fragmentary, disarranged, and distorted elements of an ancient fertility-cult liturgy, celebrating the sexual union of a god and a goddess. From this standpoint the book's acceptance in the canon would present no problem, since it would have been a religious book from the very beginning. The only problem would have been to eliminate the pagan elements so as to make it acceptable in Israelite circles.

According to one theory representative of this view the book portrays the sacred marriage between Ishtar and Tammuz. It is argued that certain features of the song are far more suitable for a goddess seeking to renew her marriage to a dead-and-risen deity than for a simple village peasant girl pursuing a rustic lover. The woman is aggressive (3:1-4) and warlike (6:10). She boldly refers to premarital relations (2:4-6, King James Version; cf. 1:6). And there are strange mythological-geographical features. Though the fertility-cult interpretation has been ably defended by several capable scholars, their views have failed to win general acceptance. For one thing, it seems difficult to explain how such a liturgy could have found entrance into Israelite worship—or why anyone would have thought it worth while to expurgate and preserve it.

The view most widely held by scholars today is that the book is simply a loose collection of lyrics—an anthology of songs. There is no special theme other than that of love between the sexes. It is this view that forms the basis of the following commentary. It must be acknowledged, however, that other interpretations may have elements of truth in them. Quite possibly the collection was preserved because many of the songs were used at weddings, though not necessarily in accordance with any fixed pattern. Possibly also some of the songs—which are admittedly difficult to understand as expressions of simple peasant boy-and-girl emotions—originated in the pre-Israelite fertility cult, or at least in a pagan mythological context. Preserved among the common people because of their antiquity and intrinsic beauty, they would gradually lose their original associations and be given a harmless secular meaning. The history of the individual lyrics, as well as of the book as a whole, is undoubtedly far more complex than is usually realized.

Value

The religious significance of the song is twofold. First, its inclusion in the canon is a symbol of the church's blessing on marriage and sexual love. It is a continual reminder that simple human joys, the pleasures of love, and the delights of the natural world have their honored place among the people of God. In the second place it must be recognized that the tradition of allegorical interpretation was not entirely wrong. There is a real analogy between such love as the song describes and the love of the spirit. It is only from a profound knowledge of human love, in all its manifestations, that people can rise to an understanding of the love that unites God with humanity.

Commentary

1:1. *Title.* On the name of the book and the attribution of authorship see Introduction.

1:2-4. *A Girl's Invitation to Her Lover.* The girl speaks, perhaps only in imagination, to her beloved. She longs to be united with him in marriage. **Wine** and perfumed **oils** are connected with feasting and joy. The love of her lover brings to the girl an even greater joy. The Hebrew word translated **love** in verse 2 is one reserved for sexual love alone; the verb **love** in verse 3 is from a more common root. **Name** in common Semitic usage connotes the reputation of a man, also his essential nature, his personality. Verse 4*b* should probably be translated "Bring me, O king, into thy chambers." The practice of treating the bridegroom as a king is fairly widespread. Advocates of the fertility-cult interpretation see here a real **king**, who enacts the role of the god in the sacred marriage.

1:5-6. ***A Girl's Defense of Her Beauty.*** A peasant girl is speaking to girls of the city, who despise her. She insists that her attractions have not been diminished by her daily exposure to **the sun** and the darkening of her complexion. **The tents of Kedar** are the black goat's-hair tents of the bedouins. **The curtains of Solomon** are unknown. Parallelism suggests that "Solomon" might be a deliberate substitution for the similar-sounding name of some bedouin tribe. The girl's job was to guard the vineyard when the grapes were ripening. While doing so she lost her heart (her **vineyard**) to a man. Her brothers, who—as in oriental society today—would have great authority, are **angry**.

1:7-8. ***A Shepherd Girl's Search for Her Lover.*** In her imagination the girl begs her shepherd lover to **tell** her where he has gone. Apparently others advise her just to take care of her **flocks** and not bother with him if she does **not know where he is.**

1:9–2:7. ***A Colloquy of Lovers.*** The speeches here alternate in a formal way, but there is no real conversation. Several brief dialogue songs have perhaps been joined. In verses 9-11 the lover praises his beloved's beauty. In verses 12-14 she praises him in return. The description is full of the imagery of pleasant odors. **En-gedi** is an oasis on the western shore of the Dead Sea. In verse 15 the lover speaks, in verse 16*ab* his **beloved**. In verses 16*c*-17 they speak together of their nuptial **couch**, decorated with **green** branches.

2:1-7. The lover's dialogue continues. In verses 1-3 they compare their beauty to various spring flowers and blossoms. She likens herself to one of the little flowers of the coastal Plain of **Sharon** or to a **lily**. Just what flowers are meant can no longer be certain. In verse 2 he echoes the comparison. In verse 3 she compares him, in his strength and beauty, to a blossoming **apple tree** whose **fruit** she has already tasted. **Banqueting house** means probably the bridal chamber. **Raisins** and **apples** were in antiquity regarded as exciting sexual desire. The intense eroticism of verses 6-7 is unmistakable. Advocates of the fertility-cult interpretation see in these verses the consummation of the sacred marriage of two deities such as Ishtar and Tammuz.

2:8-17. ***The Joy of Love in the Spring.*** The appreciation of nature exhibited in this book is unparalleled elsewhere in the Old Testament. It reaches a climax in this famous passage. The girl speaks of her lover's coming to her, **bounding** with joy, calling to her through the **windows,** asking her to come into the lovely countryside. Verse 15 appears to be a fragment without context. It is one of two passages (the other being 8:8-10) which cannot by any stretch of imagination be given a fertility-cult interpretation. Its meaning is uncertain, but it may be a plea from young girls for protection from **foxes** (cf. our term "wolves") who would take advantage of their innocence. Verses 16-17 contain the girl's response to her lover's plea. She will gladly spend the night with him among the fields and hills. With verse 16 cf. 6:3 and 7:10.

3:1-5. ***The Girl Dreams of Her Lover.*** In her dream the girl wanders through the narrow **streets** of the town and passes a band of **watchmen** (cf. 5:7) while seeking her lover. When she finds him, she brings him back to her home. Some scholars find in this passage a typical theme of the fertility cult: the goddess seeking for her dead, yet-to-be resurrected lover. Verse 5 is identical with 2:7 and similar to 8:4.

3:6-11. ***A Solemn Procession.*** This song is entirely unique. It is only here that **Solomon** (if the name is original) appears in his own person. In 1:5 and 8:11-12 he is mentioned only incidentally and for purposes of comparison. Some scholars think this is a processional ode actually composed for the marriage of Solomon to some princess. Others believe that the name of Solomon has been substituted for the name of a god who was carried in procession—perhaps a god with a name such as Shelem or Shulman, which might easily be altered to Solomon.

The **column of smoke**, it has often been noted, suggests the coming of Yahweh from Sinai. The strange Hebrew word translated **palanquin** seems actually to be Greek, although some scholars regard it as Iranian; but this word may, of course have been introduced only in the latest version of the text. Not until the last verse does it become evident that the procession is connected with a **wedding**. Defenders of the fertility-cult interpretation naturally find here a god being borne to the temple for the sacred marriage.

4:1-7. ***Description of the Girl.*** Descriptive love songs of this type are characteristic of the modern Arabic-speaking Orient as well as the ancient Near East. From antiquity there are numerous examples from both cultic and secular sources.

Some of the similes seem merely grotesque to the modern western reader. This is because in making a comparison with only one feature, an extended description is given of the object which is being compared. For example, in verse 1 the only point of comparison between the girl's **hair** and a **flock of goats** is that both are black. In verse 2 her **teeth** and the freshly washed **ewes** are both white. The fact that the goats are walking down a mountainside east of the Jordan is included only to bring the picture of the flock more vividly to the mind of the reader. The observation that the ewes **bear twins** and **not one among them is bereaved** marks them merely as healthy specimens. In verse 4 the girl's **neck is like the tower of David** only with respect to its height and delicacy. The **arsenal** with its **bucklers** and **shields** is wholly irrelevant to the image. Verse 6 is similar to 2:17. If it is original here, it expresses the lover's desire for the physical consummation of his love.

4:8–5:1. ***A Colloquy of Love.*** It is probable that this section contains three originally independent poems, or fragments of poems, which have been brought together to form an artificial unit. Note the five-times repeated words **my bride** or **my sister, my bride** and the three references to **Lebanon**.

4:8. This is the most clearly mythological passage in the book. The Canaanite-Phoenician setting is unmistakable. **Lebanon . . . Amana . . . Senir . . . Hermon** are all mountains in Syria. It has been suggested that the original speaker was Adonis, inviting his beloved to join him in the hunt which, according to legend, resulted in his death.

4:9-11. The lover praises the kisses and other charms of his beloved. The curious reference to the beloved as **my sister** can also be found in other ancient oriental sources, especially the Egyptian.

4:12-15. The lover declares his beloved is a **locked** garden—inaccessible, a virgin. The comparison of a wife to a **fountain** is also found in Proverbs 5:15-18. **Orchard** in verse 13 is a Persian word and shows that in its present form the book cannot be older than the Babylonian exile.

4:16. The girl begs the winds to entice her lover into the garden.

5:1. He accepts her invitation. The concluding words, **Eat, O friends . . .**, are presumably addressed to guests at a wedding, although in their original pagan form they may have been an invitation to worshipers to join in the fertility cult.

5:2–6:3. ***A Nocturnal Search for the Lover.*** Verses 2-8 have a dreamlike quality. Indeed they may be intended only as the description of a dream (cf. 3:1-5). The lover knocks on the girl's door after she is asleep (verses 2-4). When she rises to admit him, he is **gone** (verse 6). As she seeks him through the dark streets, the night watch find and beat her (verse 7), perhaps because they take her for a prostitute. The search theme is characteristic of the fertility cult. Those who hold to this interpretation think of the watchmen as the guardians of the underworld, where the fertility god is held a prisoner.

5:9-16. In response to a query by the **daughters of Jerusalem** (verse 16) the girl enumerates the charms of her lover.

Advocates of the fertility-cult interpretation point out how easily verses 14-15 might be taken as describing the statue of a god.

6:1-3. In answer to a second query the girl announces that she knows where her lover may be found. It is not certain whether her reply is to be understood metaphorically—as referring to the delights of physical love—or literally—as a picturesque account of the present whereabouts of her shepherd lover. With verse 3 cf. 2:16 and 7:10.

6:4–7:9. *Praise of the Girl's Beauty.* This section may well include several originally independent songs. All except 6:11-12 are unified in their present context by being addressed to the girl in praise of her loveliness.

6:4-10. The use of **Tirzah** in parallelism with **Jerusalem** suggests that it is regarded as capital of the northern kingdom of Israel. Because the city had this position only in the period up to Omri (I Kings 16:23-24), many commentators assume the poem must be very early. This may be true. But one must not overlook the possibility of deliberate archaizing—especially since Jews of the postexilic period abhorred Samaria, the later northern capital. Also, the possible symbolic meaning of Tirzah is "delight." Verses 5*c*-6 repeat 4:1*e*-2. Verses 8-9 mean that among any number of women—even **queens** and ladies of the court—the beloved would be the most beautiful.

The strange combination of **fair** with **terrible as an army** in verse 10 suggests to the adherents of a fertility-cult interpretation the common ancient view that certain goddesses were patrons of both love and war (cf. verse 13). Whether this verse belongs with what precedes it or with what follows it is uncertain.

6:11-12. The Revised Standard Version assumes the girl to be speaking in both these verses. Some commentators believe verse 11 to be a speech of the lover. The Hebrew of verse 12 is almost untranslatable. The Septuagint reads instead of **my prince** a proper name, "Aminadab."

6:13. The girl is invited to perform a **dance.** Since a dance by the bride is a common feature of oriental weddings, it is often assumed that this is its function here. Some doubt is thrown on this interpretation by the fact that she evidently dances naked or nearly so and that the dance is apparently described as a war dance (**before two armies**). The term **Shulammite** is often associated by commentators with Abishag the Shunammite, David's concubine (I Kings 1:3). But it is perhaps more natural to connect it with Shulmanitu, a Semitic goddess of war and love who was the counterpart of Shulman (see above on 3:6-11).

7:1-5. The similes are in the style of those in 4:1-7 (see comment). In this instance it is the dancing **feet** that first attract attention. The description then moves upward. **Heshbon** is a city in Transjordan. **The gate of Bath-rabbim** is unknown. **Lebanon** is a mountain in Syria, of which **Damascus** was the capital. Mt. **Carmel** is on the seacoast of Palestine. On the use of **king** for the lover see above on 1:2-4.

7:6-9. The lover, longing for fulfillment, compares his beloved to the stately and nourishing palm tree.

7:10-13. ***The Invitation of the Girl.*** This may originally have been an independent lyric. But its position here gives the passage the effect of an answer to verses 6-9. Verse 10 is similar to 2:16 and 6:3; line *b* resembles Genesis 3:16*d*. The girl invites her lover to taste the full delights of love in the spring-filled countryside (cf. 2:10-14). **Mandrakes** were used to arouse sexual desire.

8:1-4. ***The Girl's Longing for Her Lover.*** The girl wishes that she could always have her lover near her, **like a brother**, so that she could freely express her affection. The emotion she feels, however, is not sisterly but passionately sensual (verse 3; cf. 2:6). Verse 4 appears to be some kind of refrain (cf. 2:7 and 3:5). Its relation to the context is not clear.

8:5. ***A Mythological Fragment.*** The meaning of this verse is obscure. There may be some allusion originally to the birth of a god or other mythological figure. The first line is reminiscent of 3:6.

8:6-7. ***The Power of Love.*** The girl is the speaker. She affirms in general language that nothing is stronger or to be more highly valued than love. The **seal** is a signet, a carved stone cylinder for impressing in clay the equivalent of a modern signature. It was usually carried on a cord about the neck and thus hung over the **heart.** The seal on the **arm** may refer to a signet ring—or possibly to an armlet, though no example of this type has been found. **Jealousy** might better be translated "passion." **Death . . . grave . . . flashes . . . many waters** have mythological associations in ancient Semitic thought (see comment on Psalms 18:7-18 and 65:5-8).

8:8-10. *The Walls of Innocence.* All recent commentators agree that this passage has no mythological or fertility-cult significance (see above on 2:8-17). They are not agreed, though, as to whether the speakers in verses 8-9 are the girl's suitors playfully threatening to lay siege to her, or her brothers determined to protect her from all who would take advantage of her innocence (for **sister** in this sense see above on 4:9-11). Verse 10 indicates that she has a mind of her own! The **peace** which she would bring to her lover here means "satisfaction." The Hebrew word (*shalom*) suggests a play on the name **Solomon** (*Shelomo*) in the following line and Shulammite in 6:13.

8:11-14. *Three Fragments.* In the first fragment (verses 11-12) the lover says that, valuable as is the **vineyard** of **Solomon,** his own **vineyard**—meaning his beloved—is far more valuable to him. Nothing is known of **Baal-hamon.** In verse 13 apparently a lover is speaking to his beloved, but the context of the speech is unclear. Verse 14 seems to be a fragmentary variant of 2:17*cd.* Some commentators think of these as the girl's words for which the lover of verse 13 is waiting. However, this interpretation is hardly a natural one.

FOR FURTHER STUDY

THE BOOK OF JOB

E. G. Kraeling, *The Book of the Ways of God*, 1939. Anthony and Miriam Hanson, *The Book of Job*, 1953. H. W. Robinson, *The Cross of Job*, 1955. Samuel Terrien in *Interpreter's Bible*, 1954; *Job: Poet of Existence*, 1957. N. H. Tur-Sinai, *The Book of Job*, 1957. M. H. Pope in *Interpreters Dictionary of the Bible*, 1962. Roger Carstensen, *Job: Defense of Honor*, 1963. B. Zuckerman in *Interpreter's Dictionary of the Bible Supplement*, 1976.

THE BOOK OF PSALMS

W. O. E. Oesterley, *The Psalms*, 1939. Elmer A. Leslie, *The Psalms*, 1949. John Paterson, *The Praises of Israel*, 1950. Samuel Terrien, *The Psalms and Their Meaning for Today*, 1952. Artur Weiser, *The Psalms*, 1962; the best commentary in English. Sigmund Mowinckel, *The Psalms in Israel's Worship*, 2 volumes, 1963.

THE PROVERBS

W. O. E. Oesterley, *The Book of Proverbs*, 1929. A. Cohen, *Proverbs*, 1945. C. T. Fritsch in *Interpreter's Bible*, 1955. E. D. Jones, *Proverbs and Ecclesiastes*, 1961. S. H. Blank in *Interpreter's Dictionary of the Bible*, 1962. R. B. Y. Scott, *Proverbs; Ecclesiastes*, 1965. R. N. Whybray, *Wisdom in Proverbs*, 1965, and in *Interpreter's Dictionary of the Bible Supplement*, 1976.

ECCLESIASTES

G. A. Barton, *The Book of Ecclesiastes*, 1908. A. L. Williams, *Ecclesiastes*, 1922. R. Gordis, *Koheleth: the Man and His World*, 1951.

THE SONG OF SOLOMON

W. H. Schoff, editor, *The Song of Songs: A Symposium*, 1924. M. Jastrow, *The Song of Songs*, 1954. H. H. Rowley, "The Interpretation of the Song of Songs" in *The Servant of the Lord*, 1952. T. J. Meek in *Interpreter's Bible*, 1956. N. K. Gottwald, "Song of Songs" in *Interpreter's Dictionary of the Bible*, 1962. W. F. Albright, "Archaic Survivals in the Text of Canticles" in D. W. Thomas and W. D. McHardy, editors, *Hebrew and Semitic Studies*, 1963. R. E. Murphy, in *Interpreter's Dictionary of the Bible Supplement*, 1976.

ABBREVIATIONS AND EXPLANATIONS

ABBREVIATIONS

D — Deuteronomic; Deuteronomist source

E — Elohist source
Ecclus. — Ecclesiasticus
ed. — edited by, edition, editor
e.g. — *exempli gratia* (for example)
ERV — English Revised Version
esp. — especially

H — Holiness Code

J — Yahwist source
JPSV — Jewish Publication Society Version

L — Lukan source
LXX — Septuagint, the earliest Greek translation of the Old Testament and Apocrypha (250 B.C. and after)

M — Matthean source
Macc. — Maccabees
MS — manuscript

N — north, northern
NEB — New English Bible

P — Priestly source
p. — page
Pet. — Peter
Phil. — Philippian, Philippians
Philem. — Philemon
Prov. — Proverbs
Pss. Sol. — Psalms of Solomon
pt. — part (of a literary work)

Q — "Sayings" source

rev. — revised
RSV — Revised Standard Version

S — south, southern

trans. — translated by, translation, translator

viz. — *videlicet* (namely)
Vulg. — Vulgate, the accepted Latin version, mostly translated A.D. 383-405 by Jerome

W — west, western
Wisd. Sol. — Wisdom of Solomon

QUOTATIONS AND REFERENCES

In the direct commentary words and phrases quoted from the RSV of the passage under discussion are printed in boldface type, without quotation marks, to facilitate linking the comments to the exact points of the biblical text. If a quotation from the passage under discussion is not in boldface type, it is to be recognized as an alternate translation, either that of another version if so designated (see abbreviations of versions above) or the commentator's own rendering. On the other hand, quotations from other parts of the Bible in direct commentary, as well as all biblical quotations in the introductions, are to be understood as from the RSV unless otherwise identified.

A passage of the biblical text is identified by book, chapter number, and verse number or numbers, the chapter and verse numbers being separated by a colon (cf. Genesis 1:1). Clauses within a verse may be designated by the letters *a, b, c,* etc. following the verse number (e.g. Genesis 1:2*b*). In poetical text each line as printed in the RSV—not counting runovers necessitated by narrow columns—is accorded a letter. If the book is not named, the book under discussion is to be understood; similarly the chapter number appearing in the boldface reference at the beginning of the paragraph, or in a preceding centered head, is to be understood if no chapter is specified.

A suggestion to note another part of the biblical text is usually introduced by the abbreviation "cf." and specifies the exact verses. To be distinguished from this is a suggestion to consult a comment in this volume, which is introduced by "see above on," "see below on," or "see comment on," and which identifies the boldface reference at the head of the paragraph where the comment is to be found or, in the absence of a boldface reference, the reference in a preceding centered head. The suggestion "see Introduction" refers to the introduction of the book under discussion unless another book is named.